SMALL PARROTS
(Parrakeets)

BY

DAVID SETH-SMITH, F.Z.S.,

Curator of Mammals and Birds to the Zoological Society of London; Member of the British Ornithologists' Union; Member of the Royal Australasian Ornithologists' Union; Hon. Corresponding Fellow of the American Ornithologists' Union; Hon. Fellow of the New York Zoological Society; Hon. Member of the Société National d'Acclimatation de France; Editor of the *Avicultural Magazine*, etc,

1979 Edition
Revised by
Dr. Matthew M. Vriends
ISBN 0-87666-978-X

© 1979 by T.F.H. Publications, Inc. Ltd.

Distributed in the U.S. by T.F.H. Publications, Inc., 211 West Sylvania Avenue, P.O. Box 427, Neptune, N.J. 07753; in England by T.F.H. (Gt. Britain) Ltd., 13 Nutley Lane, Reigate, Surrey; in Canada to the book store and library trade by Beaverbooks, 953 Dillingham Road, Pickering, Ontario L1W 1Z7; in Canada to the pet trade by Rolf C. Hagen Ltd., 3225 Sartelon Street, Montreal 382, Quebec; in Southeast Asia by Y.W. Ong, 9 Lorong 36 Geylang, Singapore 14; in Australia and the South Pacific by Pet Imports Pty. Ltd., P.O. Box 149, Brookvale 2100, N.S.W., Australia; in South Africa by Valiant Publishers (Pty.) Ltd., P.O. Box 78236, Sandton City, 2146, South Africa; Published by T.F.H. Publications, Inc., Ltd., The British Crown Colony of Hong Kong.

Contents

INTRODUCTION TO THE 1979 EDITION
INTRODUCTION
SYSTEMATIC INDEX...........................xi
PARRAKEETS.................................1
APPENDIX..................................255
INDEX.....................................285
INDEX OF UPDATED NOMENCLATURE.......296

INTRODUCTION TO THE 1979 EDITION

David Seth-Smith's book, originally published as **PARRAKEETS, A HANDBOOK TO THE IMPORTED SPECIES**, in 1926, was a best-seller in its time. It quickly went out of print in the 1920's and has languished all these years because of the Great Depression of the 1930's and the wars of the 1940's. After these unnatural catastrophes, conservationists and alarmists cried for the ban on the importation of parrots from all over the world, thus the 1950's, 1960's and most of the 1970's were bad years for the parrot lover. But it soon became apparent that birds were being depleted in Nature by man's "civilizing" activities and encroachment upon the limited ranges of many parrots ... and the collectors of birds had little impact upon natural bird populations.

During the course of aviculturists' enchantment with parrots, many species were bred. Zoological gardens and public aviaries became the depository for many species and varieties which either never existed in Nature or were eventually declared as "Endangered Species."

The English had an especial fondness for parrots and many exotic introduction experiments were carried out with vast numbers of parrots being released into the British forest with hopes of their "taking." Unfortunately, the gentlemen hunters shot them down as fast as the bird lovers released them and nothing ever came of these noble experiments.

But the great experience of the aviculturists, coupled with unbridled enthusiasm and access to the huge British Empire (then!), enabled British experts to write books such as this one which have never been duplicated in terms of individual experiences with parrots in captivity.

The present edition of **PARRAKEETS** has had its name changed because American aviculturists often use the term "parrakeet" referring to the Australian Shell Parrakeet, *Melopsittacus undulatus*. There is really no special name for the group of birds properly called "parrakeets," so *"small parrots"* or *"dwarf parrots"* is the commonly used term.

The original Seth-Smith book contained 20 full colored lithographs which have been reproduced in the original size in this volume. An additional 12 full color photographic plates of popular parrots have been added to the 1979 edition.

In addition, a separate index showing both the common and taxonomic names by which the birds are identified in this volume and their *currently* accepted taxonomic and common names has been added.

Dr. Matthew M. Vriends.

INTRODUCTION.

THERE is no definite distinction between a "Parrot" and a "Parrakeet," the latter word being purely a popular term used for the smaller Parrots. It cannot be applied to any particular family, or subfamily, nor to those species with long or short tails. The gigantic Macaws are never called Parrakeets, but they are closely related to the Conures and possess the long tails that one generally associates with Parrakeets. The title of this work must, therefore, be interpreted in the sense in which it is generally used by aviculturists—that is, to mean the smaller Parrots, whether they possess short tails or long, whether they have ordinary or filamented tongues.

It has been the aim of the author to make the present book a complete monograph of the imported species of Parrakeets; and it is hoped that the information contained in its pages may be regarded as perfectly reliable. A few species have been included which probably have never reached this country alive, but which it has been thought well to mention in case they should be brought over. It is, however, impossible to obtain exact information as to what species have been imported and what have not, as extremely rare birds are occasionally brought home by travellers without any record being published. Moreover, one never knows what may turn up in the way of rare birds.

The classification adopted in the following pages is that of Dr. Sharpe's *Hand List of Birds,* which has been found most useful in the preparation of this volume. Count Salvadori's volume on the Parrots, in the *Catalogue of Birds in the British Museum*, has also been constantly used for reference, especially in the descriptions of the species. Besides these, Gould's *Handbook* and magnificent folio volumes on the *Birds of Australia*, Mr. A. J. Campbell's *Nests and Eggs of Australian Birds*, Dr. Mivart's *Monograph of the Loriidæ*, *The Avicultural Magazine*, &c., have been frequently referred to. The author is most grateful to several kind friends who have supplied him with information on Parrakeets in their possession.

Three of the plates in the present work have previously appeared in the *Avicultural Magazine,* and some explanation of this fact is desirable. The coloured engraving of *Trichoglossus ornatus,* was first published in the above-mentioned journal in March, 1897; and as the block was available it was borrowed for the present work, and the author is indebted to the Avicultural Society for its loan. The original drawing of *Platycercus browni* was made at the present writer's expense, but permission was given to the Society to reproduce it first in their journal, which they did in August, 1902. The plate of *Ptilosclera versicolor* was produced at the joint expense of the above-mentioned Society and the writer of this book, and it appeared first in the *Avicultural Magazine* for July, 1903.

The main part of the present volume was first published in 1902 and 1903, but it has been brought up-to-date (1926) by the addition to the Appendix of some 24 pages, which commence on page 261, with an account of the Solitary Lorikeet.

For very many years Parrakeets have been among the most popular of foreign birds, and it has been the great aim of aviculturists to induce the rarer species to breed and rear their young in aviaries, and many species have been bred successfully, though only one may be said to have become so firmly established in Europe as to make further importations unnecessary.

The Australian Budgerigar (*Melopsittacus undulatus*) has proved itself so well adapted to a captive life that it is now bred annually in thousands, and if it should ever become extinct in its native country, it is not likely to cease to be a favourite aviary and cage bird in Europe, either in its normal green dress, or the blue, yellow or other hues in which it now appears. But there would seem to be no reason why other species should not be established in this country if only aviculturists would combine together to not only encourage the breeding of a species but, by exchanging specimens for a change of blood, to keep the species going without the necessity of further importations. Some half-century ago the Turquoisine (*Neophema pulchella*) was a comparatively common aviary bird, which bred freely in captivity, and the stock might have been kept up until to-day if only it had been treasured with as much care as some prize breeds of dogs are at the present time. Instead of this being the case, the bird is practically extinct as an aviary bird and very scarce in its native country.

Regarding the keeping and breeding of Parrakeets in captivity, it may be stated as a general rule that each pair of birds should occupy a compartment of an aviary to themselves. They will sometimes agree with birds belonging to a different class to themselves, such as doves, finches or quails, but rarely with other species of Parrakeets. The exceptions to this rule that occur to one are perhaps the Cockatiel, which may safely be kept with Budgerigars, and the Budgerigar, which, being naturally a gregarious species, does best when several pairs are kept in the same aviary.

The type of aviary most favoured for Parrakeets consists of a covered portion or shed, built of brick or double boarding of some ten feet square and about the same height, well lighted and communicating with an outside flight of not less but preferably greater dimensions, though the height need not be more than eight feet. Strong half-inch mesh wire netting should be used and the flight laid down with turf, which must be renewed annually, while for perches natural branches are best.

The Marquis of Tavistock, who has for some years been very successful in keeping and breeding the rarer species of Parrakeets, is strongly in favour of movable aviaries which can be shifted bodily, by the help of rollers, on to fresh ground each year. These aviaries are about 24 feet long, 8 feet high, and 8 feet wide, each aviary being intended for one pair of Parrakeets only. The whole structure, including the floor, is covered with $\frac{1}{2}$-inch mesh wire netting, and where the larger Parrakeets are kept there is an inner lining of one-inch mesh netting of stout gauge. Grass soon grows through the netting that is on the ground. The bottom frame of the structure is made specially strong to stand the strain of lifting the aviary on to rollers for moving when necessary. A shelter-shed, about three feet wide, is formed at one end of the aviary, the end being completely boarded and lighted by means of small windows protected with wire netting, and the floor of the shelter provided with three sliding zinc trays filled with sand. The roof of the shelter is covered with felt, over which is corrugated iron.

A feeding door is provided at the back of the shelter, and near to this is a zinc-lined box communicating with the shelter and made of a sufficient size to contain, when necessary, three good-sized brooder lamps for warming purposes. One lamp is enough to prevent the temperature falling below freezing point except in exceptionally cold weather, while two maintain a comfortable warmth, and three can be used if the weather is very severe.

Lord Tavistock claims for these aviaries much greater fertility and stamina in his birds. He says that practically every hen goes to nest that might be reasonably expected to do so, and the young birds are never deformed. Ring-necked Parrakeets bred in these aviaries come into breeding condition when ten months old and nest when two years old, although the cocks are still in immature plumage.

The great advantage of such aviaries is that they can be moved on to fresh ground at least once a year, but it is obvious that the site must be a very level one, otherwise the moving of such bulky structures would be extremely difficult, and it may be suggested to those who wish to follow Lord Tavistock's practice of moving his birds on to fresh ground each year, but who cannot manage the moving of these large aviaries, that they should have their aviaries built in sections, which could be fastened together by means of iron bolts. These could then be taken apart, section by section, and re-erected on a new site with far less labour than would be involved by the moving of such aviaries as above described.

The aviculturist who wishes to induce his Parrakeets to lay and rear their young in his aviaries is often at a loss to know the best type of nesting box to provide, and it is a fact that some species are very particular in the choice of a site for a nursery. Some birds prefer a horizontal type of nesting box, such as is described on page 23, but perhaps a still better type is the vertical one, made of one-inch board, some sixteen inches high by nine inches square (outside measurements). The bottom of this should be made of wood of some two to three inches in thickness and hollowed out like a saucer so as to avoid the possibility of the eggs rolling to one side and getting chilled. A small handful of sawdust placed in the depression forms all the nesting material required. The entrance-hole should be near the top, and of two inches diameter, and a short perch should project from just below the entrance-hole, on the outside. The top should be hinged to open, to allow of inspection. In order to allow the young birds to climb out of the nest when they are old enough, it is advisable to fasten a piece of wire netting on the inside of the nesting-box, below the entrance-hole. This should be stapled closely against the side of the box, where it will form, as it were, a ladder.

Some species, such as Kings and Crimson-wings, require a very deep nesting-box, and a distance from the entrance-hole to the bottom of some four to five feet is none too great. But with these deep boxes the provision of some form of " ladder " inside is essential, and wire netting fastened to the inside of all four sides answers the purpose. The size of the entrance-hole must be judged by the size of the bird, and for Kings, three inches would be about correct. In these deep boxes an inspection door should be provided near the bottom of the box.

D. SETH-SMITH.

SYSTEMATIC INDEX.

	PAGE
Family Loriidæ	1
Genus Calliptilus, Sunder	261
1. *solilarius* (Lath.)	261
Genus Trichoglossus, Vig. and Horsf.	4
2. *hæmatodes* (Linn.)	4
3. *forsteni*, Bp.	4
4. *cyanogrammus*, Wagl.	5
5. *nigrigularis* (Gray)	263
6. *mitchelli* (Gray)	6
7. *novæ-hollandiæ* (Gm.)	6
8. *rubritorques*, Vig. and Horsf.	10
9. *rosenbergi*, Schl.	264
10. *ornatus* (Linn.)	11
11. *johnstoniæ*, Hartert	262
Genus Psitteuteles, Bp.	13
12. *euteles* (Temm.)	13
13. *weberi*, Buttikofer	264
14. *chlorolepidotus* (Kuhl.)	14
Genus Ptilosclera, Bp.	255
15. *versicolor* (Vig.)	255
Genus Glossopsittacus, Bp.	16
16. *concinnus* (Shaw)	17
17. *porphyrocephalus* (Dietr.)	265
18. *pusillus* (Shaw)	265
Genus Charmosyna, Wagl.	265
19. *stellæ*, A. B. Meyer	265
Genus Hypocharmosyna, Salvad	266
20. *wilhelminæ* (A. B. Meyer)	266
21. *placens* (Temm.)	266
Genus Charmosynopsis, Salvad	266
22. *pulchella* (Gray)	266
Family Cacatuidæ	20

Systematic Index

	PAGE
Subfamily Calopsittacinæ	20
Genus Calopsittacus	20
23. *novæ-hollandiæ* (Gm.)	20
Family Psittacidæ	25
Subfamily Nasiterninæ	25
Genus Nasiterna, Wagl.	25
Subfamily Conurinæ	26
Genus Conurus, Kuhl.	28
24. *acuticaudatus* (Vieill.)	28
25. *hæmorrhous* (Spix)	28
26. *guarouba* (Gm.)	30
27. *solstitialis* (Linn.)	32
28. *jendaya* (Gm.)	33
29. *auricapillus* (Kuhl.)	35
30. *nenday* (Vieill.)	36
31. *weddelli*, Deville	266
32. *whitleyi*, Kinnear	267
33. *rubrolarvatus*, Mass. and Souancé	37, 267
34. *wagleri*, Gray	38
35. *leucophthalmus* (P.L.S. Müll.)	39
36. *holochlorus*, Scl.	39
37. *rubritorques*, Scl.	40
38. *aztec* (Souancé)	41
39. *cactorum* (Kuhl.)	41
40. *æruginosus* (Linn.)	44
41. *pertinax* (Linn.)	46
42. *aureus* (Gm.)	47
43. *canicularis* (Linn.)	48
Genus Conuropsis	48
44. *carolinensis* (Linn.)	48
Genus Cyanolyseus, Bp.	53
45. *patagonicus* (Vieill.)	53
46. *byroni* (Childr.)	57
Genus Henicognathus, Gray	57
47. *leptorhynchus* (King)	57
Genus Microsittace, Bp.	58
48. *ferruginea*, (P.L.S. Müll.)	58
Genus Pyrrhura, Bp.	59
49. *cruentata* (Neuwied)	59
50. *vittata* (Shaw)	60, 258
51. *chiripepe* (Vieill.)	269
52. *leucotis* (Kuhl.)	61

Systematic Index

	PAGE
Genus Pyrrhura—*continued.*	
53. *picta* (P.L.S. Müll.)	62
54. *perlata* (Spix)	62
Genus Myopsittacus, Bp.	63
55. *monachus* (Bodd)	63
Genus Bolborhynchus, Bp.	71
56. *lineolatus* (Cass.)	71, 258
Genus Psittacula, Ill.	72
57. *cœlestis* (Less.)	72, 270
58. *passerina* (Linn.)	73
59. *guianensis* (Sw.)	269
60. *cyanopygia*, Bp.	270
Genus Brotogerys, Vig.	77
61. *tirica* (Gm.)	79
62. *chiriri* (Vieill.)	79
63. *virescens* (Gm.)	80
64. *pyrrhopterus* (Lath.)	81
65. *jugularis* (P.L.S. Müll.)	82
66. *tuipara* (Gm.)	83
67. *chrysopterus* (Linn.)	85
68. *tui* (Gm.)	85
Subfamily Palæornithinæ	90
Genus Geoffroyus, Bp.	270
69. *aruensis* (Gray)	270
Genus Tanygnathus, Wagl.	90
70. *luzonensis* (Linn.)	91
71. *megalorhynchus* (Bodd.)	91
72. *muelleri* (Temm.)	93
73. *everetti*, Tweed	271
Genus Palæornis, Vig.	93
74. *eupatria* (Linn.)	96
75. *nepalensis* (Hodgs.)	98
76. *indoburmanica*, Hume	99
77. *magnirostris*, Ball	100
78. *eques* (Bodd.)	100
79. *torquata* (Bodd.)	101
80. *docilis* (Vieill.)	104
81. *cyanocephala* (Linn.)	104
82. *rosa* (Bodd.)	106
83. *schisticeps*, Hodgs.	107
84. *finschi*, Hume	109
85. *peristerodes*, Finsch.	109

Systematic Index

Genus Palæornis—*continued*.

	PAGE
86. *calthropæ*, Blyth	271
87. *derbyana*, Fraser	111, 273
88. *fasciata* (P.L.S. Müll.)	112
89. *alexandri* (Linn.)	114
90. *caniceps* (Blyth)	115
91. *modesta*, Fraser	116
92. *nicobarica*, Gould	117
93. *tytleri*, Hume	119
94. *longicauda* (Bodd.)	120

Genus Polytelis, Wagl. .. 121

| 95. *barrabandi* (Swains.) | 121 |
| 96. *melanura* (Vig.) | 123, 258 |

Genus Spathopterus, North .. 124

| 97. *alexandræ* (Gould) | 125 |

Genus Ptistes, Gould .. 129

| 98. *erythropterus* (Gm.) | 129 |

Genus Aprosmictus, Gould .. 131

99. *cyanopygius* (Vieill.)	132
100. *chloropterus*, Ramsay	273
101. *amboinensis* (Linn.)	274
102. *sulaensis*, Reichen.	274

Genus Pyrrhulopsis, Reichenb. .. 134

103. *splendens* (Peale)	135
104. *tabuensis* (Gm.)	136
105. *taviunensis*, Layard	274
106. *personata* (Gray)	136

Genus Psittinus .. 138

| 107. *incertus* (Shaw) | 138 |

Genus Agapornis, Selby .. 139

108. *cana* (Gm.)	141
109. *taranta* (Stanley)	275
110. *pullaria* (Linn.)	143
111. *fischeri*, Reichen.	276
112. *lilianæ*, Shelley	277
113. *nigrigenis*, W. L. Sclater	279
114. *personata*, Reichen.	280
115. *roseicollis* (Vieill.)	145

Genus Loriculus, Blyth .. 150

116. *vernalis* (Sparrm.)	151
117. *chrysonotus*, Scl.	153
118. *indicus* (Gm.)	154

Systematic Index

Genus Loriculus—*continued.*
119. *galgulus* (Linn.) 155
120. *sclateri*, Wall. 157
Subfamily Platycercinæ 157
Genus Platycercus, Vig. 158
  121. *mastersianus*, Ramsay 158, 258
  122. *elegans* (Gm.) 159
  123. *adelaidæ*, Gould 162
  124. *flaveolus*, Gould 163, 259
  125. *flaviventris* (Temm.) 164
  126. *pallidiceps*, Vig. 165
  127. *amathusia*, Bp. 168
  128. *browni* (Temm.) 168
  129. *erythropeplus*, Salvad. 170, 259
  130. *eximius* (Shaw) 172
  131. *splendidus*, Gould 177
  132. *icterotis* (Kuhl) 178
Genus Porphyrocephalus, Reichenow 179
  133. *spurius* (Kuhl) 179
Genus Barnardius, Bp. 183
  134. *barnardi* (Vig. and Horsf.) 183, 260
  135. *semitorquatus* (Q. and G.) 187
  136. *zonarius* (Shaw) 189
Genus Psephotus, Gould 191
  137. *hæmatorrhous*, Bp. 191
  138. *xanthorrhous*, Bp. 193
  139. *pulcherrimus* (Gould) 197
  140. *chrysopterygius*, Gould 202, 281
  141. *dissimilis*, Collett 206, 281
  142. *multicolor* (Kuhl) 206, 260
  143. *hæmatonotus*, Gould 211
Genus Neophema, Salvad. 214
  144. *bourkei* (Mitch.) 214
  145. *venusta* (Temm.) 216
  146. *elegans* (Gould) 219
  147. *chrysogastra* (Lath.) 221
  148. *petrophila* (Gould) 222
  149. *pulchella* (Shaw) 223
  150. *splendida* (Gould) 226
Genus Cyanorhamphus, Bp. 227
  151. *unicolor*, Vig. 227
  152. *novæ-zealandiæ* (Sparrm.) 229

Systematic Index

Genus Cyanorhamphus—*continued.*

153. *cooki*, Gray	284
154. *saisseti*, Verr. and Des Murs	234
155. *auriceps* (Kuhl)	234
156. *malherbei*, Souancé	239
Genus Nymphicus, Wagl.	240
157. *cornutus* (Gm.)	240
158. *uvæensis*, Layard	241
Genus Nanodes, Vig. and Horsf.	242
159. *discolor* (Shaw)	242
Genus Melopsittacus, Gould	244
160. *undulatus* (Shaw)	244, 284
Genus Pezoporus, Illig.	249
161. *terrestris* (Shaw)	249
Genus Geopsittacus, Gould	252
162. *occidentalis*, Gould	252

PARRAKEETS

Family LORIIDÆ.

LORIKEETS.

PARROTS are amongst the most brilliantly coloured of feathered creatures, and the *Loriidæ*, or Brush-tongued Parrots, are some of the most gorgeous of the tribe. It is only proposed to deal here with the Sharp-tailed Lories, popularly known as Lorikeets; which bear the same relationship to the Broad-tailed, or true Lories, as do the Parrakeets proper to the true Parrots.

Lorikeets are some of the most lively and engaging of birds, and, when suitably treated in captivity, make most delightful and interesting aviary occupants. They are not so well adapted for cage culture; for, being exceedingly restless and active birds, their plumage very soon becomes rubbed and broken if kept in too small an abode; and, moreover, being soft-food eaters, they are, in consequence, decidedly dirty birds, and a small cage becomes objectionable in a very short time. In an aviary they are charming birds, always on the move, performing the quaintest of antics amongst the branches, wrestling and playing with one another like so many gorgeously-attired acrobats.

It is unwise to trust Lorikeets in an aviary with

other birds, especially other kinds of Parrakeets, as they are inclined to be spiteful and treacherous, so that a pair should always have a compartment to themselves.

In a wild state the Lorikeets are strictly arboreal, feeding upon the nectar and pollen of flowering trees, especially the different species of *Eucalyptus*, various fruits and unripe seeds. In captivity they will often live upon a diet of seed for a time, but this treatment invariably results in death from fits sooner or later. The food most suitable for Lorikeets in captivity is, unquestionably, milk-sop (slightly sweetened), ripe fruit and seed (canary, hemp and millet), although very little of the latter is eaten.

Many aviculturists have proved this treatment to be the only successful one for the Brush-tongued Parrakeets; so fed, they are long lived, and always in the brightest of plumage. This is the treatment adopted at the Zoological Gardens, where Lorikeets generally do remarkably well, often surviving for a number of years, albeit their cages are painfully small for such active birds.

I must not omit to say that the milk-sop for Lorikeets must always be made with *boiling* milk, poured on to either crumb of bread or plain biscuit, and slightly sweetened with sugar. Needless to add, this must be given fresh daily, as well as such fruit as soft apple, pear, grapes or banana. Sweetened, stewed apple has been recommended for these birds, but I have never tried this food, though I should have no hesitation in doing so.

It is strange that bird-dealers should almost invariably advise a diet of seed only for Lorikeets; possibly they imagine that all of the parrot tribe require the same treatment; or if they have ever tried milk-sop as the staple food, this has probably not been made with *boiled* milk, and has, naturally, turned sour, with the inevitable result.

Like other Parrots the Brush-tongues breed in holes, generally high up in hollow branches or trunks of trees, the decayed wood being gnawed away until the shape of the hollow is to the birds' liking. The number of eggs laid to a clutch seems to vary with the species, some laying but one, others two to four; probably the latter number is the most usual.

One or two species have bred successfully in captivity, though such an event is rare. Curiously enough the males seem ready and anxious enough to breed, but for some unknown reason, possibly from our climate being too cool, the females rarely appear to be in breeding condition, and eggs are seldom laid. However, if suitably located, in an outdoor aviary, with more or less natural nesting sites, and, providing the summer should be a warm one, there would seem to be no reason why these engaging and lovely birds should not reproduce their kind.

Many of the Lorikeets are, when once established in captivity, comparatively hardy birds if properly treated, and may, with perfect safety, be put out-of-doors for the summer months. They are fond of bathing, and should have access to water for this purpose.

The sexes are, so far as I am aware, alike in plumage in all of the Lories, but, in most cases at least, the females are slightly less in size than the males, and possess a smaller and more effeminate-looking head.

Genus TRICHOGLOSSUS, Vig. and Horsf.

THE BLUE-FACED LORIKEET.

Trichoglossus hæmatodes (Linn.).

This Lorikeet is about the same size as, and in many respects closely resembles, the well-known Swainson's Lorikeet (hereafter described). It is, however, readily distinguished from that species by the lesser amount of blue on the head, and by the absence of red on the breast, which is entirely yellow. The abdomen also differs in being green instead of blue.

This species is very rare in this country, but has been occasionally represented at the Zoological Gardens, where a fine specimen is now (May, 1902) on view.

T. hæmatodes has its habitat in the Island of Timor.

FORSTEN'S LORIKEET.

Trichoglossus forsteni, Bp.

The influx of Forsten's Lorikeet to the bird-market within the last few years is somewhat remarkable, seeing that ten years ago, or less, there was not a single specimen in the National Collection, Count Salvadori's description in the "Catalogue" being taken from a specimen in the Rothschild Museum at Tring. The Zoological Society received their first specimen in 1896, in which year the species became almost as common in the bird-market as Swainson's Lorikeet. The first examples I ever saw were exhibited at the Crystal Palace Bird-show in February of that year, when they caused quite a sensation, being "something

quite new." In the Calcutta Bird-Market, Mr. Frank Finn tells us that since 1894 this has been quite the most commonly imported Lory, and has bred in the Calcutta Zoological Gardens. (*cf. Ibis*, 1901, p. 439).
The following is a description of *T. forsteni*. Head purple-brown, slightly tinged with blue on the front and lores, and faintly tinged with green on the crown; back, wings, and tail green; a band of greenish-yellow on the nape; the feathers of the upper back edged with purple-brown, and with more or less concealed red spots; breast bright red; throat and a patch on the abdomen dark purple; vent, under tail-coverts and flanks yellow, the feathers being broadly tipped with green; under wing-coverts red.

This species is about 10 inches in length. It inhabits the island of Sumbawa.

Illustration from living specimen in the Zoological Society's Gardens.

THE GREEN-NAPED LORIKEET.

Trichoglossus cyanogrammus, Wagl.
Coloured figure, MIVART'S *Loriidæ*, Pl. XXX.

I am not aware of this species ever having appeared in the open English bird-market, but it has been exhibited at the Zoological Gardens. It inhabits the Amboyna group of islands and Western New Guinea. The forehead and chin are blue; top of head greenish; occiput, ear-coverts, and throat purple-black; a band on the nape is yellowish-green, the feathers of this band having a concealed red central band; the back, wings, and tail green, the feathers of the upper back having more or less concealed red markings on them; throat and breast bright red, each feather being edged with dark purple : a patch on the abdomen green ; under tail-coverts and flanks yellow, splashed with green. Length about 11 inches.

"In various parts of its wide habitat," writes Dr. Mivart, "it is very common. It frequents (we learn from Salvadori) the smaller branches of coppices and the tops of low trees, and nourishes itself on *casuarina* seeds, fruit and nectar. It is a quarrelsome and noisy bird."

MITCHELL'S LORIKEET.

(*Trichoglossus mitchelli*, Gray).

Coloured figure, MIVART'S *Loriidæ*, Pl. XXXIII.

This species need only be briefly mentioned here, as it is hardly likely to be met with by aviculturists. Two specimens have lived in the London Zoological Society's collection, and another in the Amsterdam Zoological Gardens, but these appear to be almost, if not quite, the only known examples of the species, the habitat of which is uncertain.

The back, wings and tail are green ; head brownish-purple, tinged with blue on the front and lores ; nape yellowish-green ; breast bright red, the feathers faintly edged with green ; abdomen green, tinged with dark purplish-brown. Total length 9 inches.

SWAINSON'S LORIKEET.

Trichoglossus novæ-hollandiæ (Gm.).

Coloured figure, MIVART'S *Loriidæ*, Pl. XXXV.

This species, popularly termed the "Blue-mountain Lory," is by far the best known of the *Trichoglossi*, and is often imported in considerable numbers.

The back, tail and wings are green; the head dark blue, there being also a patch of this colour on the abdomen. The breast is yellow, suffused with red. In some old specimens the red colour spreads over nearly the entire breast, except the sides, which are yellow, although many of the feathers are slightly edged with red. Where the breast-feathers approach the abdomen they are often edged with blue. Flanks red and yellow, edged with green, and merging into green on the thighs. Under tail-coverts red, yellow and green; under wing-coverts red. There is a greenish-yellow band on the nape. The bill is red, shading off to yellow at the tip. Some specimens show a number of red and yellow markings on the upper back, whereas in others very few or none appear.

I know of no positive method of determining the sex of Swainson's Lorikeet, except from the fact that the male is generally slightly larger than the female, and this, I think, applies to all of the Lories. The plumage varies considerably in different individuals, some possessing far more red on the breast than others; but this I believe to be entirely due to age, the breast feathers becoming redder every year. Length about 12 inches.

"The flowers of the various species of *Eucalypti*," Gould informs us, "furnish this bird with an abundant supply of food, and so exclusively is it confined to the forests composed of those trees, that I do not recollect to have met with it in any other." Mr. Campbell writes of this species: "As a flock of these splendid Lorikeets wheel simultaneously in mid-air, the flashing splendour of the deep crimson under the surface of the wings, intensified by the light of a slanting sun, is a sight to be remembered. But there are other sights. During February, 1896, thousands of these grand Lorikeets visited a vineyard about four acres in extent, near Marchison, on the Goulburn River, and feasted for three days on grapes. They remained in one vineyard, although others were near. The unduly favoured vigneron was so exasperated, not only at the depre-

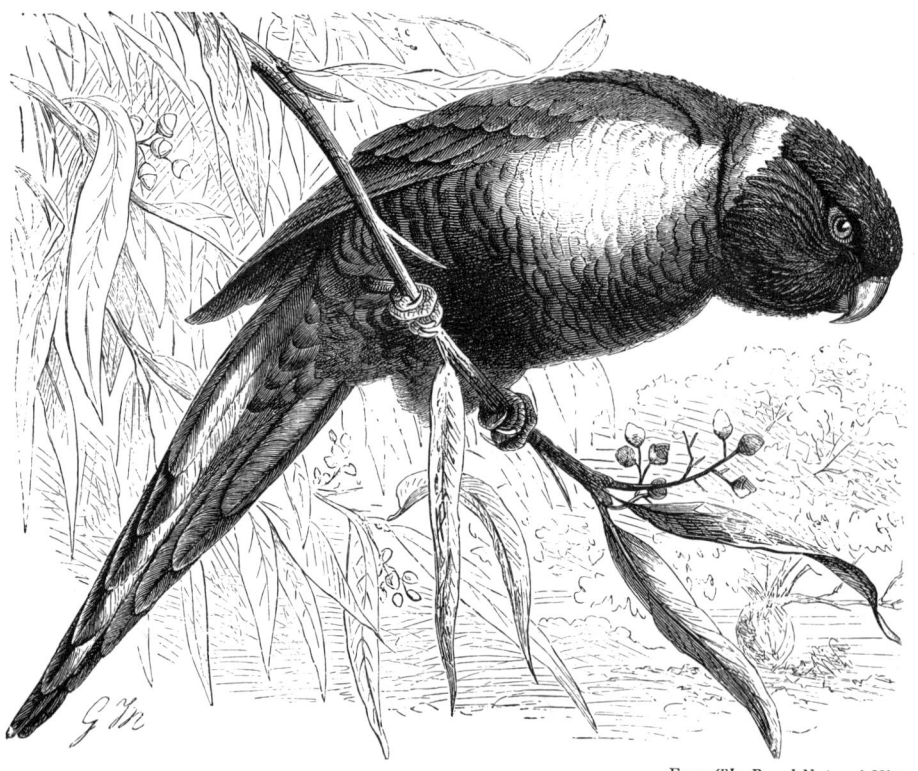

From *The Royal Natural Hist*

SWAINSON'S LORIKEET, *Trichoglossus novæ-hollandiæ*.

dations committed, but with the terrible din of the multitudes of harsh, screeching voices, that in one day he shot no less than seventy birds."

The late Dr. Russ mentions two or three cases in which this species has bred in Germany, and Dr. Greene states that "these birds have frequently bred in confinement, sometimes in a hollow log, like the rest of the Parrot race (with one certain and a few doubtful exceptions), and sometimes on the ground, behind a brick or a piece of board." I have, however, been able to find but one record of young having been reared by Swainson's Lorikeet, in this country. In *Notes on Cage Birds* (second series) a correspondent, who signs himself "Cheshire," writes: "I think it may interest a few readers of "Bird Notes" to know that a pair of Blue-mountain Lories reared two young in a small aviary (probably 5 feet square) in the Aquarium at Blackpool. The hen laid two eggs on some old sods on the floor of the cage, and I went nearly every day to see if she were sitting well. As the place began to be very crowded, being the height of the season, a large stone was placed before her to prevent her being disturbed. I left a few days after they were hatched, but managed to get a peep at them when the hen was off once. I heard a few weeks after of their being alive and well, but do not know anything further."

A pair owned by the writer frequently paired, and the hen often spent the greater part of the day in her nest-box, but no eggs were laid.

The voice of this species is, at times, exceedingly harsh and unpleasant, and if caged in a small room, would be almost unbearable; in an outdoor aviary, however, it seldom indulges in unpleasant noises, especially if kept in pairs. It is not safe to keep any of the Lorikeets with other Parrakeets, although they are often harmless towards small birds.

Swainson's Lorikeet is a native of Eastern Australia.

THE RED-COLLARED LORIKEET.

Trichoglossus rubritorques, Vig. and Horsf.

This is another very uncommon Lorikeet in this country, and beautiful as it is rare. It inhabits the northern parts of Australia, where it takes the place of its congener, *T. novæ-hollandiæ*, of the more easterly parts. In their habits the two species seem to be identical. Gilbert, quoted by Gould, remarks that "this species is abundant in all parts of the Cobourg Peninsula and the adjacent islands, and is an especial favourite with the natives, who carefully preserve the heads of all they kill, for the purpose of ornamenting their persons by slinging them to the arm a little above the elbow. It is generally seen in large flocks, feeding on the summits of the loftiest trees. Its flight is rapid in the extreme. Like the other *Trichoglossi*, its food consists of honey and the buds of flowers."

The Red-collared Lorikeet may readily be distinguished from Swainson's by the brighter blue of its head, the orange-red band on the nape, and by the breast being orange instead of yellow and red, and the abdomen dark green instead of blue.

The following is a complete description of this fine Lorikeet :—

Whole of head bright blue; the breast and a band on the nape reddish-orange; below this band comes another band of blue; under wing-coverts and sides vermilion; a patch on the abdomen dark-green; flanks yellow, splashed with green; under tail-coverts yellow and green; back, wings and tail green; the feathers of the upper back more or less marked with orange-red; bill red. Total length about 12 inches.

Illustration from living specimen in the Zoological Society's Gardens.

THE ORNATE LORIKEET.

Trichoglossus ornatus (Linn.).

This is perhaps the most wonderfully coloured of the *Trichoglossi*, gorgeously as each and every member of that genus is arrayed. This splendid species is not very frequently imported, but it now and then arrives in some numbers, and is at times sold at a reasonable figure. A great many were imported in 1895, and for some time after they were common in the bird-market, but at the present time (March, 1902), it is a scarce species in this country. Dr. Meyer, quoted by Dr. St. George Mivart, writes of this Lorikeet: " I got it at all times and everywhere in the Minahassa, from January till July ; at the end of March, 1871, it suddenly appeared in large flocks near Limbotto ; near Gorontalo in September ; on the Togian Islands in August ; and in South Celebes in October and November. They live in flocks and fly very quickly, with much noise and quick strokes of the wings ; they have a short and shrill cry, and do not sit quiet a long time at one spot, but climb all over the tree. At midday, in the heat, they sit in flocks in the shadow of the leaves, chattering and scratching each other's heads. In cool weather they are on the wing nearly the whole day."

Dr. C. S. Simpson wrote of a pair of Ornate Lorikeets in his possession, which were kept in an indoor aviary :[1]—" On the approach of spring, the male bird's attentions to his lady became marked and demonstrative ; he constantly drove her about the aviary and for a time she would fly from him, then relenting, would rest tranquilly on a bough, while he

---

[1] *Avicultural Magazine*, vol. iii., p. 83.

performed the most grotesque antics, which she, doubtless, thought charming. His love-making consisted of a peculiar dance, or rather a series of jerky movements of the head and body, puffing out his body feathers, putting out his tongue, and uttering various clucking and hissing noises. During the time of courtship he would never, if he could prevent it, allow the hen to feed herself. Whenever she tried to reach the food-vessels, he drove her away, and after helping himself, called her to him and fed her with regurgitated food. I watched them closely, and I believe for days together the hen received nothing but what the cock gave her; but as she remained plump and well, there seemed no reason for interference.

"When I thought the pair ready to nest, I provided them with a small barrel artistically covered with bark, hung rather high and secluded by surrounding branches. They at once set to work on this, pulled off every atom of bark, and bit every twig off the surrounding boughs. They took possession of the barrel and spent much of their time scuffling about inside it; the hen always spent the night in it, the cock usually roosting on the top, or in the entrance-hole.

"To my great disappointment, they never got any further than this; both birds were in splendid health and condition, they paired, and during the whole of the summer appeared to be on the point of nesting, but no eggs were laid, and on the approach of autumn their manifestations of affection became less demonstrative, though they still appeared greatly attached to each other."

The following is a description of the adult:—

Nape, back, tail, wings and abdomen green; top of head and ear-coverts purplish-blue; a band of red, with transverse lines of bluish-black, on the occiput; a yellow band from the occiput downwards on each side of the neck; throat, cheeks and breast bright red, the breast-feathers being barred with bluish-black; flanks greenish-yellow, barred with yellow; under tail-coverts greenish-yellow; quills blackish on the inner web. Total length nearly 9 inches.

The Ornate Lorikeet inhabits Celebes, Buton and the Togian Islands.

Genus PSITTEUTELES, Bp.

The members of this genus only differ from the *Trichoglossi* in colour, being almost entirely green or greenish-yellow.

THE PERFECT LORIKEET.

Psitteuteles euteles (Temm.).

A pair of this beautiful little Lorikeet were deposited in the Zoological Society's collection in 1896, where they still live (May, 1902) in the most perfect health and condition, which speaks well for the treatment they receive. They have been from the time of their arrival beautifully tame, and will upon one's approach, come at once to the side of their cage and gently nibble at one's finger, without the slightest fear. They play with one another, often while hanging by their feet from the roof of their cage, and hiss and chatter to each other in precisely the same way as do the *Trichoglossi*.

This species is *very* seldom imported alive, in fact, I think the charming couple now on view at the

Zoological Gardens is the first pair ever exhibited alive in this country; but let us hope it will not for long be such a rarity, for it seems to be quite the nicest of imported Lorikeets, though comparatively soberly clad; and one cannot help feeling that the pair above referred to are wasted in their small cage in the Parrot house. In a large aviary they would be perfectly charming.

The prevailing colour of this species is green-yellowish on the under parts; the head yellowish-olive; bill yellow. Total length about $10\frac{1}{2}$ inches.

The Perfect Lorikeet is found in the islands of Timor, Flores, Wetter, Lettie, Babbar and Timorlaut. Specimens from Flores, Count Salvadori informs us, are darker than those from the other islands.

Illustration from living specimen in the Zoological Society's Gardens.

THE SCALY-BREASTED LORIKEET.

Psitteuteles chlorolepidotus (Kuhl.).

Coloured figure, MIVART'S *Loriidæ*, Pl. XLIII.

This species, although not very commonly imported, is fairly well known amongst English aviculturists. It is 10 inches in total length; of a bright grass-green above, and yellow below, the yellow breast-feathers being margined with green. Some of the feathers of the upper back are also yellow, margined with green. A few of the feathers of the throat and sides tinged with red; under wing-coverts red; bill red.

"To give any detailed account of its habits and mode of life," writes Gould, "would be merely repeating what I have said respecting the *Trichoglossus multicolor* [Swainson's Lorikeet], with which it frequently associates and even feeds on the same branch; it is, however, not so numerous as that species, nor so generally distributed over the face of the country. The brushes near the coast, studded here and there with enormous gums, towering high above every other tree by which they are surrounded, are the localities especially resorted to by it.

" Its principal food is honey, gathered from the cups of the newly expanded blossoms of the *Eucalypti*, upon which it feeds to such an excess, that on suspending a fresh-shot specimen by the toes, a large teaspoonful of liquid honey will flow from the mouth. A proper attention to the diet of these birds, by supplying them with food of a saccharine character, would doubtless enable us to keep them as denizens of our cages and aviaries, as well as the other members of the family."

" At Coomooboolaroo," writes Mr. Campbell, "this Lorikeet lays a single egg, sometimes two. Out of nine nests found there, two only contained pairs, the rest having a single egg each."

In captivity this species seems to take more kindly to a diet of canary-seed than do most of the Lorikeets, but probably, examples fed entirely upon seed would not long remain free from fits, or would very soon lose the natural brightness of their plumage. They will certainly do better if treated as recommended in the chapter on Lorikeets in general, than if fed upon seed alone.

On page 170 of *Notes on Cage Birds* (published in 1899), a correspondent signing himself " H. J." records the successful breeding in captivity of this species in an unheated aviary during the winter. Unfortunately, neither the date of this interesting event, nor the name of the successful breeder, are recorded ; he writes :—" Readers will be interested to, know that I have now obtained perfectly fledged young birds of the Scaly-breasted Lorikeet. The hen began to sit about December 21. The nest is, or rather the nestlings are, in a cocoa-nut husk, in a perfectly detached and open unheated wooden erection, where the water has been frozen almost every night, and sometimes all day, during the severest cold weather." Further on the same writer proceeds :—" I would say that these rare birds, which I consider to be the most beautiful and charming of all aviary pets, have the run of the aviary food, including sopped bread (these are not soft-food eating birds, however), but their principal diet is canary-seed, of which they eat a great deal, in fact, they touch little else ; hemp seed is poison to them —except in the extreme of cold and wet weather it is sure to bring on fits. One youngster came out of the nest on February 26, the other on March 4."

This species ranges through the southern half of Queensland to South Australia and New South Wales.

Genus GLOSSOPSITTACUS, Bp.

The genus *Glossopsittacus* contains five species, inhabiting Australia, New Caledonia and New Guinea. Living specimens of but one of these, however, the Australian representative of the genus, appear to have been imported.

THE MUSKY LORIKEET.

Glossopsittacus concinnus (Shaw).

Although not brilliantly coloured like the *Trichoglossi*, this is a very beautiful species, and one of the most attractive of the Lorikeets. It is a common bird in the eastern parts of Australia and is at times imported to this country in some numbers, although until recently it was rarely to be had.

The prevailing colour is bright green, the head being ornamented with bright red patches on the ear-coverts, lores, and forehead. The top of the head is decidedly tinged with blue. The back is olive-brown, and the sides of the breast greenish-yellow.

Although the sexes are, practically, alike in plumage, the bluish tinge on the head is much more apparent in the male than in the female. It is slightly over $8\frac{1}{2}$ inches in length.

Of the wild life of this bird Gould writes:—
"Like every other species of Lorikeet, the present bird is always to be found upon the *Eucalypti*, whose blossoms afford it a never-failing supply of honey, one or other of the numerous species of that tribe of trees being in flower at all seasons of the year. . . . It is a noisy species, and with its screeching note keeps up a perpetual din around the trees in which it is located. During its search for honey it creeps among the leaves and smaller branches in the most extraordinary manner, hanging and clinging about them in every possible variety of position. It is so excessively tame that it is very difficult to drive it from the trees, or even from any particular branch. Although usually associated in flocks, it appears to be mated in pairs, which at all times keep together during flight, and settle side by

side when the heat of the sun prompts them to shelter themselves under the shade of the more redundantly-leaved branches.

"The eggs, which are dirty white and two in number, are of a rounded form, 1 inch in length and ⅞ of an inch in breadth. Those I obtained were taken from a hole in a large *Eucalyptus* growing on the Liverpool range." "These Lorikeets (Mr. A. J. Campbell writes) have also cultivated a taste for fruit. During the summer (February and March) of 1889, the Muskies were very troublesome in the apple orchards of South Brighton."

The Musky Lorikeet has the reputation of being very subject to fits in captivity. This is probably owing, however, to its proper treatment being imperfectly understood. Bird-dealers nearly always advise seed only, for this and all other Lorikeets, and on a seed-diet alone all are subject to fits sooner or later. If fed as I have recommended when treating of Lorikeets in general, the present species may be kept in health for several years. A fine male Musky Lorikeet, owned by my friend, Mr. Reginald Phillipps, lived in his aviary for over four years without the least ailment; it became, however, somewhat spiteful towards his other Parrakeets (a failing possessed by most male Lorikeets), and he very kindly presented the bird to me. It lived in my possession for another year, but suddenly commenced to ill-treat a Golden-fronted Parrakeet (*Brotogerys tuipara*) with which it was kept, so that I was obliged to part with it. Of this specimen Mr. Phillipps wrote as follows in the *Avicultural Magazine*:—"That this Lorikeet should have lived over four years in my possession is, I suppose, remarkable, for of all the Lorikeets the Musky has perhaps the worst record for fits. A lady, who was many years in Australia, told me that the

Colonists seldom attempt to keep it. One she herself had tried in Australia soon died in a fit. Even at the London Zoological Gardens (I am writing this without book, but I think correctly), where with some of the Lorikeets they have been very successful, they seem to be rather the reverse with this species, judging by the dates of receipt given from time to time in the Parrot house. I need hardly say that my Musky was not fed on seed, to which, indeed, he always had access, but which he never touched so far as I know."

I have never noticed the musky odour that this species, in common with several others of the family, is said to possess.

Illustration from living specimen in the Zoological Society's Gardens.

Family CACATUIDÆ.

Subfamily CALOPSITTACINÆ.

THE COCKATIEL.

Calopsittacus novæ-hollandiæ (Gm.).

Coloured figure, GREENE'S *Parrots in Captivity*, Vol. I.

This species is the sole representative of the subfamily which it occupies, and may be said to bear the same relationship to the Cockatoos, as do the true Parrakeets to the true Parrots.

So well is this Parrakeet known, even to the veriest tyro in aviculture, that a description seems almost unnecessary, but for the sake of the few of my readers who may not know it, I may state that the male is dark grey (some specimens being much darker than others) with bright yellow face, cheeks and crest, and brick-red ear-coverts.

The female is much paler and browner than the male, the face being only tinged with yellow. The underside of the tail is yellow, barred with dark grey. The Cockatiel is about $12\frac{1}{2}$ inches in length. The young, on leaving the nest, resemble the adult female. Gould found this species "breeding in all the apple-tree (*Angophora*) flats of the upper Hunter, as well as on all similar districts on the Peel, and other rivers, which flow to the north-west." " I have seen," he wrote, " the ground quite covered by them while engaged in procuring food, and it was not an unusual

From *The Royal Natural History.*

COCKATIEL (Male), *Calopsittacus novæ-hollandiæ.*

circumstance to see hundreds together on the dead branches of the gum-trees in the neighbourhood of water, a plentiful supply of which would appear to be essential to their existence."

Mr. H. W. Ford, F.G.S., quoted by Mr. A. J. Campbell, remarks that "the Grey and Yellow Top-knotted Parrot ('Quarrion,' native name among bushmen) flies round about water-holes for some time, then settles on a tree near the water. Another would fly round screeching all the time, and down to the edge of the water, take one gulp and off as if all the hawks in creation were after it, screeching all the time."

With the exception of the Budgerigar (*Melopsittacus undulatus*), the Cockatiel is by far the commonest Australian Parrakeet with English aviarists, and scores are reared in this country annually. It will breed readily in any aviary, and even in a cage sometimes, laying four or five eggs, which are frequently all hatched. Often four or more broods are produced during the spring and summer, so that it can well be imagined that a pair of Cockatiels will soon add very considerably to the population of an aviary. A pair kept by the writer a few years ago reared sixteen young birds between March and September, brood after brood being produced in the same nest-box, the female often commencing to lay again before the young left the nest, in which case it was necessary, as soon as the young had flown, to carefully remove and wash the eggs, replacing them after cleaning out the nest-box. Cockatiels do not seem to mind their nest being examined, or, if necessary, cleaned out; true, they make a good deal of noise while this is being done, but they rarely if ever desert the nest, as many other species undoubtedly would do.

Young Cockatiels are uncommonly ugly little creatures while in the nest, and on being inspected, raise their stump-like crests and rock their bodies from side to side, all the while hissing like so many serpents. Cockatiels commence to incubate with the first or second egg, so that the first hatches several days before the last, and a brood consists of young of various sizes. Unlike other Parrakeets, the male shares in the task of incubation, sitting during the daytime while his wife takes duty at night.

As to the best form of nest for Cockatiels, opinions differ, some aviculturists preferring the artificial log-nest often sold for Parrakeets, while others advise a box with a hollowed out bottom. Personally, I have never found that Cockatiels, or in fact any species of Parrakeet, care much for the usual type of log-nest, which is too smooth and artificial, being bored out, apparently on a lathe. To be of any practical use log-nests should be perfectly natural, partially decayed, hollow logs, with the natural rotten wood inside, which the birds can gnaw into shape. Such logs are not easily obtained, but are undoubtedly the most perfect nesting sites for Parrakeets in captivity. The next best form of nest is, in my opinion, a box, say 12 inches long, by 6 or 7 inches wide and about the same height, made of rough and not too new-looking wood, of about $\frac{3}{4}$ of an inch in thickness, with an entrance hole at one end, near the top, and with the bottom formed so that it gradually slopes down to a saucer-shaped hollow at the end farthest from the entrance hole. Small barrels, hung up horizontally, have been recommended, but I do not think they are so suitable as the boxes above described, for Parrakeets like to get as far back in the nest as possible, and in a barrel the lowest part would be in the centre.

A portion of the lid of the nest-box should be hinged on, so that the nest can be cleaned out after each brood has flown.

The Cockatiel is not a specially interesting bird in captivity, being wild and noisy, and the young birds are exceedingly foolish creatures, dashing wildly about the aviary and screeching loudly on any one's entrance; nevertheless for the novice in aviculture, who wishes to commence with a hardy species, and one that will readily reproduce its kind in his aviary, there is perhaps no more suitable bird than this. If the young are taken from the nest and reared by hand they are said to make delightful pets, and even to learn to repeat words distinctly.

A mixture of oats, hemp and canary-seed, supplemented with green food such as chickweed, groundsel, dandelion and the like, forms a suitable diet for the Cockatiel; but when young are being reared stale bread, soaked in water and squeezed nearly dry, is much appreciated, and is a great help in the arduous task of rearing a large family.

The Cockatiel is distributed over the whole of Australia, excepting the north-east of Queensland.

Family PSITTACIDÆ.
Subfamily NASITERNINÆ.

THE PIGMY PARROTS.

Nasiterna, Wagl.

Coloured figures, ROWLEY'S *Ornithological Miscellany*, Vol. I.

No living specimen of this subfamily has ever been imported, so far as I am aware, but such beautiful

From *The Royal Natural History*.
PIGMY PARROT, *Nasiterna pygmæa*.

little birds are they, and such charming subjects would they be for aviculturists, if only they could be brought to this country alive, that I cannot resist the temptation to mention them here, albeit, strictly they are outside the scope of this work.

Nine species of Pigmy Parrots are known, ranging throughout New Guinea and the surrounding islands. They are exceedingly small in size, being mostly about $3\frac{1}{2}$ inches in total length, and the males are brilliantly coloured. The sexes differ somewhat both in size and markings, the males being the larger and more highly coloured birds. Of the habits of these minute Parrots very little is known, except that they spend most of their time amongst the thick foliage of trees, rarely descending to the ground, are very shy and difficult to observe, and breed in holes in trees, as do most Parrots. That the Pigmy Parrots feed chiefly upon seed there can be little doubt, seeing that the bill very closely resembles that of the Cockatoos in shape. The curious elongation of the shafts of the tail-feathers is well shown in the annexed cut, which illustrates the type species.

Subfamily CONURINÆ.

CONURES.

The Conures constitute a numerous race of Parrakeets, inhabiting Central and South America, and the West Indies; while one species ranges far into North America. They are a hardy, noisy and mischievous race, and are not especial favourites with aviculturists in this country; their piercing shrieks are frequently uttered and become almost unbearable in a house; while, with their strong bills, they seem to take a special delight in gnawing their cages or aviary to pieces. Moreover, they have the reputation of being decidedly spiteful towards other birds if kept in a mixed collection, so that it is not advisable to keep them with other birds. But they have their good points; they are some of the longest-lived and hardiest of the Parrot tribe, become wonderfully tame and fond of their owners, especially if procured young; and some make good talkers. Many are, again, very beautiful; and, on the whole, they are decidedly intelligent birds.

The sexes are, outwardly, alike in the Conures, although the males are slightly larger than the females. They breed in holes, either in trees or rocks, laying three or four white eggs. All kinds of seed, fruit, and probably the young shoots of various trees and plants form the diet of the Conures in a wild state. They are most destructive to grain crops of all kinds, and are hated by farmers.

In captivity several species have reproduced their kind; but they do not always make good parents, and have been known to mercilessly slay their offspring just before, or at the time of, leaving the nest.

Their food in captivity is of the simplest description; canary-, hemp-, and millet-seed, and oats, forming the staple diet; while green food, such as chickweed, flowering grass, groundsel and fruit, should be added, freely in the summer and sparingly in winter. Sunflower seed is also appreciated by some species.

Genus CONURUS, Kuhl.

THE SHARP-TAILED-CONURE.

Conurus acuticaudatus (Vieill.).

This is a rarely imported Conure, but has been exhibited amongst the Zoological Society's fine collection. It closely resembles the Blue-crowned Conure, the next described, so that it is quite possible it may have occasionally been mistaken for that species.

The prevailing colour is green, the breast having a somewhat bluish tinge. The crown, lores, cheeks and ear-coverts are dull blue. The underside of the tail is olive, the base of the lateral feathers being brownish-red on the inner-webs. The bill has the upper mandible whitish with a black tip, and the lower mandible blackish. Length about 14 inches.

Of the wild life of this Conure little seems to be known; Mr. E. W. White wrote of it near Andalgala in Catamarca:—" This species is not very abundant here, but flies very swiftly in flocks of seven or eight, screeching continually when on the wing. I shot my specimen out of a number perching on a tala tree, as they were devouring the young shoots." (P.Z.S., 1882, p. 621.)

The Sharp-tailed Conure inhabits Bolivia, Paraguay, Northern Argentina and Uruguay.

THE BLUE-CROWNED CONURE.

Conurus hæmorrhous (Spix).

This species very closely resembles *C. acuticaudatus*, but the blue on the head is less extensive, the forehead and crown only being of that colour. Both mandibles are whitish, and the general plumage is brighter green than in the species last described. It is about 13 inches in length. The Blue-crowned Conure is very seldom imported into this country, but the Zoological Society has possessed several examples at various times and some have found their way to other collections. It appears to be a most desirable species from an aviculturist's point of view.

Mr. Schmalz, of Vienna, quoted by the late Dr. Russ, writes of some examples of this species in his possession:—" Even in a few days they became accustomed to my presence, although they were at first very shy, and I was then enabled to convince myself that they were Parrots of a high degree of intelligence. One had a festering wound from a bite, which I was obliged to clean and wash out daily with a sponge. The bird at first fluttered as if mad; but by the fourth day it was completely tamed, and soon I did not need to take it in my hand at all; for when it saw me coming with the sponge, it voluntarily held its head bent forward. When it was quite well it began to fly about the room madly, by which it in no small degree disquieted the other birds; but when I called 'Ara!' it stopped at once, and when I showed it the sponge it immediately flew to the place where I had always washed its head, and let me take it quietly in my hand. Now it is thoroughly tame, and allows itself to be laid on its back, &c. Formerly a dreadful screamer, and especially noisy in the morning, it has now been trained, by a few cross words and light taps on the beak, to abstain entirely from its cries. It is, moreover, charmingly affectionate, and has learnt without any particular teaching to say 'Ara! Good Ara!' and 'Cockatoo!' just as plainly as any Grey Parrot. A female (for such it proved later on by laying eggs) of this species became just as tame, and learnt to say exactly the same words, but pronounced them more softly."

The Blue-crowned Conure occurs from Bahia to Cujaba in the interior of Brazil.

THE GOLDEN CONURE.

Conurus guarouba (Gm.).

Coloured figure, GREENE'S *Parrots in Captivity*, Vol. III.

This, the so-called Queen of Bavaria Parrakeet, is one of the most beautiful of the Conures, being bright lemon-yellow in colour with dark green quills. The bill is whitish, and the feet flesh-coloured. It is about 14 inches in length.

Very little appears to be known of the wild life of this Conure. Messrs. Sclater and Salvin tell us that it is "rare in the neighbourhood of Pará, where it appears once a year, when a particular fruit is ripe." Dr. A. R. Wallace says that these birds are called Imperial Parrots in Pará, "because their colours are those of the Brazilian flag—yellow and green."

In captivity it is exceedingly rare, but the Zoological Society has possessed two or three at different times. The only living specimen I remember to have seen, was in the Jardin d'acclimatation in Paris, where a very fine example was on view in September, 1900. Probably this was the bird of which Mr. O. E. Cresswell wrote in the *Avicultural Magazine* for April, 1897: "I had gathered that the general tint of plumage was light canary, the reality far exceeded my visions of it. The general body-colour is of the most splendid amber, and it seems as if one looks through the rather downy plumage to richer depths of amber below. The green, too, of the primary and secondary wing-feathers is vivid beyond description. The figure of the bird is not very

From Cassell's *Book of Birds*.

GOLDEN CONURE, *Conurus guarouba*.

elegant, but of this one cannot judge fairly in a cage, deplorably cramped for so lovely an inmate."

The Hon. Canon Dutton, writing of the Conures in the *Avicultural Magazine*, says: "The one really fascinating Conure I have seen was a specimen of *luteus*, or as the British Museum Catalogue calls it, *guarouba*. This was a specimen which was deposited at the Zoological Gardens, and was for sale for £10. It was extraordinarily tame. You could swing it about by one leg or by the tail; it would lie on its back in your hand, and delighted in being played with; it was said to be a good talker." The sexes of this species are outwardly alike, as with all the Conures. According to the British Museum Catalogue, the young have the "cheeks and upper wing-coverts with scattered green feathers;" but Canon Dutton mentions two that were at the Zoo. as "nearly all green."

The Golden Conure is an inhabitant of North Eastern Brazil.

THE YELLOW CONURE.

Conurus solstitialis (Linn.).

Coloured figure, GREENE'S *Parrots in Captivity*, Vol. III.

This is another very beautiful but rarely imported Conure; known in its native country as the "Kessi-kessi."

The prevailing colour of this Parrakeet is bright orange-yellow, inclining to deep reddish-orange in some specimens. The greater wing-coverts are green, tipped with yellow. The primary-coverts, primaries and secondaries bluish-green; tail green at the base and becoming blue towards the tip and at the sides. The young of this species are much greener than the adults, and resemble adult Jendaya Conures (next described), from which they may, however, be distinguished by the yellow edges to their wing-coverts, and a yellower tinge on the back.

The Hon. Canon Dutton writes:—" I had in my charge for some time four specimens of *Solstitialis*. These certainly were beautiful, all four slightly different in colour, which may have been owing to their being young birds. They resembled Jendayas, but were of a more brilliant orange and red. Bechstein says they learn to speak easily and well. Russ makes no remark upon their qualities as pets. These were noisy and wild, and though I put them under the charge of a woman who was particularly fond of animals, they never became tamer as long as I had them." (*Avicultural Magazine*, vol. iv., p. 173.) Dr. Russ, however, in his *Speaking Parrots*, mentions a specimen that "was exceedingly tame, and chattered some words most charmingly."

The Yellow Conure inhabits Guiana and Rio Branco.

THE YELLOW-HEADED CONURE.

Conurus jendaya (Gm.).

Coloured figure, GREENE'S *Parrots in Captivity*, Vol. III.

This Conure is much more frequently imported than the last, and is a very handsome and desirable species. It inhabits the eastern parts of Brazil, where it is said to be very numerous. Mr. W. A. Forbes writes[1]:—" This Parrakeet, called by the Brazilians 'Jendaia,' may often be seen tamed in houses, and to this species no doubt belonged most of the *Conuri* that I continually saw flying in small flocks of from four to twenty or so, both at Parahyba and between Quipapá and Garanhuns. These birds, however,

---

[1] *Ibis*, 1881, p. 351.

were so wary that I only succeeded in at all making out what they were by means of a glass, which clearly revealed their yellow undersides. At other times they were invariably high in the air, far out of gun-shot and almost out of sight; indeed their presence was usually first indicated by their cries, which were audible long before they themselves became visible. Only once, in a patch of forest near Quipapá, did I get anywhere within shot of these birds, and then they were off directly they became aware of the presence of a stranger."

That the Yellow-headed Conure has bred successfully in captivity, on one occasion at least, is shown by the following extract from a letter which appears (unfortunately without date) in *Notes on Cage Birds* (Second Series, p. 173). The writer, who signs himself "Blue Robin," remarks :—"Last Christmas-time a pair of these birds in my possession made determined attempts to perpetuate their species ; but, considering the severity of the season, failure was not surprising. A third attempt was made in June, with the result that two fine young birds are now disporting themselves, with their parents in close attendance, in the aviary. . . .

"I suppose it would be about three months from the period of incubation before they left the nest— a hollow log—upon the top of which they used to sit and nibble their toes and chatter fully a fortnight before they ventured to take flight into the wide world before them. They are very fairly treated by the numerous inmates of the aviary, though, as a rule, new-comers are not received with favour."

"Of Jendayas generally," the same writer proceeds: "I have nothing but good to record ; if only they would not scream they would be perfect. Hardy, amusing, intelligent, and peaceable—never dull or sleepy like the more dignified *Platycerci*—but climbing and whittling away at the long-suffering boughs when they can find nothing else to amuse them." The same writer goes on to say, in another letter: "I could fill a chapter on the subject of these truly delightful Parrakeets. They are handsome, hardy, and without exception the most amusing and audacious birds I ever kept. Like all the Conures, they are noisy, wasteful, and confirmed 'whittlers,' but their intelligence is second to none of the Parrot tribe, and far in advance of the stately, well-mannered and more elegant *Platycercus*. They are excellent mimics of sweeter-voiced birds, so that their noise is not altogether confined to the screaming they are all too fond of resorting to."

The following is a description of the adult: Head and neck bright yellow, more or less tinged with orange-red on the forehead, throat and round the eyes; back, scapulars and upper wing-coverts green; underparts and lower back orange-red; primaries and secondaries blue, the former with the base of the outer webs green; tail above blue, merging into olive-green at the base, and black below. The total length of this bird is about 12 inches.

THE GOLDEN-HEADED CONURE.

Conurus auricapillus (Kuhl.).

This species is very much like the last described, the chief difference being that the green of the back extends to the top and sides of the head, the throat and upper breast.

It inhabits Eastern Brazil, and is rarely imported to this country.

THE BLACK-HEADED CONURE.

Conurus nenday (Vieill.).

This Conure was first received at the Zoological Gardens in May, 1870, when it was considered an exceedingly rare species, and Dr. Sclater described the specimen received as the first example he had ever seen alive (*cf.* P. Z. S., 1870, p. 383). At the present time, however, it is one of the most freely imported of the Conures, and is generally offered for sale as the Nandy or Nenday Parrakeet. It is not a popular species with aviculturists, although there does not seem to be very much difficulty in inducing it to breed in captivity, providing a true pair can be selected; and it is said to be harmless in a mixed collection, which certainly is not the case with most of the Conures.

In *Notes on Cage Birds* (p. 171) a writer, signing himself "Norton," remarks:—"It may interest some of your readers to hear how successful I have been with my Black-headed Conures (Nandy Parrakeets). I have had them in my out-door aviary for nearly two years, and last year they had a nest, but no young were hatched. This year, I am happy to say, there are two young birds fully fledged; one is already out of the nest and nearly as big as the old birds. They both appear to be strong and healthy." Mrs. Johnstone, of Bury St. Edmunds, Suffolk, in a letter published in the *Avicultural Magazine* of September, 1901, writes as follows, of a pair of Black-headed Conures in her aviary:—"They nested some weeks ago, and had five fine fully-fledged young birds. I expected daily to see them fly, and, wondering at their non-appearance, looked into the nesting-log and found that one young Parrakeet, fully-fledged and quite fat, had been killed by a piercing blow at the back of the skull, completely smashing the head. The remaining four birds are well, and, I should say, may fly any day."

Conurus nenday inhabits Paraguay, where it is said to be very common in certain districts, congregating in large flocks (*cf. Ibis*, 1901, p. 229). The prevailing colour is green, becoming yellowish on the rump and underparts; head blackish-brown; primaries, secondaries, and primary-coverts blue, the latter edged with green on the outer web; thighs red; tail olive-green, becoming blue towards the tip. Length about 12 inches.

Illustration from living specimen in the Zoological Society's Gardens.

THE RED-HEADED CONURE.

Conurus rubrolarvatus, Mass. and Souancé.

This fine Conure is rarely imported into this country, albeit it has been represented at the Zoological Gardens on several occasions, and Mr. Goodchild has drawn the accompanying coloured figure from a specimen now living there.

Mr. Walter Goodfellow met with large flocks of this species on his journey through Colombia and Ecuador, and gave the following interesting account in the *Avicultural Magazine* (vol. vi., p. 69). "Another bird common all along the western side of Ecuador, and exceedingly common in parts of Cauca, in Colombia, is the Red-faced Conure (*C. rubrolarvatus.* . . . These birds I saw offered for sale in Guayaquil at 5d. each, and no doubt at half that price they could have been bought. Being rather large birds, they show off their colours to advantage. I imagine, though, they must be rather noisy birds to keep, for they have a disagreeable shriek. They ought not to be at all delicate, for we shot specimens near the Volcano of Puracé, by Popayan in Colombia, at an altitude of over 8,000 ft.

"In passing through the little village of Carmen (still in Colombia) on our ride from Buenaventura to Cali, we saw the same birds in immense clouds, coming from their feeding grounds in the high mountain forests, to pass the night in the little sheltered valley below. Carmen could boast of little else in the way of vegetation but bamboos, which grew in great thickets, and every branch of these giant grasses was literally weighing down with its burden of *C. rubrolarvatus*. The noise was simply deafening! Those we shot by the acid waterfall of Paracé, in the month of May, 1898, were undoubtedly nesting in the crevices of the perpendicular cliffs there, for on the report of our firearms, numbers of them flew screaming from the holes and ledges around. I noticed, too, that the plumage of some was draggled, evidently by sitting on their eggs."

Prevailing colour bright green, paler on the underparts; nearly the whole of the head, edge of the wings, under wing-coverts and thighs red. Total length about $13\frac{1}{2}$ inches.

The Red-headed Conure inhabits Colombia, Ecuador, and Peru.

WAGLER'S CONURE.

Conurus wagleri, Gray.

This species inhabits Venezuela and Colombia. Mr. C. W. Wyatt met with it in large flocks between Ocaña and Bucaramanga (*cf. Ibis*, 1871, p. 381). It is practically unknown in this country, although it has been represented in the Zoological Society's collection.

C. wagleri may be described as follows: Prevailing colour green, paler on the underparts; forehead and crown red; red markings, more or less pronounced, on the throat; bill yellowish-white. Total length about 14 inches.

THE GREEN CONURE.

Conurus leucophthalmus, (P.L.S., Müll.).

The Green Conure is another of those uncommon and not particularly interesting species that one very rarely sees in captivity except in Zoological Gardens. It is almost entirely green, paler on the underparts; the edge of the wing and smaller under wing-coverts red. The bill is yellowish-flesh-colour. Total length about $13\frac{1}{2}$ inches.

Very little has been written respecting the wild life of this Conure, which does not appear to differ in its habits from its congeners. It inhabits Guiana, Trinidad, Colombia, Peru, Bolivia and the north of Brazil.

THE MEXICAN CONURE.

Conurus holochlorus, Scl.

This species inhabits Central America, from Mexico to Nicaragua. It is not often imported to Europe, but has been represented in the Zoological Gardens on more than one occasion.

Mr. O. Salvin came across this Conure at Coban and Dueñas, where it is known as "El Chocoyo." "It frequents," he writes, "the patches of maize (*Zea mais*), which cover the hill-sides, and commits serious damage on the crops. It may constantly be seen flying over the plains and low country at all hours of the day, in flocks varying from two birds to twenty or thirty in number. When any large number fly together, they usually, I may say almost always, divide themselves into couples, though these do not preserve regular order like a flock of Geese." (P.Z.S., 1860, p. 44.)

The Mexican Conure is green, paler on the underparts; and generally has no red feathers whatever, although sometimes a few appear, scattered about the throat and upper breast, which has led ornithologists to confound it with the next described, which, however, has now been proved to be distinct.

THE RED-THROATED CONURE.

Conurus rubritorques, Scl.

This rare Conure was named by Dr. Sclater from a specimen living in the Zoological Society's Gardens. When writing the British Museum Catalogue, however, Count Salvadori considered this to be merely a variety of *C. holochlorus*. Subsequently Messrs. Salvin and Godman received a series of ten specimens from Nicaragua, all of which had the red throat as in the type specimen, and Count Salvadori agreed that *C. rubritorques* must be recognised as a species (*cf.* Bull, B.O.C., vol. i., p. 11).

The Red-throated Conure is only distinguishable from the Mexican Conure by the red band on the throat. It inhabits Nicaragua.

THE AZTEC CONURE.

Conurus aztec (Souance).

This is another Central American species, inhabiting the district from Southern Mexico to Costa Rica. Mr. A. Boucard found this Parrakeet abundant in all parts of Yucatan, but the greatest number was met with in Western Yucatan, flocks of from four hundred to eight hundred individuals being seen. "In November and December," he writes, "they were feeding upon the seeds of a plant which grows very abundantly in that part of this State. The sharp piercing cry of these birds is almost deafening when in large flocks." (*P. Z. S.*, 1883, p. 455.)

The Zoological Society has possessed living examples of the Aztec Conure.

The plumage of this species is as follows:—

Upper parts green, which extends to the cheeks and ear-coverts; quills blue, tipped with black, and green at the base of the outer webs; a narrow band of orange-yellow between the nostrils; the throat and upper breast olive-brown, with shaft stripes of a darker shade of the same colour; lower breast and abdomen olive; thighs, flanks and under tail-coverts green; tail green, tipped with blue above, and golden-olive below. Total length about 9½ inches.

THE CACTUS CONURE.

Conurus cactorum (Kuhl).

This charming little Conure inhabits the eastern parts of Brazil, and is frequently imported alive to Europe. Of its wild life, however, very little has been recorded. Mr. W. A. Forbes, writing on the birds of North-eastern Brazil, remarks: "Numerous living specimens of this little Parrakeet (*C. cactorum*) were brought to me by the natives at Garanhuns, who called it simply 'Perriquito.' I have already noticed the abundance of large *Cacti* in the sandy districts around Garanhuns, and on these, no doubt, these Parrakeets largely subsist. I never succeeded in identifying the bird in a wild state, though I every day saw or heard flocks of a *Conurus* flying high in the air around Garanhuns." (*Ibis*, 1881, p. 352.)

In captivity this species becomes wonderfully tame and familiar, but it possesses one fault, shared by the rest of the Conures, namely, its irrepressible voice, which soon becomes almost unbearable. Concerning a pair of these Conures, Mr. O. E. Cresswell writes: "I have had them about five years; they do not talk, but are always merry and bright, and seem to have great capacity for enjoying life. At any time they will go into a strange sort of ecstasy, jabbering and fluttering and rushing towards me if I come up to the cage or aviary (for I have at times turned them into an aviary), but if any one else is too near they are shy and won't do this. When, however, I have been away for any time, and then reappear, their delight knows no bounds, all shyness goes, and before any company they continue their jabbering and fluttering as long as I will look at them." (*Avicultural Magazine*, vol. iv., p. 176.)

Miss R. Alderson, of Worksop, has kindly sent me the following notes on some Cactus Conures in her possession:—

"Like every other kind of bird they vary in temperament. I have three that are all that can be desired, while two others are just the reverse. Of the first four I purchased three are still alive; the fourth died from injuries, caused, it is supposed, by a

Tovi Parrakeet. All four birds were extraordinarily tame from the first, though I believe they were newly imported. The very day they arrived they all ran in a body across the aviary floor to meet me, and some of them even took biscuit from my fingers. If a large bird attacked them they joined forces, and it was most amusing to see them beat off a formidable opponent by sheer force of numbers. The three are named respectively 'Ping,' 'Pang,' and 'Jock.' The first two are, I think, a pair, and are devoted to each other. Jock is allowed to play with them, and they are very kind to him. He is the funny man of the party, and goes through the most amusing antics and grimaces for the benefit of the other two. They are all very bright and affectionate little birds, and love to sit in a row on my arm eating pea-nuts and biscuits. Before I leave the aviary I have to look round to make sure they are all there, for they are very fond of flying on to my back, and are so light that I might easily carry one out by mistake. They watch for me passing the aviary, and there is a shrill chorus of disappointment if I do not go inside. I tried keeping the two new ones with the original trio, but these chased the new comers about so that I was obliged to separate them. The operations were conducted in a most business-like way, all three acting in unison to expel the intruders. Cactus Conures are fairly hardy, easy to keep, and cost but six or seven shillings a pair. Mine have been for some time in the same aviary as my tiny waxbills, with no bad results."

I have been unable to find any record of this little Conure having bred in the United Kingdom, but it has been known as a cage-bird for a great many years, and it is exceedingly probable that it has reproduced its kind in captivity.

The Cactus Conure is coloured as follows :—

Above green; top of the head, cheeks, lores, throat,

sides of the neck, and upper part of the breast pale brown; below the eyes a yellow line; ear-coverts green; abdomen and lower breast dull orange; thighs, flanks, and under tail-coverts greenish-yellow; primaries bluish; quills tipped with blackish; tail-feathers bluish towards the tips. Total length about $10\frac{1}{4}$ inches.

Illustration from skins in the British Museum and a living example in the Zoological Society's collection.

THE BROWN-THROATED CONURE.

Conurus æruginosus (Linn.).

As will readily be seen from the accompanying coloured plate, the present species differs but slightly in appearance from the Cactus Conure. In its habits, also, it appears to be almost identical with its congener, being found in a wild state amongst cactus thickets, upon the seeds of which it doubtless feeds. (*Cf. Ibis*, 1871, p. 381.)

Writing on the birds of Margarita Island, Mr. Austin H. Clark remarks of this species: "Very common in the flat coast region, and also in the cassava fields on the mountain sides. On the coast by Parlamar, where it was much more abundant than anywhere else, its loud screeching could be heard on all sides as the flocks flew about searching for food. When in the trees, however, they were quite quiet; a whole flock would seem to disappear on alighting, every member becoming instantly still, and, for a time, motionless; but, on being startled, the whole flock would screech louder than ever, and fly swiftly away.

"While in Parlamar I noticed many flocks of these birds flying very high in air over the town towards the mainland. As none were seen to fly back again, I judged it to be a migration. Possibly the birds resorted to the island to breed, and were now leaving, as the breeding season was about over. . . . . I saw one belonging to a friend in Trinidad which would imitate any word or sentence said to it immediately, even copying emphatic noddings of the head." (*Auk*, July, 1902, p. 262.)

The Brown-throated Conure is frequently imported as a cage bird, but I am not aware of its having reproduced its kind in captivity. The Baroness von Schlechta, quoted by Dr. Russ in his *Speaking Parrots*, mentions one specimen as "an affectionate and merry bird, which has often cheered me with its simple song, and cried out in a very amusing manner, clawing its beak with its foot, 'Pretty Poll! pretty Poll! there! there! there! there!' In other respects it was very clever, but often very wild."

The Brown-throated Conure inhabits Guiana, Venezuela, Colombia and Rio Negro.

The following is a description of the adult: Above green, the crown tinged with blue; an orange-yellow circle round the eye; forehead, lores, cheeks, ear-coverts and throat brown; breast, abdomen and under tail-coverts greenish-yellow; middle of the abdomen orange; quills blue; tail bluish towards the tips of the central feathers.

The young are similar to the adults, but their colours are much duller. Total length about $9\frac{3}{4}$ inches.

The illustration is from skins in the British Museum and a living specimen in the Zoological Gardens.

THE ST. THOMAS' CONURE.

Conurus pertinax (Linn.).

This species is slightly larger in size than the Brown-throated Conure, being just 10 inches in length. It is found in the islands of St. Thomas and Curaçao, being restricted in the former to the hills on the eastern side of the harbour. (*Cf. Ibis*, 1859, p. 374.) Mr. Hartert states that in the Island of St. Thomas these birds "are no longer caught for sale, while formerly they were brought to the steamers by the negroes. On Curaçao it is very numerous in the western parts of the island, but not so common, although by no means rare, in the eastern. The nests are mostly built in large ants' nests placed in trees, into which they dig holes. The negroes take the young ones from the nests and keep them in cages. Large numbers are sold to the sailors." (*Ibis*, 1893, p. 320.)

The St. Thomas' Conure is not so often seen in captivity as either the Cactus or Brown-throated Conures, but it is probably sometimes mistaken for one of these species. Mr. O. E. Cresswell writes of a specimen in his possession: "He is tame and funny, and is said to say a few words very plainly, but he has not said them to me yet. I must confess he is noisy, especially when he is in my library and can just hear a party of other parrots out of doors, and another contingent in another room. .... The Latin epithet for this species, *pertinax*, sounds strange, but I am inclined to think was not rashly conferred. Through many mornings my bird screeches with real pertinacity." (*Avicultural Magazine*, vol. iv., p. 176.)

The following is a description of the adult: The forehead, chin and sides of the head are yellow-orange; top of the head bluish; upper parts bright green; throat and upper part of breast olive; lower part of breast and abdomen greenish-yellow, inclining to orange on the middle of the abdomen; quills blue, edged towards the tip with black; tail green above, the central feathers being blue towards the tips; under-side of tail golden-olive.

Habitat, St. Thomas, St. Croix and Curaçao.

THE GOLDEN-CROWNED CONURE.

Conurus aureus (Gm.).

Coloured figure, GREENE'S *Parrots in Captivity*, Vol. II.

Specimens of this Conure frequently find their way to the English bird-market, where it is generally termed by bird dealers the "Half-Moon Parrakeet."

The back of the head, nape, and upper parts generally are green; forehead and crown orange-yellow; a ring of orange-yellow encircling the naked skin round the eye, and this is again surrounded by a bluish band which extends over the top of the head. The cheeks and throat are orange; under-parts greenish-yellow; the wings green above with the exception of the secondaries, which are blue; bill blackish. Total length nearly 11 inches.

Dr. Russ, in his *Speaking Parrots*, says that this is "among the most anciently known of the Parrots, as well as being one of the earliest to be imported alive." He also credits it with being an excellent talker, and mentions one example which was remarkably gifted in this direction. "A bird of this species in my own possession," he writes, "became tame without any trouble on my part, and when I went into the aviary would fly at once on to my shoulder, or climb upon my outstretched finger. It may, I think, take precedence of all its congeners in teachableness and gentleness."

I have been unable to find any record of this species having bred in captivity.

The Golden-crowned Conure inhabits Paraguay, Brazil, Bolivia, Guiana, and the Amazon Valley.

PETZ'S CONURE.

Conurus canicularis (Linn.).
Coloured figure, GREENE'S *Parrots in Captivity*, Vol. III.

This small Conure inhabits Central America, from Mexico to Costa Rica. It is about $9\frac{1}{2}$ inches in total length; bright green on the back and tail; olive-green on the cheeks; throat and breast olive; abdomen, under wing-coverts, and under tail-coverts yellowish-green. The forehead is orange; the top of the head and lores bright blue. The secondaries are blue.

Petz's Conure is not very frequently met with in captivity, but most writers give it a good character. I can find no record of young having been reared in the United Kingdom.

Genus CONUROPSIS, Salv.

THE CAROLINA CONURE.

Conuropsis carolinensis (Linn.).
Coloured Figure, GREENE'S *Parrots in Captivity*, Vol. II.

This species, the only North American Parrot, has been separated from the typical Conures (*Conurus*) by Count Salvadori, on the ground of its differing from these in one or two essential points. In the true Conures the fourth primary is attenuated, and the nostrils are exposed; whereas in the Carolina Parrakeet the fourth primary is not attenuated, the cere is feathered, and the nostrils hidden.

From *The Royal Natural History.*

CAROLINA CONURE.

At one time this fine Conure was exceedingly numerous, its range extending from Florida and the Gulf States to the Great Lakes, Iowa and New York. It is now, however, restricted to the Gulf States and the Mississippi Valley, and is said to be very local. There appears to be every prospect of its sharing, in the near future, the fate of the Passenger Pigeon.

In his interesting work on North American birds, entitled *Bird Studies* (1898), Professor W. E. D. Scott remarks: "So far as is now known, the birds are found only in a few localities in the Indian territory, and in parts of Florida. Even the last twenty-five years has shown a marked decrease in the birds in Florida. During the winter of 1875 and 1876, which I spent in Sumpter County on Panasoffkee Lake, I saw large flocks of these birds daily, and also noticed many flocks the same year in passing up and down the Ocklawaha River. In the winter of 1879 and 1880 I saw only two flocks, and these were small. During the years from 1885 to 1892 I was in Florida for at least half of each year, and in 1886 the entire year, but I find only one record of Paroquets in these years, a small flock seen at a place called Linden. As my travels were taken to study the birds of the region, and as they extended to every point of the Gulf Coast from Cedar Keys to the Dry Tortugas, and also well into the interior, I conclude that but a small remnant of these birds exists, and while doubtless man is directly responsible for their actual destruction, yet I cannot but believe that the more subtle indirect influences growing out of the settlement of the country are far more responsible for the results than the actual slaughter, great as it has been, which has occurred."

Mr. Henry Nehrling, in his book entitled *Our Native Birds of Song and Beauty*, writes respecting this Conure: "When I visited Florida in April, 1886, I saw small flocks in the woods near Lake Apopka. In Orlando and Sanford freshly caught Parrakeets were offered for sale in large numbers. In March,

1891, a pair of these birds were obtained for the Public Museum of Milwaukee, near Gotha, Orange County, Fla. The small flocks which I saw proceeded with an astonishing rapidity and swiftness through the air. Their flight was very graceful and somewhat undulating, reminding me strongly of that of the Passenger Pigeon. I saw the birds only in the extensive hammock woods and cypress swamps.

"The food of this Parrakeet, before the country was extensively settled, consisted of the seeds of the cocklebur (*Xanthium strumarium*), of the seed contained in the round balls of the sycamore, pecan and beech nuts, seeds of the magnolia, and tulip trees, fruits of the popan (*Asimia triloba*), wild cherry, mulberry, &c. It has also been observed that they consumed the seeds of the sand spar or burr-grass (*Cenchrus echinatus*), one of the vilest and most troublesome weeds in existence. They have also been known to visit the corn fields, where they indulged in eating the sweet milky seeds. According to Mr. Frank M. Chapman, they eat the milky seeds of a species of thistle (*Cirscium lecontie*). He saw them feeding among the thistles in March, 1890, on the Sebastian River in Florida."

It is sad indeed to think of this Parrakeet so soon being wiped off the face of the earth, and being numbered with the species that have been. But it seems to have submitted patiently to its fate, for we read of whole flocks being shot down without the least trouble, as when one bird was killed or wounded the remainder of the flock would not leave their dead or dying companion, but kept flying round with loud cries until the whole flock was killed.

When so numerous the Carolina Conure was undoubtedly one of the worst enemies the farmers had to contend with, and there was little chance of good corn crops where these birds existed in any numbers; but it is sincerely to be hoped that the small scattered bands that still exist in isolated localities may be strictly protected from the fate with which they are threatened.

It is curious that no reliable information as to the nesting of this species in a wild state appears to have been published, but there is little doubt that they breed in holes in trees, either in the trunk or limbs.

In captivity this species is, as might be expected, very rarely seen now-a-days, although formerly it was common. As long ago as Beckstein's time it was frequently brought to Europe, and Dr. Russ, in his *Speaking Parrots*, mentions it as one of the commonest Parrots in the bird market. "The experience and observation of years," writes the author just mentioned, "has convinced me that a Carolina Parrakeet, caught when old, is never susceptible of taming and training, but always remains stupidly shy, obstinate and untamable; though a very young bird, which happens to fall into the hands of a judicious trainer who treats it properly, becomes as completely tame and familiar as any of its congeners. As regards capacity for speech, certainly it can only attain to second or third rank, and even if it becomes unusually tame and affectionate, it will at the best be wearisome by reason of its intolerable screaming. . . .

"The various attempts made at breeding have in but few cases produced any satisfactory result. In the Zoological Gardens the only effect was the laying of eggs; but in my aviary the young have become fledged, and Dr. Nowotny has met with similar success."

I do not believe the Carolina Conure has ever been bred in England; at any rate I can find no published record of such an event, although Dr. Greene, in his *Parrots in Captivity*, states that it "will breed freely in a large aviary."

The following is a description of the adult: Prevailing colour bright green, much paler and yellower on the underparts; the forehead, cheeks, lores and region round the eyes deep orange; the remainder of the head yellow; the tips of the wing-coverts yellowish; quills dark bluish; edge of the wings and thighs tinged with orange.

The immature birds have the head and neck entirely green, except the forehead and lores, which are dull orange-red (*Ridgway*).

Genus CYANOLYSEUS, Bp.

THE LESSER PATAGONIAN CONURE.

Cyanolyseus patagonicus (Vieill.).

This species inhabits Uruguay, Argentina and Northern Patagonia. It is a fine large bird, in fact, with the exception of the slightly larger form known as *Cyanolyseus byroni* of Chili, this is the largest of the Conures, its total length being $17\frac{1}{2}$ inches.

Of this Parrakeet in a wild state Mr. W. H. Hudson writes:[*] " In habits it differs somewhat from most of its congeners, and it may be regarded, I think, as one of those species which are dying out, possibly owing to the altered conditions resulting from the settlement of the country by Europeans. It was formerly abundant on the southern pampas of La Plata, and, being partially migratory, its flocks ranged in winter to Buenos Ayres, and even as far north as the Paraná river. When, as a child, I lived near the capital city (Buenos Ayres), I remember that I always looked forward with the greatest delight to the appearance of these noisy dark green winter visitors. Now they are rarely seen within a hundred miles of Buenos

---

[*] *Argentine Ornithology*, vol. ii., p. 41.

Ayres; and I have been informed by old gauchos that half a century before my time they invariably appeared in immense flocks in winter, and have since gradually diminished in numbers, until now in that district the Bank-Parrot is almost a thing of the past. Two or three hundred miles south of Buenos Ayres city they are still to be met with in rather large flocks, and have a few ancient breeding-places, to which they cling very tenaciously. When there are trees or bushes on their feeding ground they perch on them; they also gather the berries of the *Empetrum rubrum* and other fruits from the bushes; but they feed principally on the ground, and, while the flock feeds, one bird is invariably perched on a stalk or other elevation to act as sentinel. They are partial to the seeds of the giant thistle (*Carduus eariana*) and the wild pumpkin, and to get at the latter they bite the hard dry shell into pieces with their powerful beaks. When a horseman appears in the distance they rise in a compact flock, with loud harsh screams, and hover above him, within a very few yards of his head, their combined dissonant voices producing an uproar which is only equalled in that pandemonium of noises, the Parrot House in the Zoological Gardens of London. They are extremely social, so much so that their flocks do not break up in the breeding season; and their burrows, which they excavate in a perpendicular cliff or high bank, are placed close together; so that when the gauchos take the young birds—esteemed a great delicacy—the person who ventures down by means of a rope attached to his waist is able to rifle a whole colony. The burrow is 3 to 5 feet deep, and four white eggs are deposited on a slight nest at the extremity. I have only tasted the old birds, and found their flesh very bitter, and scarcely palatable."

Mr. E. W. White writes: " At Guazan this

Parrot is found in large flocks, and settles usually on bare trees. By the natives it is called 'Loro Barranquero,' as it builds its nest in holes in the barrancas or cliffs. When one is shot of a flock flying over, the rest will continue to whirl round the spot long enough to give the sportsman time to kill nearly the whole; and at every shot, as the victims tumble, the rest redouble their screams, so that the noise, always great, becomes at length deafening.

"At Cosquin, in the neighbourhood of Cordoba, I had more opportunity of observing them. They are extremely abundant throughout the sierras there, and are very destructive to crops.

"On each patch of ground sown with wheat or maize a boy is stationed as a scarecrow; and the shouts of these, the whole length of the valley, some leagues, almost rival in intensity the Parrot chorus.

"The warfare between the birds and their tormentors, however, is invariably in favour of the former, as they have a habit of gliding unseen to the bottom of the stems, which they bite through, so that the stalk falls and they consume the grain at leisure.

"In the winter, fallen fruit kernels of the woods afford them sustenance. They breed in deep holes on the cliff faces; and the attempt to sack their nests is very hazardous. Four or five eggs are usually found in a clutch." (*P. Z. S.*, 1882, p. 620.)

The Lesser Patagonian Conure is not a rare bird in captivity in this country. It is a hardy and intelligent species, readily becoming tame, and sometimes learning to repeat a few words distinctly. I am not aware of its ever having bred in captivity. It is usually kept singly, as a cage-bird, although it will readily withstand the rigours of an English winter in an outdoor aviary.

In an interesting paper on Parrakeets, which

appeared in the *Feathered World* of October 11, 1895, Mr. O. E. Cresswell gives the following account of a Patagonian Conure in his possession: " He has never been sick or sorry, is extraordinarily hardy, and his great imitative powers are a constant source of amusement. Not only can he say many things, and call many names—always strictly parliamentary ones —but he mimics various odd sounds to perfection, and we fancy goes through a kind of Punch and Judy drama in a foreign tongue. . . .

" The Conure was for a long while very shy; it was months before he ever uttered his own name, 'Cockie.' Then he began to imitate odd sounds, not always a desirable accomplishment. The valve of a stove in the bird room squeaked horribly; as one advanced to open it he anticipated the squeak with wonderful metallic precision. Then for a while he lived in a room within sound of the wood house. He soon imitated sawing to perfection; scraping up and down the bars of his cage, and rendering the occasional squeak of the saw with his voice. He is full of likes and dislikes, and would always say more for the youngest of the three attendants of the aviaries than for anyone else. He soon learnt abbreviations of the names of all three, taking particular pains with, to him, the difficult utterance of 'Frank.' Private whistle signals was his next accomplishment; which he sometimes screams out of the window with puzzling accuracy as servants pass. He is a capital judge of people, and equal to any watchdog. If a tramp approaches the house he screams in a particular key till someone comes, but takes no notice of well-dressed visitors or carriages, unless a dog accompanies them, when he shrieks for protection. Jealousy is a powerful passion with most parrots, and when he is wayward and won't talk, if his attendant gets a bantam or pigeon and kisses it, Cockie almost always speaks lest the other bird should speak first."

The following is a description of the adult: Upper parts, including the whole of the head, dark olive-green, darker on the forehead; lower back yellow; throat and breast greyish brown; an irregular whitish band crosses the upper part of the breast; abdomen yellow, with a large patch of red in the centre; thighs red; primary coverts and quills blue; tail above olive-green, below brown.

The illustration is from a living example in the Zoological Society's collection.

THE GREATER PATAGONIAN CONURE.

Cyanolyseus byroni (Childr.).

This large Conure is not often imported alive to Europe, but it has been represented in the Zoological Society's collection, and from its similarity to the last described may have passed for that species on some occasions. It is considerably larger than *C. patagonicus*, measuring 20 inches in total length, and the whitish breast-band is much more clearly defined. In other respects the two species are identical.

C. byroni inhabits Chili.

Genus HENICOGNATHUS, Gray.

THE SLIGHT-BILLED PARRAKEET.

Henicognathus leptorhynchus (King).

This remarkable species is the sole representative of its genus, and is at once easily distinguishable from all other species by its long and comparatively straight upper mandible. It inhabits Chili, where it is said to be numerous, inhabiting the forests for the greater part of the year, and visiting the cultivated districts when the grain crops are ripe. Although practically unknown in this country in a living state, the Slight-billed Parrakeet has been represented in the Zoological Society's unparalleled collection.

H. Grönvold, del.

Henicognathus leptorhynchus. ¾.

The prevailing colour of this species is dull green, brighter on the top of the head, where each feather has a dusky edging; the forehead, lores, and a ring round the eye, crimson; a faint patch of dull crimson on the abdomen; primaries and primary-coverts tinged with blue; tail dull red, becoming greenish towards the tip; iris orange; feet and bill lead colour. Total length about 15 inches. The sexes are alike.

Genus MICROSITTACE, Bp.

THE CHILIAN CONURE.

Micrositace ferruginea, P. L. S. (Müll.).

This is another of those Parrakeets that are only to be met with on rare occasions in Zoological Gardens, or may perhaps be brought home privately by travellers. It inhabits Chili and the Straits of Magellan, and is the sole representative of the genus.

The sexes are alike, and are coloured as follows: Prevailing colour dull green, each feather having a dusky margin; crown tinged with blue, and with black edges to the feathers; forehead and lores dull reddish-brown, and a patch of this colour on the abdomen; primaries and primary-coverts green, with a bluish tinge; tail reddish-brown, with greenish tips to the feathers. Total length about 13 inches.

Genus PYRRHURA.

This genus contains some twenty-three known species of small, and for the most part very beautiful, Conures, in which the nostrils are exposed, and the tail is frequently, more or less, reddish brown. The genus ranges from Costa Rica to Southern Brazil and the north of the Argentine Republic. So far as I am aware, but five species have been imported as cage birds, at any rate within the last thirty or forty years. The sexes are alike, as in all of the Conures.

THE RED-EARED CONURE.

Pyrrhura cruentata (Neuwied).

This rare species inhabits the south-east of Brazil, from Bahia to Rio Janeiro. It has been represented in the Zoological Society's menagerie, but is almost unknown in private collections.

Prevailing colour green; top of head and nape brownish-black, each feather edged with yellowish; frontal edge, lores, ear-coverts, and a ring round the eyes, reddish-brown; an orange-yellow patch on the side of the neck; cheeks green; throat blue, and a narrow collar of the same colour on the hind neck; a reddish patch on the rump and on the abdomen; bend of wing crimson; wing-coverts green, tinged with blue; outer primaries blue; inner primaries and secondaries green; tail above olive, tinged with reddish-brown on the inner webs; below reddish-brown. Total length, $11\frac{1}{2}$ inches.

THE RED-BELLIED CONURE.

Pyrrhura vittata (Shaw).

This is another of the rarely-imported Conures. Specimens have, however, been exhibited at the London Zoological Gardens on various occasions. It inhabits, like the preceding species, the south-eastern parts of Brazil.

Mr. J. F. Hamilton writes: "I met them frequently in the neighbourhood of maize-plantations, on which they commit great havoc. Along the Saõ-Paulo railroad flocks were frequently seen flying overhead." (*Ibis*, 1871, p. 308.)

Prevailing colour green; a chestnut band on the forehead; cheeks green; throat and breast olive, with dusky bars on the edges of the feathers; a reddish-brown patch on the lower back, and a patch of the same colour on the abdomen; outer primaries blue; tail green, becoming coppery-red towards the tip. Total length about $10\frac{1}{2}$ inches.

Count Salvadori remarks that "in some specimens there are hoary spots, edged with dusky, more or less distinct, on the occiput and nape."

THE WHITE-EARED CONURE.
Pyrrhura leucotis (Kuhl).

This is another of the Brazilian Conures, and one that is far more often imported into this country than any other member of the genus (*Pyrrhura*). It is said to inhabit the wooded region near the coast, and to congregate in flocks, now and then paying visits to the cultivated fields and committing sad havoc among the grain crops.

P. leucotis is one of the prettiest of the Conures, and from an aviculturist's point of view a desirable species so long as it is not allowed to associate with other birds. It is exceedingly spiteful and mischievous, and Dr. Greene mentions a case in which a nest of young Cockatiels were wantonly attacked by a pair of these Conures, and most of the young killed or maimed. (*Cf. Feathered Friends*, p. 213.)

This species has probably bred in captivity both in England and on the Continent, but I can find no record of young having been *successfully* reared.

In *Notes on Cage Birds* (Second Series, p. 181), a correspondent signing himself " E. J." writes: " With the exception of Cockatiels, the only other parrots that have bred with me this year are White-eared Conures. Four young were hatched during the first week in August (1887), and lived some time, but grew very slowly. Two entirely disappeared; one had his head eaten off and the other was bitten about the body."

The Hon. and Rev. Canon Dutton writes: " I had a pair of White-eared Conures, which were given to me because one picked itself. They were turned into an aviary, but they showed no sign of wishing to breed, and as they were wild and uninteresting I parted with them." (*Avic. Mag.*, vol. iv., p. 173.)

Prevailing colour green; top of the head blackish-brown; cheeks chestnut; ear-coverts white; hind neck blue; throat dull bluish; upper breast greenish, each feather having two bands at the tip, one whitish-grey, the other blackish on the edge; lower back dark red; abdomen dark red; bend of the wing red; primaries mostly blue; tail above reddish-brown; tail below coppery brown-red; bill horn-brown. Total. length, slightly over 8 inches.

The illustration is from a living specimen in the Zoological Society's Gardens.

THE BLUE-WINGED CONURE.

Pyrrhura picta (P. L. S. Müll.).

This species inhabits Guiana and Trinidad, and is very rarely brought alive to Europe. It has been represented at the London Zoological Gardens.

The following is a description of the adult: Prevailing colour green; top of the head and nape black; upper part of cheeks chestnut; forehead and lower part of cheeks and a faint band on the nape blue; ear-coverts grey; throat brown, upper breast greenish, the feathers of both being margined with light greyish edges, producing a scaly appearance; lower back and abdomen dark red; bend of wing red; primaries mostly blue; tail above reddish-brown; below coppery-red. Total length, $9\frac{1}{2}$ inches.

THE PEARLY CONURE.

Pyrrhura perlata (Spix).

This Conure is but rarely imported. It inhabits Lower Amazonia. The Zoological Society has possessed a pair.

Prevailing colour green; forehead, hind neck, cheeks, upper breast, sides, vent and tail-coverts bluish; top of the head and nape brown; ear-coverts greyish-brown; throat and breast brown, each feather being lighter on the edges; middle of the abdomen reddish-brown; primaries blue; bend of the wing red; tail above and below reddish-brown, darker below. Total length, $9\frac{1}{2}$ inches.

The illustration is drawn from skins in the British Museum.

Genus MYOPSITTACUS, Bp.

This genus contains but two known species, but it is one of the most interesting in the whole Parrot family from the fact that these are the only nest-building parrots known, with the exception of the Love-birds (*Agapornis*), which line their nest-hole with the pliant pieces of bark from green twigs, and may therefore be termed nest-building parrots. *Myopsittacus*, however, builds a large nest of sticks amongst the branches of tall trees which no other parrots, so far as is known, ever do.

THE GREY-BREASTED PARRAKEET.

Myopsittacus monachus (Bodd.).

Coloured Figure, GREENE'S *Parrots in Captivity*, Vol. III.

This species, which is also known as the Quaker or Monk Parrakeet, inhabits Argentina, Paraguay, Uruguay, and Bolivia. It is gregarious, always living in flocks, which sometimes number many thousand individuals.

Darwin came across flocks of these Parrakeets while travelling down the Parana River, during the voyage of the "Beagle," and he tells us that it appears to prefer the tall trees on the islands to any other situation for its building-place. "A number of nests," he writes, "are placed so close together as to form one great mass of sticks. These parrots always live in flocks, and commit great ravages on the cornfields. I was told that near Colonia two thousand five hundred were killed in the course of one year."

By far the best account that I can find of these Parrakeets in a wild state is that given by Mr. E. Gibson in the *Ibis* (1880, p. 3). His observations were made in the neighbourhood of Cape San Antonio, in Buenos Ayres, where these birds are termed "Loros," and, although his account is long, it is well worth quoting here. He writes: "In thousands. All the woods are full of their great nests, with their bright-coloured talkative denizens; all day long rises their noisy chatter, drowning almost every other sound in wood and garden; and, lastly, all the apples, pears, peaches, and medlars in the garden meet with their but too thorough appreciation.

"This species . . . is gregarious, feeding in flocks and building in communities.

"It is one, too, that I have rather an animosity against; for, like the Lapwing (*Vanellus cayennensis*) in the plains, it plays the part of sentinel to all its feathered neighbours. One steals gently through the underwood, stalking some wary bird of prey or flock of tree-building Teal, and glancing up in a deprecatory way at the Parroquets' nests—but all in vain: the subdued chatter suddenly becomes an ominous silence (sufficient betrayal in itself);

hundred pairs of black beady eyes survey the intruder from the nests and neighbouring branches; and then there follows the whirring of as many wings, while

From *The Royal Natural History*.

GREY-BREASTED PARRAKEET, *Myopsittacus monachus*.

a row arises that would put all the rooks that ever 'caw'd' to shame. Gone is the warned quarry, while the exasperated writer of these notes makes a hasty calculation as to which is the largest group of Perroquets, and knocks over half-a-dozen accordingly, 'to encourage the rest.'

"The nests are frequented all the year round; and it is of rare occurrence to find any large one totally deserted during the day.

"During the summer and autumn the thistle is the principal food of *B. monachus*. In the former season the flowering thistle-heads are cut off, and generally carried to the top of the nearest tree, there to be pulled to pieces for the sake of the green kernel. In the autumn, when the ripe seeds have fallen, they are sought for on the ground.

"Every morning, just between daybreak and sunrise, is the favourite hour for their depredations in the garden, though scores frequent it during the day also. They never carry off the fruit, but gnaw it as it hangs, abandoning one apple for another, and that for a third, in a most destructive manner.

"To show how little does shyness enter into their constitution, I have known seventy-five to be shot in the garden in the course of the forenoon, the fowler standing in the open, close to a dead tree which formed their favourite perch on arriving from the surrounding woods. The Basques and Italians who come from the neighbouring township for a day's Perroquet-shooting scorn to fire at any group that will not yield four or five dead birds at least, and, indifferent shots as they are, kill as many as they can carry. . . . .

"The flight of *B. monachus* is rapid, with quick flutters of the wings, which seem never to be raised to the level of the body, nor yet brought sufficiently forward. Like *Conurus patagonus*, too, the straight unexpanded tail fails to keep the bird on an even keel, as it were, first one side rising higher and then the other.

"While the presence of Carancho or Chimango is ignored, any other bird of prey is generally mobbed when it first appears in the woods. All the Perroquets rise in a regular crowd, and hover over and above it, screaming and chattering angrily.

"Young birds are sometimes taught to speak; but their articulation is, as a rule, indistinct. I remember hearing of one, however, which was seized and carried off by a Carancho, giving utterance to its despair in a singularly appropriate exclamation—'Ay de mi, ay de mi' (alas! alas!). One, which had escaped from its owner, long retained the hoarse 'Pretty Poll' it had acquired in its captivity, no doubt to the envy of its uneducated relatives, and to my frequent bewilderment as I strolled through the wood it frequented.

"*Breeding-Notes.*—The nests are generally suspended from the extremities of branches, to which they are firmly built or woven in. The new nests consist only of two chambers, the porch and nest proper, and are built and inhabited by a single pair of birds. These become gradually added to, till plenty of them come to weigh perhaps a quarter of a ton each, and are of a bulk enough to fill a large cart. Thorny tala twigs (no branches), firmly interlaced, form the only material; and there is no lining to the chambers, even in the breeding-season. Some old forest trees have seven or eight of these huge masses suspended to their branches, while the ground underneath is strewn with twigs and the remains of fallen nests. The entrance to the chambers is almost invariably underneath, or, if on the side, is protected by the overhanging eave, doubtless in both cases as a safeguard against the attacks of the opossum (*Didelphys aurita*). These entrances lead into a porch or outer chamber; and the latter communicates with the breeding chamber. There is no interior communication between these sets of apartments; and each set is inhabited, in the breeding-season at least, by one pair of 'Loros.' The number of pairs perhaps never exceeds a dozen, even with the largest nests. Repairs are carried on all the year round; but additions and new nests are only formed towards the spring.

"Opossums are frequently found in one or other of the upper chambers, the entrance having been made too high, and so affording access. But though they take up their abode there, they cannot force their way into the remainder of the nest; and the Perroquets refuse to be driven away. In fact, the latter are most aggravatingly obstinate on the question of their manorial rights. Notwithstanding all our efforts, two or three nests are now established in the garden itself, in some fine old pine trees; and there the birds sit all day and hack off the twigs, or descend on to the fruit-trees and eat peaches. I have picked off these squatters through the day, and banged whole handfuls of shot into the nests at night, besides frequently pulling down the latter; but the 'Loros' could give Bruce's famous spider heavy odds in the perseverance line of business, and beat it then; so it is not surprising that they have had the best of the warfare.

"A species of Teal breeds in the nests of *B. monachus;* and in one case I found an opossum domiciled in an upper chamber, Perroquets occupying all the others but one, in which a Teal was sitting on eggs.

"The breeding-season does not begin till about the 1st of November; but I have taken eggs as late as the 19th of December. Seven and eight are the largest clutches taken; but I have never seen more than six of these hatched out. As I said before, the eggs are laid on the thickly-matted flooring of the second or inner chamber, and without any preparatory lining."

The Grey-breasted Parrakeet is, at times, imported freely to this country, and sold at a remarkably low figure, but it cannot be said to be an especially attractive species, although one sometimes hears of individuals being singularly gifted with the power of speech, and becoming very tame. As an instance, the following quotation from *Notes on Cage Birds* (Sec. Series, p. 184), will interest my readers. "T. P. B." writes: "My bird is an excellent talker; its longest sentence is:—

> Merrily danced the Quaker's wife,
> With all her bairns about her.

But it can say a large variety of things, most of them picked up by itself without teaching. It also does tricks to order. At the command 'Act daft!' it ruffles up all its feathers, puts one leg up, opens its beak wide, and nods its head, imitating an idiot very well; 'Act proud!' it turns its beak against its breast and draws up its head.

"The bird is most affectionate to its owners, but rather a terror to visitors. She is never confined at all in the daytime, and likes hanging by her feet over the door, and pulling off the servants' caps as they enter, and then laughing at them. In fact, she is as full of tricks as a monkey, and as intelligent as most human beings, understanding all that is said in her presence. Her courage is wonderful; she is afraid of nothing whatever, except, curiously enough, a ladder. She will 'go' for strange dogs or cats, which generally flee for their lives, terrified by her audacity. I put her in a paper bag or under my coat sometimes, as she cannot be frightened. Now and then she demands a bath, by a peculiar squawk, and when a large basin of lukewarm water is brought in and put on the floor, she goes into it and enjoys herself. So entirely impervious to cold is she that I have known her to sit and dry herself on the crack between two window sashes, with a keen north-easter blowing through it. She has never had a moment's illness since I got her, except once when I trod on her by accident as she was playing with the shavings in my workroom. She moped then for a day or two, but got off safe with a slight twist in one wing, which impedes her flight in some degree.

"Her staple food is canary and hemp seed. She will not touch nuts of any sort, but comes down on the table at meals and nibbles everything—curry, fish, potato, bread, &c. Her favourite dish is plum-pudding. She is very fond of tea, and can climb on the edge of a cup without upsetting it."

I can find no record of young having been reared by this species in an English aviary, although it will sometimes build huge, untidy nests if provided with plenty of twigs. Mrs. C. Buxton, however, quoted by Dr. Greene in his *Parrots in Captivity*, records the successful rearing of two broods of Quakers in a nest built "on the top of a slender fir" in the open.

The Grey-breasted Parrakeet possesses a very powerful bill, and is quite capable of gnawing a hole in the woodwork of any but an unusually strongly-constructed aviary, or of biting through thin wire, and this fact should be taken into consideration by those who would keep Quakers.

Canary, millet, and hemp seed, oats, sunflower seed, and other small corn, should form the staple diet of these Parrakeets in captivity; and fruit of all kinds should be added in season.

The prevailing colour of this species is green, yellower on the abdomen, flanks, and under tail-coverts; the face, throat and breast grey, most of the feathers having a lighter margin, which presents a scaly appearance; quills bluish; tail green above, bluish below. Total length, $11\frac{1}{2}$ inches.

Genus BOLBORHYNCHUS, Bp.

The range of this genus extends from Mexico to Northern Chili and the Argentine Republic. There are seven known species, but examples of only one, so far as I am aware, have been imported alive to this country.

THE LINEOLATED PARRAKEET.

Bolborhynchus lineolatus (Cass.).

This curiously-marked little Parrakeet inhabits Central America, from Southern Mexico to Panama, and perhaps Venezuela.

Mr. Salvin remarks: "Mr. Godman and I discovered a small flock in the Volcan de Fuego, at an elevation of about 8,000 feet above the sea level. We saw them in a tree overhanging the track to Acatenango, above the Indian huts of Calderas, and succeeded in securing three or four specimens before the rest took flight and flew away." (*Ibis*, 1871, p. 94.)

In captivity this species is said to be tame and gentle. It is somewhat delicate, and should never be subjected to a lower temperature than 60° Fahr.

Canary and millet seed and ripe fruit should form its staple diet.

The prevailing colour is dull green, the top of the head being brighter; forehead, cheeks, and under parts yellowish-green; almost the entire plumage barred and spotted with black. Total length about 7 inches. The plumage is alike in the sexes.

Genus PSITTACULA, Ill.

The present genus, which contains the Parrotlets, the smallest members of the sub-family (*Conurinæ*), ranges from Mexico through the northern parts of South America to Bolivia.

As the members of this genus have frequently been termed "Love-birds," and thus confounded with the true Love-birds (*Agapornis*), it may be well to point out that, although at first sight the Parrotlets appear to resemble the Love-birds, they differ very considerably from them in several important points. In the first place the true Love-birds actually carry building material to their nest-hole, which they line with this, whereas the Parrotlets lay their eggs on the decayed, bare wood in the hole of some tree, like other Parrakeets. The tail-feathers of the Parrotlets, although short, are pointed, not rounded as in *Agapornis*. I believe that one species only has been imported alive to this country, which is to be regretted, as there are many far more beautiful species than the common *P. passerina*. Mr. Walter Goodfellow in his journey through Ecuador met with the lovely *P. cœlestis*, and thus describes it: "Around Guayaquil, and especially on the Island of Puná at the mouth of the river, the tiny *Psittacula cœlestis* was fairly common, and at times could be bought in the town for twopence or threepence each. These are lovely little birds, and would make a grand addition to our aviaries at home. Its total length does not exceed 4 inches. The head, throat and cheeks are bright light green, and there is a brilliant blue spot by the eye; the nape is greyish-blue, but the back is rather a difficult colour to describe, being what I call a greenish stone colour. The wings are sapphire with a green edging to the primaries. The tail is bluish-green with the upper tail-coverts turquoise, and the rump bright sapphire-blue. The breast and under parts are light green. It will be seen by those who are unacquainted with the bird that it has a lovely arrangement of colouring. The back is particularly soft looking, and the shade of sapphire one of the richest that could be found in any bird." (*Avic. Mag.*, vol. vi., p. 123.)

THE PASSERINE PARROTLET.

Psittacula passerina (Linn.).

Coloured Figure, GREENE'S *Parrots in Captivity*, Vol. II.

This species, frequently but erroneously termed the "Blue-winged Love-bird," is at times imported to this country in large numbers, and sold at a very low price. It inhabits Brazil, where it is said to be very common. Mr. W. A. Forbes, writing on the birds of North Eastern Brazil, remarks: "I first saw the South American 'Love-bird' on the road between Iguarassu and Olinda, and subsequently in nearly every place I stayed at. In the interior it is very abundant, flying about in large flocks, often in company with the Brazilian Canary (*Sycalis flaveola*), generally frequenting the gardens or plantations round houses, especially where there are castor-oil (*Ricinus*) trees. Its flight, though quick, is not prolonged. You see two or three alight on a bush or small tree, which sit there quietly till they are joined by two or three more; then perhaps a few more arrive, and so on, till twenty or thirty assemble

From *The Royal Natural History.*
PASSERINE PARROTLET, *Psittacula passerina.*

in the same tree, and after a while they fly off, together or in small batches, as they arrived.

"Mr. Weaver, at Quipapá, told me that a few weeks before my visit these Parrakeets were immensely numerous there, and that the numbers we then saw were nothing to what there had been previously, before the greater part had gone more inland towards the Sertoes, as they do towards the commencement of the dry season. The Brazilians call it 'Perriquito Tapacú.'" (*Ibis*, 1881, p. 353.)

In captivity this species is said to have bred frequently in Germany and elsewhere on the Continent, but there are very few records of young being successfully reared in the United Kingdom. This is strange, as the bird is so frequently imported, and seems to be ready enough to breed if suitable surroundings are provided for it. The following account of a pair of Passerine Parrotlets breeding in a bell cage, 21 in. high and 13 in. in diameter, is of great interest, and shows how very accommodating these little birds are. Mr. O. E. Cresswell writes: "In the summer of 1892 I bought a pair of these sweet little Parrakeets. It never occurred to me that they might breed in a cage, and, so far as I can recollect, I never gave them a cocoanut husk till the following year. Their cage, through the winter, was kept in a comfortable bird-room, but its inmates were very quiet and undemonstrative. Through the lovely summer of 1893 I changed their residence, and the cage was daily carried out into the garden. They became very lively, and were specially excited at hearing the sound of swallows overhead, whose chattering much resembles their own; and I saw some signs of breeding. However, in the middle of September I went abroad, but heard later on that the hen had laid an egg. She laid five and sat well, but soon after my return in October she was disturbed and deserted the nest. Examination showed that her eggs were all fertile, and ought to have hatched. The birds then showed no signs of breeding again, and spent the winter as before. The summer of 1894 was far less hot, and it was only in the later summer months that the cage was carried out of doors. They then at once showed signs of breeding, and actually incubated while the cage was carried in and out; but no eggs hatched, though several were fertile.

"In 1895 I had their daily outdoor airing begun earlier, and the result was that the hen laid her first egg in July. At irregular intervals she laid seven, but one was thin-shelled and broke, and I had to regularly overhaul the nest—this she now allows me to do with perfect composure. I took away three clear eggs and left three apparently good. In due time one was hatched, and exactly a week after another; by this time the first-born had grown immensely and I fancy suffocated the younger, which was soon found dead. The survivor, in its earlier stages, was certainly a most hideous little creature. Its head was about the size of the rest of its body, and that looked like a lump of raw meat. For four weeks it showed no sign of down, then all at once specks of green appeared, and the feathers developed so fast that in another fortnight it was fledged and scarcely distinguishable from the mother. All through the time of incubation the cock diligently fed the hen, and at night slept in the cocoanut with her; and both parents fed the baby. Before it emerged from the cocoanut I heard cracking, which I discovered to be that of hemp, which apparently the parents had carried up whole. I used to throw in more, and the nestling quickly ate it. A tiresome stage ensued, when the little creature used to scramble down to the ground and could not climb up again, but this only lasted three or four days." (*Avic. Mag.*, vol. ii., p. 144.)

Blue-winged Parrotlets should always be kept in pairs, as they are most affectionate one towards the other, and in this respect resemble the true Lovebirds. Their staple food should be canary- and millet-seed, and hemp may be given sparingly. Green food, such as chickweed and flowering grass, should be freely supplied during the summer months.

The male is coloured as follows: Bright green; under-parts paler green; rump, most of the secondaries, primaries, primary-coverts, and wing-coverts bright ultramarine blue.

The female is entirely green, paler below, with no blue whatever in her plumage; the rump is bright emerald-green.

Total length about 5 inches.

Genus BROTOGERYS, Vig.

The last genus of the present sub-family contains twelve known species, of which eight at least have been imported alive into this country. Most of them become tame remarkably quickly if kindly treated, and make delightful pets.

These little Parrakeets are only moderately hardy, and should therefore never be subjected to a lower temperature than 55° or 60° Fahr., although they may not at first seem to feel the cold.

When first imported they very often have the quill feathers cut quite short, which is very annoying if they are intended for a large aviary, as it renders them incapable of flight. Before purchasing these birds, therefore, it is advisable to examine their wings.

Their food should consist chiefly of canary-seed and ripe fruit, but white and spray millet may be added in small quantities, and plain biscuit, given in strict moderation, is much appreciated by some species.

None of the members of this genus make good talkers, but some will occasionally learn to repeat a few words, and most will readily learn to imitate sounds, such as the notes of other birds, especially other Parrots.

The sexes are outwardly alike, but the males are, as a rule, slightly larger than the females.

The range of this genus extends from Central America to Brazil, Peru and Bolivia.

From The Royal Natural History.

ALL-GREEN PARRAKEET, *Brotogerys tirica.*

THE ALL-GREEN PARRAKEET.
Brotogerys tirica (Gm.).

This species, the largest of the genus, inhabits Eastern Brazil, where it is said to be exceedingly common, associating in large flocks, and committing serious injury to the grain crops.

It has lately been imported into this country in some numbers, and may occasionally be purchased at a remarkably low figure. It is a gentle bird, and may safely be kept in an aviary with small birds. Miss R. Alderson writes: "The All-greens are said to become very tame, but so far mine are rather shy, though not so nervous as when I obtained them. The pair always keep together, and seem very inoffensive towards other birds."

This species does not appear to have bred in captivity, in the United Kingdom at any rate.

As its name implies, this Parrakeet is green, the forehead, sides of the head, and under-parts being paler yellowish-green. The primaries and their coverts are blue, and the two central tail-feathers are tinged with this colour.

The total length of this species is about 10 inches, the tail measuring 5 inches.

THE CANARY-WINGED PARRAKEET.
Brotogerys chiriri (Vieill.).

This species inhabits Central and South-eastern Brazil, Bolivia, Amazonia and Eastern Peru. It is said to frequent the river banks in flocks, and to breed in the white ants' nests, laying five or six white eggs. (*Cf. P. Z. S.*, 1873, p. 300.)

The Canary-winged Parrakeet is not a common

cage-bird in this country, although at certain times small consignments reach the bird-dealers. It is a very desirable species, though somewhat noisy.

Prevailing colour green, lighter on the underparts; the bastard-wing and outermost wing-coverts bright yellow; primary coverts blue. Total length about 9½ inches.

THE WHITE-WINGED PARRAKEET.

Brotogerys virescens (Gm.).

This Parrakeet is decidedly rarer in captivity than the preceding species, which it closely resembles in appearance. It inhabits the Amazon valley, and Mr. Wallace found it in flocks of several hundreds in the island of Mexiana. (*Cf. P. Z. S.*, 1867, p. 588.)

My friend, Mr. R. Phillipps, possessed a male of this species in 1897, which became very tame, and was at that time said to be the only living specimen in Europe. (*Cf. Avic. Mag.*, vol. iv., p. 18.) The species had, however, been represented in the Zoological Society's collection prior to that date, and Mr. Goodchild has drawn the accompanying figure from a specimen now living in their gardens.

The prevailing colour is green, the forehead and cheeks being tinged with blue; primaries mostly white; primary-coverts blue; secondaries white, with a yellowish tinge; greater wing-coverts yellow. Total length about 8¾ inches.

THE ORANGE-FLANKED PARRAKEET.

Brotogerys pyrrhopterus (Lath.).

This little Parrakeet would make the most charming pet imaginable if it were not so noisy. I have never seen a really wild one. They always seem to be perfectly tame when imported, and will often allow themselves to be carried about on one's finger from the first. But their noisy chatter is most trying and is the one objection to them. A few years ago they were considered great rarities, but at the present time are imported in considerable numbers, although they still command a fairly high price, as the bird-dealers are fond of selling them as ladies' pets.

Mr. Walter Goodfellow met with vast flocks of these Parrakeets in the neighbourhood of Guayaquil, where, he tells us, they commit considerable damage in the banana plantations. In the latter town any number of these birds, which are locally known as "Paviches," could be purchased at 2½d. each. (*Cf. Avic. Mag.*, vol. vi., p. 68.)

I have never heard of an instance of this species having bred in captivity.

Prevailing colour green, paler, and more yellowish on the under-parts; top of the head bluish-green; forehead, chin, and sides of the head greyish; primary coverts blue; under wing-coverts orange. Total length about 8 inches. The male is slightly larger than the female.

This species inhabits the north-west of Peru and the west of Ecuador.

THE TOVI PARRAKEET.

Brotogerys jugularis (P. L. S., Mull.).

This is the most frequently imported of the genus, and can generally be purchased at a very moderate price. Like most of its congeners, it very soon becomes perfectly tame if kindly treated, and soon follows its owner about the aviary, and will readily chum up with any other species of *Brotogerys*. A specimen now in my possession has formed a close friendship with a female *B. tuipara*, and the two are always close together, either preening one another's feathers or having a heated argument with a pair of Rosy-faced Lovebirds in the next aviary.

The Tovi Parrakeet inhabits Mexico, Central America, and Colombia. Mr. Goodfellow tells us that the Archidona Indian women carry them about on their shoulders when employed in their household duties, and seem particularly fond of them. (*Avic. Mag.*, vol. vi., p. 125.)

A pair of these Parrakeets belonging to Mr. Phillipps became positively spiteful towards their owner. He writes: " The female was a spiteful little wasp, and would seize hold of any exposed piece of flesh she could reach, my ears and neck being her favourite morsels; and the male, excited and incited to evil by this Jezebel, would join in most heartily. The more I dodged about and tried to beat them off the more waspish and Jezebelish would they become, shrieking all the while at the top of their voices like a couple of infuriated women. The male was really a good-hearted fellow, but was superbly chivalrous, always standing up for his wife. For some years, off and on, a six-foot flight cage in my dining-room was their home, and the end two-foot door I would innocently open and would attend to the food, the male sitting perfectly still on a perch opposite and rather below me, the female being on her eggs at the other end. On one such an occasion the male suddenly dashed at my forehead almost with the weight and violence of a thrown-up cricket ball, half stunning me and making quite a respectable wound, although the beak did not readily catch hold of the tightly-drawn skin. For a few days I was very cautious, but, finding him quite quiet, once more gave him an opportunity, of which he promptly availed himself. Darting straight at me like a bolt from a cross-bow, without cry or the slightest warning, he seized me sideways across the centre of the upper lip, a little below the nose, and hung on like a bulldog." (*Avic. Mag.*, vol. vi., p. 144.)

The Tovi Parrakeet does not appear to have been successfully bred in captivity in this country, although Mr. Phillipps mentions eggs.

The prevailing colour of this bird is green, becoming yellowish on the under-parts, with a slight bluish tinge on the abdomen; a spot of orange on the chin; interscapular region olive-green; greater wing-coverts and quills bluish-green; primary coverts blue; tail green, with the central feathers tinged with blue. Total length about $7\frac{3}{4}$ inches. The sexes are alike in colour, but the male is the larger bird.

THE GOLDEN-FRONTED PARRAKEET.

Brotogerys tuipara (Gm.).

This species inhabits Lower Amazonia, and is very rarely met with in captivity; I have only seen one living specimen—a female, which is now in my possession. This bird, with another—also a female—

was purchased by my friend, Mr. Reginald Phillipps, on March 17, 1894, so that it has now (October, 1902) lived in captivity more than eight years. While in Mr. Phillipps' possession it paired with a male Musky Lorikeet (*Glossopsittacus concinnus*), and laid four clear eggs, which Mr. Phillipps describes as "round ovals of large size, larger than those of the Golden-shouldered Parrakeet, but not exhibiting the slight inclination to quince-shape of most of the eggs of the Tovi with which I was favoured some years ago" (*Avic. Mag.*, vol. vi., p. 142). The Tuipara came to me on March 31, 1900, together with the Musky Lorikeet, who very soon developed the bad habit of plucking out his wife's feathers, so that she became a most disreputable looking creature. The birds were separated, with the result that the Tuipara gradually regained her plumage, and has now long been very sleek and well. She has recently been presented with a husband in the form of the Tovi Parrakeet mentioned in the preceding chapter, and the two birds are devoted to one another, and always close together. The Tuipara imitates the notes of other Parrakeets very faithfully; recently I quite thought a Brown's Parrakeet (*Platycercus browni*) had escaped into the aviary occupied by the Tuipara, as I distinctly heard, as I thought, the Brown's call-note rapidly repeated; I soon discovered, however, that the notes proceeded from the Tuipara, a species whose natural notes are very unlike those of any of the *Platycerci*.

The Tuipara, like other members of the genus, is exceedingly fond of fruit, and will eat any amount of this if it can get it. During the summer months she lives in a large aviary, and when I enter she is often hidden amongst the leaves of some tree or shrub, but if I happen to have a plum or pear in my hand she immediately makes her appearance, although she has never become tame enough to take it from my hand. She is also very fond of soaked bread or biscuit, and if this is given dry she takes it to the nearest water dish and soaks it before she eats it. She never flies straight to the food, but climbs down the nearest branch or wirework, and then runs along the shelf on which the food is placed. None of the *Brotogerys* Parrakeets descend to the ground if they can help it, and their food should always be placed on a ledge at a distance from the ground.

The Golden-fronted Parrakeet is bright green, somewhat paler on the under-parts; the top of the head is tinged with blue; a narrow band on the forehead, and the chin, orange; quills mostly blue; primary coverts bright orange, most conspicuous in flight; the feet flesh-colour; iris very dark brown. Total length about $7\frac{3}{4}$ inches.

THE GOLDEN-WINGED PARRAKEET.
Brotogerys chrysopterus (Linn.).

This species inhabits Guiana, Venezuela and Trinidad. It has been represented on two occasions at least in the Zoological Society's collection, but is practically unknown to aviculturists. It is somewhat smaller, but very much like *B. tuipara*, the only difference in colouring being in the forehead and chin, which are brown instead of orange. Total length about $6\frac{3}{4}$ inches.

THE TUI PARRAKEET.
Brotogerys tui (Gm.).

The Tui Parrakeet occurs in Western Brazil, Upper Amazonia, Eastern Ecuador and Eastern

Peru. Mr. Walter Goodfellow found it breeding in the month of July near the mouth of the Napo. "They were exceedingly plentiful," he writes, "but at that season were mostly seen in pairs only. Stopping one day on the river bank for a few minutes, just after we entered the Marañon (as the highest part of the Amazon is called), our Indians, I think, must have seen one of these birds enter a tree overhead, or I do not know what would have caused them to suspect there was a nest there. At any rate one of them quickly mounted the tree and produced six young ones from a hollow in the bend of a branch 20 feet above the ground. There was the greatest difference imaginable in their sizes, some being almost feathered, while others were only about half the size and scarcely a feather showing. They were quite willing at once to feed on masticated banana from the Indians' mouths. The yellow on the forehead was already conspicuous in those that were most feathered. I brought a pair from this nest home with me, and still have them in perfect health. I did not trouble to feed mine from the mouth, for small as they were I found they would eat the banana readily by themselves, and would eat all day long if they were kept supplied with fruit. This diet they lived on solely, until we almost reached England. I had, however, laid in a small stock of canary-seed in Parà, in case my bananas gave out on the way, which they did a day or two before we reached Madeira. I found, however, that they took as readily to the seed as if they had never fed on anything else. . . . I believe they could with ease be taught to speak, because mine imitate all sorts of sounds, and the notes of many birds, so that they constantly deceive us in this way. . . . I can heartily recommend these birds as pets, for they are most affectionate, and although I have no time to pay any special attention to mine now, they remain just as tame as when they were with me nearly all day long out in South America." (*Avic. Mag.*, vol. vi., p. 126.)

I think that all aviculturists who have studied the genus *Brotogerys* agree that this, the smallest species, is the most charming as a pet. Mr. Phillipps has probably studied them more than any other aviculturist, and he has most kindly acceded to my request to write a short account of this delightful Parrakeet for this book. He writes:—

" I do not know that there is any member of the Parrot family that may so safely be recommended as a pet as the little Tui Parrakeet. Many Parrots, and practically all the species in the genus *Brotogerys*, make charming pets, but their voices and mandibles are alike trying. This can hardly be said of the Tui. Its voice is not loud and does not worry one, and except when separated from its fellow is seldom noticeable ; it is a timid little bird, and very sociable, and does call out when it finds itself alone, but its worst does not amount to much. For a Parrakeet its beak is feeble. When loose in the aviary or birdroom it does but little damage, excepting to growing trees ; when badly handled it will sometimes lay hold of one's finger, if it be not too large, but nothing more. I have kept the Tui for many years, and have never been *bitten* by one yet. Moreover, I have never known a Tui hurt another bird—generally it is just the other way round, for it has neither the pluck nor the power to defend itself from the attacks of others.

" Like all the species of the genus, and many Conures and others, the Tui *does* like a companion. If it can get a fellow of its own species—good ; if of the opposite sex—better still ; but if it can get neither the one nor the other it will chum with a member of any species of its own genus, or with any small Conure. In a mixed aviary, however, a male Tui has to put up with a good deal when he has a female for a companion. Birds, like the Fair Maid of Perth and her sex generally, in spite of all their talk, do not really admire meekness, gentleness, and such like 'unmanly' virtues; they infinitely prefer a good 'knock-me-down' ruffian; and so my poor Tuis have generally been deserted in favour of some more powerful bird. I do not know what the author has to tell us of a certain female Tuipara now in one of his aviaries. That bird was once the bride of an old Tui of mine. But a bloodthirsty Musky Lorikeet, a regular rake, a right down bad character, after trying to murder his own wife—who would not go to nest—eloped with the Tuipara, by whom he had four clear eggs, now in my collection. Poor old Tui! To save his life I had to shut him up. How many wives have been snatched away from him at various times, and who, alas! deserted him only too willingly, it would be difficult to say.

"The Tui is but a little bird, the smallest and most delicate of all the genus. It may be distinguished at a glance by the patch of Canary yellow on the forehead, the deep chocolate-coloured bill, and the curious yellow-white eyes. With me it has never had a fair chance. Nevertheless, although always anxious to have a mate, it has not shown any particular disposition to nest. Its timidity may have been partly the cause of this, but chiefly I suspect its sensitiveness to cold. A good healthy pair, in a quiet warm aviary, would probably nest after a while. Perhaps its backwardness in courting may at any rate be one reason why its wives so readily desert it in favour of a better man.

"When the Tui of either sex has a chum it follows it about, chatters at you when its companion chatters at you, opens its tiny mouth and protrudes its tongue and pretends to bite when its chum sets this bad example, but keeps a little in the rear. When it has not a chum, then it is that it is most engaging and will elect its owner to be its chum, following him about and stepping cautiously on to the little finger—the only one it can comfortably grasp with its tiny toes—will allow itself to be carried about the house, or anywhere; but you must be gentle, and remember that it is very nervous, and take care that it does not dart off and dash against the nearest window. If you are gentle it will become accustomed to being handled and will allow you to carry it about like a kitten.

"The Tui is a greedy bird and should not be allowed to have access to meat or any kind of soft food, *nor to hemp.* Feed it on canary seed, a tiny morsel of perfectly plain biscuit, spray millet if shut up in a cage, plenty of fruit, do not expose it to cold, and it will live for many years. The more exercise it has the better. In a good sized aviary it may safely be kept with the smallest finches.

"I have never seen a Tui fly on to the ground. If it spies anything tempting down below near a bush it will cautiously climb down head-foremost, but if there be no available shrub it will often go without its food, which should therefore be placed on a shelf or table.

"It is but a feeble talker. I have had a Tui that would utter a short word or two. But a solitary young male, kept as a constant companion, would certainly, I think, learn to talk a little, for it is very fond of imitating its owner, and will stand up to you face to face, answer you back tit for tat, and cheek you to your heart's content.

"Altogether the Tui is a charming little bird; and the more you associate with it the more engaging it will become."

The Tui Parrakeet is, unfortunately, a decidedly rare bird in captivity, although it is much less so than it was a few years ago.

The prevailing colour is green, lighter on the rump, tail-coverts and under-parts; forehead, and in adult males a streak behind the eye, yellow; some blue on the wings; bill chocolate-brown; iris yellowish; feet flesh-colour.

Total length about $6\frac{3}{4}$ inches.

The accompanying illustration is from a living specimen in the Zoological Gardens.

Sub-family PALÆORNITHINÆ.

Genus TANYGNATHUS, Wagl.

This genus is distinguished by the bill being very deep and powerful, with a very broad anterior surface to the lower mandible. It is distributed over the Philippines, Sulu and Sanghir Islands, Celebes, the Moluccas, the Tenimber Islands, the Northwestern Papuan Islands, and the north-west of New Guinea. Eleven species are known, of which living specimens of only three appear to have been imported into this country.

In captivity they should be fed on the usual seeds, nuts and fruit.

THE BLUE-CROWNED PARRAKEET.

Tanygnathus luzonensis (Linn.).

The Blue-crowned Parrakeet inhabits the Philippine Islands, Palawan and Mantanani, and also the Sulu Islands.

Mr. J. Whitehead, writing on the birds of Palawan, remarks of this species: "Very common. This Parrot is one of the first birds that attracts the traveller's attention in Palawan, as it flies swiftly from forest to forest in small flocks, screaming loudly. In flight the wings are often kept much below the level of the body. This species frequents the tops of high trees, feeding on various jungle fruits, but often during the heat of the day they hide amongst thick foliaged trees only a few feet from the ground, from which they dash out with loud screams when disturbed." (*Ibis*, 1890, p. 41.) The species is very rarely imported into this country, but has been represented in the Zoological Society's collection.

The prevailing colour is green, yellowish-green on the under-parts and interscapular region; crown and hind part of head, and sometimes the cheeks, blue; scapulars, lower back and secondaries tinged with blue; some blue on the wings; upper mandible red, lower orange. Total length about 13 inches.

The female is like the male but slightly smaller.

THE GREAT-BILLED PARRAKEET.

Tanygnathus megalorhynchus (Bodd.).

This Parrakeet has a widely-spread range, being found in Western New Guinea, the Papuan Islands, the Moluccas, Sangi and Talaut Islands, and the Togian Islands.

Dr. Meyer tells us that this species loves solitude and avoids human habitations. "In the morning and evening," he writes, "it is not easily found, as it retires into the deep forest; in the middle of the day it sleeps or sits quietly, concealed among the green foliage of high trees, and cries very loudly if any one approaches." (*Ibis*, 1879, p. 48.) This Parrakeet is very rarely imported, but if it were common I much

Tanygnathus megalorhynchus.

doubt whether it would ever be a favourite with aviculturists;—it certainly is not beautiful.

Prevailing colour green, becoming yellowish on the under-parts and on the sides; lower back blue; interscapular region green, each feather being edged with blue; scapulars black, edged with green; upper wing-coverts black, some edged with yellow; tail tipped with yellow; bill red. Total length about 18 inches.

The sexes are alike, but the male is slightly the larger bird.

MUELLER'S PARRAKEET.

Tanygnathus muelleri (Temm).

This Parrakeet inhabits the island of Celebes. It is very rare as a cage-bird in this country, but specimens are sometimes to be seen in the Zoological Gardens. In its habits it does not differ from its congeners.

The sexes are alike, and may be described as follows: Prevailing colour yellowish green, the head being less yellowish than the rest of the body; rump blue; wings green, the wing-coverts edged with blue; tail green above and yellow below; bill red in the adult and whitish in the young.

The young birds sometimes retain the white bill for a considerable time, a fact which has led some writers to consider the white-billed birds a distinct species (*T. albirostris* of Wallace).

Genus PALÆORNIS, Vig.

This genus contains no less than twenty-five known species, inhabiting Africa, from Senegambia to Abyssinia; the Seychelles, Mauritius, and Rodriguez Islands; India, Ceylon, Burma, the Andaman and Nicobar Islands, Cochin China, Hainan, Southern China, the Malay Peninsula and Sunda Islands, Borneo, Sumatra, and Java.

Parrots belonging to this genus have been known to civilisation from a very remote period, considerably longer than any other genus. Ctesias, a Greek physician and historian who lived in the fifth century B.C., described a bird which could have been no other than that now known as the Blossom-headed Parra-

94   PSITTACIDÆ

keet (*P. cyanocephala*) (*cf.* Newton's *Dictionary of Birds*, p. 685). Alexander the Great is said to have brought Parrots to Europe on his return from the

ALEXANDRINE PARRAKEET. From *Cassell's Natural History*.

conquest of India in the year 325 B.C., and his name is still applied to more than one species.

There are no Parrakeets that surpass the members

of the present genus in intelligence, and in the ease with which they learn to imitate sounds and to repeat words, and even sentences. They can also, with little difficulty, be taught to perform tricks. At the recent exhibition at Earl's Court (1902) one of the side shows consisted of some performing Indian birds, amongst which was a most accomplished Alexandrine Parrakeet (*P. nepalensis*). It loaded a small cannon, rammed in the charge, and then fetched a fuse, and climbing on to the back of the miniature gun-carriage, placed the fuse on the touch-hole and fired the cannon.

The adult plumage in this genus is not acquired until the birds are two years of age, at which time they are capable of breeding.

Several species have been successfully bred in captivity. The usual seeds—hemp, canary, and oats —should form their staple diet, to which should be added whatever fruit may happen to be in season; and when there are young to be reared, bread soaked and then squeezed nearly dry should form part of the menu.

Considerable confusion has existed in the minds of ornithologists, and still lingers in the minds of the majority of aviculturists, as to the species on which the name of the Emperor Alexander the Great should be rightly bestowed. The first four species here dealt with have long been known to amateurs and bird dealers as "Alexandrine" Parrakeets, no distinction whatever being made between these forms; and most writers on aviculture have classed them, especially the three first, as one species, either as *P. eupatria* or *P. alexandri;* the latter synonym has, however, been bestowed upon the much smaller Javan Parrakeet by scientific writers.

THE CINGHALESE ALEXANDRINE PARRAKEET.

Palæornis eupatria (Linn.).

This species is confined to the island of Ceylon, and is not so often imported alive into this country as the larger form from Central India. These Parrakeets make excellent talkers when properly trained, but they have a habit of screaming of which it is most difficult to break them. Writing on the habits of this species in a wild state, Captain Legge remarks in his *Birds of Ceylon* :—

"Large colonies of this species take up their abode in districts where cocoanut cultivation borders on forest and wild jungle, which afford an abundance of fruit-bearing trees, on the berries of which the Alexandrine Parrakeet subsists. It is also found in openly timbered country and in forest. It roosts in considerable numbers in cocoanut groves, often close to a village, pouring in about half an hour before sunset in small swiftly flying parties from all directions, which, as their numbers increase towards the time for roosting, create a deafening noise in the excitement of choosing or finding their accustomed quarters. The fronds of the cocoanut afford them a favourite perch, on which they sleep huddled together in rows. At daybreak the vast crowd is again astir, and after much ado, flying from tree to tree with incessant screaming, small parties start off for their feeding-grounds, flying low, just above the trees, and every now and then uttering their full and loud note *ke-āār ;* this sound is more long-drawn and not so shrill as that of the smaller bird, and can be heard at a great distance. Isolated birds have a habit of apparently leaving the rest of the flock and roaming off at a great height in the air, every now and then giving out a loud scream, which often attracts the attention of the traveller or sportsman for some little time before he is aware of the position of the Parrakeet, which is flying swiftly on far above his head. It is a shyer bird than its smaller congener, and rather difficult of approach when not engaged in feeding or in the business of settling down for the night ; at the latter time numbers may be shot without their companions doing more than flying out of, and directly returning to, their chosen tree. . . . They feed on grain as well as on the fruits and berries of forest-trees ; and I on one occasion captured a fine specimen which had become entangled in a species of vetch which covered the earthy portions of a rocky islet near Pigeon Island ; it had been feeding on the seeds of the plant, and while extricating them from the pod had got beneath the tangled mass and was unable to extricate itself again."

The following is a description of the adult male : Upper parts grass-green, forehead brighter, wings darker ; under-parts dull green ; a blackish stripe from the eye to the nostrils ; nape and cheeks with a faint greyish blue tinge ; broad black stripes from the lower mandible passing down and across the sides of the neck ; a rose collar round the back of the neck ; a dark red patch on the wing-coverts ; central tail-feathers blue, passing to yellowish at the tips ; bill red.

Total length about $18\frac{1}{2}$ or 19 inches.

The female lacks the black stripes on the neck and the rose collar, and is slightly smaller than the male.

THE NEPALESE ALEXANDRINE PARRAKEET.
Palæornis nepalensis (Hodgs.)

This species differs but slightly from the last described. It is rather larger, and the head is tinged with bluish grey, but this is the only difference. In all its habits the present species appears to be identical with the last. Probably *P. nepalensis* is much the most commonly imported of the so-called "Alexandrine" parrakeets.

Captain Hutton, quoted in Hume's *Nests and Eggs of Indian Birds*, remarks of this species :—" Towards the end of January and beginning of February it begins to cut a circular hole in some tree wherein to lay its eggs, which are usually two in number and pure white. The tree generally in request for this purpose is the semul or cotton-tree (*Bombax heptaphyllum* and *malabaricum*), although sometimes even the hard-wooded sál (*Shorea robusta*) is chosen ; the entrance hole is a neatly-cut circle, either in the trunk or in some thick upright branch. The trees selected by these birds are not situated in the depths of the forests but are detached on the outskirts and, what is curious in such a quarrelsome bird, there are often three or four nests in the same tree. The eggs are hatched in about twenty-one days, and in the middle of March the young birds are about half-fledged and are then removed for sale." Mr. H. J. Rainey, also quoted in Hume's *Nests and Eggs*, writes :—" During the month of June men go out bird-nesting into the interior of the forests of the Sundurbun, generally three or four of them together, and then the young birds are not quite fledged, and therefore unable to quit their nests. Great numbers of them are hauled out of their nests by the several parties who go out for them, and they find a ready sale for the nestlings.

"The young are able to leave their nests and fly away in the following month, July, and they then go to the cultivated tracts, roosting on the reed-jungle, known in the vernacular as *Nal* (*Arundo karka*, Linnæus), along the banks of streams; and as vast flocks of them congregate in the same place every night, where they remain, for about a month, if undisturbed, before dispersing themselves all over the surrounding country, they are easily caught in large numbers with bird-lime in the following manner. Slender sticks of split bamboo with the upper ends well smeared with bird-lime are placed in those parts of the *Nal* jungle where the birds are likely to settle for the night, and the next morning the flocks fly away, leaving those of their companions that have been caught with the bird-lime to captivity for life. Many are secured in this way, which is evidently profitable, for one patch of such jungle as they frequent (another may be miles away) is leased for this purpose for 20 rupees and upwards."

As previously stated, this species only differs from *P. eupatria* in its larger size and in the fact of the nape and cheeks being tinged with bluish grey.

The female lacks the black stripes and rose collar. Total length from 20 to 21 inches.

Palæornis nepalensis is confined to North and Central India.

THE INDO-BURMESE ALEXANDRINE PARRAKEET.

Palæornis indoburmanica, Hume.

This form inhabits the Indo-Burmese region, from Sikkim to Tenasserim, and eastwards as far as Cambodia; it is not, however, always easy to distinguish individuals from *P. nepalensis*.

This species is almost identical with the next described, but has a less powerful bill, and is not quite so bright in colour.

Total length about 21 inches.

THE GREAT-BILLED ALEXANDRINE PARRAKEET.

Palæornis magnirostris, Ball.

This species is confined to the Andaman Islands. It is like *P. eupatria*, but with a larger bill and a narrow, bluish collar above the rose collar. It is also somewhat brighter in colour.

Total length about 21 inches.

THE MAURITIUS RING-NECKED PARRAKEET.

Palæornis eques (Bodd).

This is the Mauritius form of the Ring-necked Parrakeet, differing from the well-known Indian bird (next described) by its darker green colour. I cannot positively state that this form has been imported alive into this country, but I think it most probable that it has been. It differs so slightly from the Indian and African birds, that it may well have been mistaken for one of these. Dr. Russ mentions a specimen which lived in his possession in Germany and "became extremely tame and affectionate, and learnt to speak well."

THE INDIAN RING-NECKED PARRAKEET.

Palæornis torquata (Bodd.).

Coloured figure, GREENE'S *Parrots in Captivity*, Vol. I.

This well-known Parrakeet inhabits Beluchistan, the whole of the Indian Peninsula, Ceylon, Burmah, and Cochin China.

Writing of this species in Burmah, Mr. Oates remarks : " The Rose-ringed Paroquet is found in flocks of considerable size, mostly in the neighbourhood of cultivation, in clearings, and on the outskirts of forests. It is more frequently caged by the Burmese than any other species of Paroquet. It breeds in January and February in the holes of trees, and lays either four or five white eggs." (*B. of Brit. Burmah*, vol. ii., p. 141.)

Captain Hutton writes: " It is known in the Dhoon as the *Szbar totah*, and is an especial favourite with the natives. It has a shrill, clamorous cry, which it utters on the wing, and is of very rapid flight, shooting past one with a rushing sound, and scarcely seen before it is gone again. In the gardens and grain fields it is very destructive, settling on the stalks of the bending corn, and not content with a few grains, it wantonly cuts off the ears and strews them in numbers on the ground.

"At the pairing season the female of this species becomes the most affected creature possible, twisting herself into all sorts of ridiculous postures in order, apparently, to attract the notice of her sweetheart, and uttering a low twittering note the while in the most approved style of flirtation, while her wings are half spread and her head kept rolling from side to side in demi-gyrations, the male sitting quietly by her side looking on with wonder, as if fairly taken a-back, and wondering to see her make such a guy of herself. I have watched them during these courtships until I have felt humiliated at seeing how closely the follies of mankind resemble those of the brute creation. The only return the male made to these antics was scratching the top of her head with the point of his beak and joining his bill to hers in a loving kiss." (*Stray Feathers*, vol. i., p. 339.)

Mr. R. M. Adam writes :—"I have, on several occasions, taken eggs from holes in neem trees during March. During courtship the manner in which the male persists in kissing the female, and between each kiss keeps letting go one foot, generally the right, from the branch on which he is sitting so as to raise his body up and down, is highly amusing." (*Stray Feathers*, vol. i., p. 372.)

In describing the nest of the Ring-necked Parrakeet Mr. A. O. Hume remarks :—"The mouth of the hole, which is circular and very neatly cut and, say, 2 inches on the average in diameter, is sometimes in the trunk and sometimes in some large bough, and not infrequently in the lower surface of the latter. It generally goes straight in for 2 to 4 inches, and then turns downward for from 6 inches to 3 feet. The lower or chamber portion of the hole is never less than 4 or 5 inches in diameter, and is often a large natural hollow three or four time these dimensions, into which the bird has cut its usual neat passage. The hole has no lining, only a few chips of wood on which the eggs rest." (*Nests and Eggs of Indian Birds*, vol. iii., p. 85.)

In captivity the Ring-necked Parrakeet will breed successfully if kept in a suitably aviary; a large outdoor aviary is the best place for these birds which, when once acclimatised, are quite hardy.

An interesting account, by Mr. G. C. Porter, of the

breeding of this species in an outdoor aviary appeared in the *Avicultural Magazine* for 1902 (vol. viii., p. 46), and the following extract from Mr. Porter's paper will interest my readers; he writes:—" The aviary is a lean-to, about a yard wide and ten feet long, and was fitted with natural branches. In this I suspended a four and a-half gallon barrel. The hen bird soon began to persecute the cock in a most cruel manner, pulling out most of his feathers and worrying him from morning till night; 'hen pecked' is a mild term to express her treatment of him. On May 19th, she had a sharp attack of egg-binding, but fortunately she dropped the egg on the bottom of the aviary. On May 22nd, she laid an egg in the barrel, which she incubated very assiduously, and brought off a fine young one on June 18th. The hen did not exhibit any anxiety when I took it out of the barrel for inspection. . . .

"Next year the hen laid again, on March 30th, but this clutch of four, although fertile, were killed by a severe late frost. The cock Ring-neck did not assist in incubation, but kept the hen well supplied with food. A small supply of sponge cake and fruit was given, in addition to hemp- and canary-seed.

"The hen laid two more eggs, from which two fine young birds were hatched on June 1st, 1901; but one, when half grown, crawled out of the hole and fell heavily on to the gravel below, the result being instantaneous death; the other emerged from the barrel in August, and was successfully reared."

Canon Dutton writes:—" This bird would be the ideal of pets, if anyone could find the way of successfully breaking it of screaming. One of the most lovely of Parakeets, its powers of talking are considerable, and its devotion to those to whom it takes a fancy is unbounded." (*Parrots in Captivity*, vol. i., p. 60.)

The male Ring-necked Parrakeet may be described as follows:—Prevailing colour green; a bluish tinge at the back of the head; a rose-coloured collar encircling the neck, except in the front; black stripes pass from the lower mandible round the sides of the neck, meeting the rosy collar, but ceasing before reaching the back of the neck; a black line from the eyes to the nostrils; central tail-feathers bluish, outer ones yellow on the inner, and greenish on the outer webs, all tipped with yellow; bill red.

Total length about 16 inches, of which the tail occupies $9\frac{1}{2}$ inches.

The female is slightly smaller and duller than the male, and lacks the black line on the lores, and the black and rosy collars; there is an indistinct green collar.

THE AFRICAN RING-NECKED PARRAKEET.

Palæornis docilis (Vieill.).

This species differs so slightly from *P. torquata* that many writers have considered it identical with its Indian relative. The only difference appears to be in the wings, which are slightly shorter, and the bill, which is somewhat smaller in the present species than in *P. torquata*.

The African Ring-necked Parrakeet inhabits West Africa (Senegambia to the Gold Coast), the Soudan, Equatorial Africa, and Abyssinia. In all its habits it appears to be identical with its congener.

THE BLOSSOM-HEADED PARRAKEET.

Palæornis cyanocephala (Linn.).

Coloured figure, GREENE'S *Parrots in Captivity*, Vol. I.

This very beautiful Parrakeet inhabits the whole of the Indian Peninsula and Ceylon. It is by no means a rare cage-bird in this country, being imported freely at certain times. In India these birds are said to confine themselves to the low-lying country, rarely ascending the hills to any height, and to avoid dense forest. Mr. Davidson informs us that "it goes about in flocks, sometimes very large, and feeds a good deal in the rice fields." Concerning a nest of this species Mr. Oates, quoted in Hume's *Nests and Eggs of Indian Birds*, remarks:—"The hole was a foot deep, very roomy, but the entrance, which had been enlarged by the bird, was only large enough to admit its body. The eggs are laid on the bare wood. Although the sitting bird was poked at with a stick, and it took fully half an hour to enlarge the hole in order to take the eggs, yet the bird could not be induced to quit the nest, and eventually had to be dragged out. When disturbed with the stick the female made a noise like the hissing of a snake. The eggs were taken on the 22nd of February."

When acclimatised the Blossom-headed Parrakeet is quite hardy and will breed freely in captivity; it is not always easy, however, to select a true pair for breeding, as the supposed hen sometimes proves to be a cock in his first year's dress.

The adult male is olive-green above, yellowish green below; the head red, tinged with what appears to be the bloom of a ripe plum on the hind part and lower part of cheeks; black stripes from the lower mandible round the sides of the neck, decreasing in width as they approach the nape; lower nape and rump bright green; a dark red spot on the wing-coverts; tail-feathers blue in the central and green in the side feathers, tipped with white; upper mandible orange, lower mandible black.

Total length nearly 15 inches.

The adult female, which is slightly smaller than the male, is duller in colour ; a yellowish collar ; no black stripes on the side of the neck ; *no red patch on the wing-coverts.*

THE ROSY-HEADED PARRAKEET.
Palæornis rosa (Bodd.).

This species inhabits the Eastern Himalayas, North-East Bengal, Assam, the Burmese Provinces and Cochin China.

Mr. Oates remarks : " This common Paroquet frequents cultivation and the outskirts of forest and clearings. It is usually seen in large flocks and, like most other Paroquets, it consumes large quantities of grain. It has a musical note, and is a very favourite bird with the natives. I have found the eggs in February and March in Pegu, deposited in the holes of trees at no great height from the ground ; they are usually four in number, and pure white." (*B. of Brit. Burm.*, vol. ii., p. 145.)

Mr. R. Thompson, quoted in Hume's *Nests and Eggs of Indian Birds,* tells us that this species "breeds from April to June, and selects usually a tree of moderate height and one somewhat decayed. They scoop out a fresh hole every year ; at least, those nests I have found have always proved to be new ones. The aperture is perfectly circular and large enough to admit of one bird entering in at a time. The decayed excrescence of a branch is invariably chosen, the birds scooping out the decayed wood, and in the form of the nest following the course of the branch in its growth from the centre to the trunk. The egg-cavity is scooped out larger than the entrance and passage, and usually contains four pure white eggs, much rounded, of about 1 inch in length and $\frac{8}{10}$ inch in the broadest part. The eggs are laid without any further preparation of a nest or lining of soft material beyond what the decayed wood furnishes as a foundation. The female usually loses her long uropygial feathers, thereby acquiring greater facilities for movements of her body in the nest. She is a close sitter, and will allow herself to be taken rather than desert the nest for a while. The young are easily tamed and soon learn to repeat a short air whistled to them. Many breed together in the same tree, and they evince, in many of their habits, a social and gregarious disposition."

This beautiful Parrakeet is not rare as a cage-bird in this country; as such, however, it is somewhat dull and uninteresting, although as an aviary subject it is delightful. It has been bred successfully in captivity in this country.

The Rosy-headed Parrakeet is very much like the last described, from which it differs in the head being much paler, rosy pink on the forehead, cheeks, and ear-coverts, changing to greyish lilac on the crown and nape; under-parts greener; a darker red spot on the wings. Total length about 13 inches, of which the tail occupies 7 inches.

The female may readily be distinguished from the female of *P. cyanocephala* by the *red spot on the wing-coverts* being present as in the male; the head is more greyish, and the yellow collar less distinct.

THE SLATY-HEADED PARRAKEET.

Palæornis schisticeps, Hodgs.

This species inhabits the Himalayas, from Afghanistan to Bhutan. It is a very beautiful Parrakeet, but one that is seldom seen alive in England.

Mr. Hume writes: "The Slaty-headed Paroquet breeds throughout the Himalayas, south of the first Snowy Range, at heights of from 4,000 to 7,000 feet. During the winter they keep much lower down, but about March they begin to come upwards to breed, and the majority lay during the latter half of March and April, though I took one nest of fresh eggs on 5th of May.

"They nest at times in natural hollows of trees; in fact, this I think is more usual, but not unfrequently in holes cut by themselves. The tree in which I have most commonly found them is the hill-oak. The eggs are often very deep down and difficult to secure, especially when, as is often the case, the tree is a sound one. The egg-chamber is at times very large, but is never less than 4 or 5 inches in diameter. They lay from four to five eggs, which are commonly placed on chips of wood; the nest has no other lining. The female sits very close and will not leave her eggs, though you may be ten minutes hacking away with an axe to get down to the nest." (*Nests and Eggs of Indian Birds*, vol. iii., p. 89.)

Adult male, green, paler and more yellowish on the under-parts; head slaty black, with a bluish tinge; black stripes from the lower mandible, passing round the sides of the neck, and joining a narrow black nuchal collar; a dark cherry-red patch on the wing-coverts; centre tail-feathers blue, with yellow tips; outer tail-feathers green, with yellow tips; under-side of tail yellow. Upper mandible red, lower yellow. Total length about $15\frac{3}{4}$ inches.

The female lacks the red wing-patch, but is otherwise like the male.

THE BURMESE SLATY-HEADED PARRAKEET.

Palæornis finschi, Hume.

Coloured Figure, Cat. Birds, Brit. Mus., Vol. XX., Pl. XII.

A specimen of this very rare Parrakeet was received by the Zoological Society of London, from Mr. E. W. Harper, of Calcutta, in November, 1900, this being the first example exhibited in the Society's collection.

This species inhabits the Burmese Provinces.

Mr. Davison writes concerning it : " I only met with this fine species in the hills to the north of Pahpoon, and from Myawadee to the foot of Mooleyit. Even in those localities it is by no means abundant. It occurs in small parties, frequenting the edges and thinner portions of the forest and the banks of streams. Its voice is very similar to that of *P. schisticeps* of India.

" In its habits it much resembles other Paroquets. I found it feeding on the large red flowers of a silk cotton tree (*Bombax*—?) north of Pahpoon, and about Myawadee on the large crimson flowers of a high creeper." (*Stray Feathers*, vol. vi., p. 119.)

Palæornis finschi is very similar in its colouring to *P. schisticeps*, from which it differs in being somewhat more yellowish, the head being more bluish, and the back more brownish. The central tail feathers are also much narrower. Total length about $16\frac{1}{2}$ inches.

The female lacks the red wing-spots.

THE MALABAR PARRAKEET.

Palæornis peristerodes, Finsch.

This curiously marked Parrakeet inhabits the South of India, and is a decidedly rare bird in captivity in this country. Of its wild life Dr. Jerdon writes:

"This beautiful Parrakeet is found only in the jungles of the Malabar Coast, from Travancore up to N. L. 17° or so, and from the level of the sea to 5,000 feet and upwards, on the slopes of the Neilgherries. It. in general, keeps to the depths of the forests, and frequents only the loftiest trees. Its flight is rapid and elegant, and it associates in small flocks. Its cry is mellow, subdued, and agreeable. It feeds chiefly on fruits of various kinds. The young birds are occasionally taken in the Wynaad by some of the jungle races there, and brought for sale to the Neilgherries." (*Birds of India*, p. 262.) Mr. F. Bourdillon quoted in Hume's *Nests and Eggs* (Oate's Edition), writes: "The nest is invariably in a hole in a tree, at a considerable height from the ground. . . . . The breeding-season seems to last from January 1st to the close of March. During April, old and young birds are very noisy; the latter learning to fly, the former showing them the way to set about it. The eggs are roundish, white and slightly polished, and the average dimensions of seven were 1·07 inch by 0·98."

The male has the head, breast and back dove-coloured; forehead, lores, and round the eye green; a bluish tinge on the top of the head, joining the green forehead; broad black stripes from the lower mandible, and a black collar; a second collar of bluish-green; lower back and upper tail-coverts bluish-green; wings dark green, with a bluish tinge; abdomen and under tail-coverts yellowish, with a greenish-blue tinge; some of the primaries blue; central tail-feathers blue, tipped with yellow; bill red. Total length $15\frac{1}{2}$ inches, of which the tail occupies $9\frac{1}{2}$ inches.

The female, which is slightly smaller than the male, lacks the green forehead, and the bluish-green collar, and has a blackish bill.

THE DERBYAN PARRAKEET.

Palæornis derbyana, Fraser.

Coloured Figure, Proceedings of the Zoological Society, 1850.

This very fine Parrakeet is one of the rarest of the genus. For a long time it was believed to be indigenous to the interior of China, but lately the Hon. Walter Rothschild has obtained two females which were said to hail from Hainan (*Cf. Bull. B. O. C.,* viii., p. lvi.), so that this is very probably its natural habitat.

The history of this rare Parrot is as follows :— A living specimen, the type of the species, by some means found its way into the aviaries of the Earl of Derby, at Knowsley, and after its death was preserved in the Derby Museum at Liverpool.

In a communication to the Zoological Society, dated November 11, 1850, which was published, together with an excellent coloured plate, by the late Joseph Wolf in the " Proceedings " of the Society, Mr. Louis Fraser wrote :—" The first specimen to which I would wish to draw the attention of the Society is a Parrakeet of large size which I propose calling *Palæornis derbyanus.* . . . .

" The specimen has been for many years in this collection, and I have chosen for its specific name that of its noble owner. The species is easily distinguished from all other members of the genus by its large size and the colours of the bill, head and breast."

Two females, probably the first seen in Europe since the specimen just referred to, were received, as mentioned above, by the Hon. W. Rothschild, in June, 1899, and were deposited in the " Parrot House " of the London Zoological Gardens, where they still (November, 1902) remain in fine condition. There was also a fine pair living in the Berlin Zoological Gardens in 1900, which may possibly have been brought home with Mr. Rothschild's specimens.

Nothing is known of this Parrakeet in a wild state, though there is every reason to suppose that its habits do not differ from those of its congeners.

P. derbyana resembles *P. fasciata* (the next described) somewhat closely; it may, however, be readily distinguished from that species by its much larger size, its lavender, instead of vinaceous red breast, and its much bluer head; moreover, the lavender colour of the breast extends lower down towards the vent than does the reddish colour of *P. fasciata*; the under wing-coverts, which are green in *P. fasciata*, are vinous in *P. derbyana*. Total length about 20 inches.

The male has the upper mandible red, whereas in the female both mandibles are black.

THE BANDED PARRAKEET.

Palæornis fasciata (P. L. S., Müll.).

The present species has a wide range, being found in the Himalayas, Assam, the Burmese Provinces, Andaman Islands, Cambodia, Cochin China and Hainan. It is often imported into this country and is a favourite cage-bird, although I have found it somewhat dull and uninteresting. Bird-dealers generally call it the "Moustache" Parrakeet, a name that is also sometimes applied to some others of the genus. I have never heard of any attempt being made to induce these Parrakeets to breed in this country, possibly because it generally arrives singly, and is usually kept purely as a cage bird. Given a large outdoor aviary, there would seem to be every prospect of a pair of these Parrakeets successfully rearing their young.

Of the wild life of this species Mr. Oates, in his *Birds of British Burmah*, remarks: "This Paroquet is found in well-wooded portions of the country, usually in small flocks, but when the paddy is ripe in immense numbers. They descend on the fields and do a vast amount of injury, cutting the stems of the rice with their bills, and then eating the half-ripened grains. During the middle of the day they sit on dead trees in clearings, uttering a variety of musical notes."

Mr. J. Armstrong writes of this species: "It is much more familiar than any other species of Parrot which I met with, and if one of a flock should happen to be wounded, its calling will bring the whole party flying round almost within arm's length, the entire number keeping up all the time an unceasing din of not unpleasing chatter." (*Stray Feathers*, vol. iv., p. 308.)

Mr. Hume remarks: "They keep in small flocks, and frequent particular trees which are in fruit, day after day, until the tree is cleared. When occupied thus feeding they are not easily disturbed. They are very difficult to see, as they crawl about the branches in a slow, stealthy way, keeping well hid by the foliage and the dense clusters of tree ferns and orchids. But when you do spy out and shoot one, if he drops dead, the others only flutter a little inside the tree, but do not fly out. I have thus, in the course of half an hour, killed five out of the same flock by patient watching and persistently staring up into the tree ; but if the bird shot is only wounded, and the poor thing falls screeching, as they do, then the flock flies off with loud outcries, but still returns within half an hour.

"It is everywhere a semi-migratory species, changing its *locale* with the seasons, according as the fruits and grains on which it feeds ripen here and there. Thus we never once saw it in the basin of Manipur, but found it abundant in the Eastern hills, while when the rice is ripe and cut it is said to swarm below and to desert the hills." (*Stray Feathers*, vol. xi., p. 55.)

The adult male may be described as follows:— Prevailing colour green; a large yellowish patch on the wing-coverts; head grey, tinged with bluish; lores greenish; broad stripes from the lower mandible to the sides of the neck, and a band from the forehead to the eyes, black; an emerald green collar on the back of the neck; back vinaceous red; central tail-feathers blue, tipped with yellowish, the outer ones bluish green. Upper mandible red, lower mandible black. Total length about 15 inches, of which the tail measures $7\frac{1}{2}$ inches.

The female may be readily distinguished by her black bill.

THE JAVAN PARRAKEET.

Palæornis alexandri (Linn.).

This is the Javan form of the preceding species, from which it differs in being slightly smaller, and in having the bill wholly red in both sexes. It inhabits Java and Southern Borneo, and in all its habits appears to be identical with its congener. It is not so common a cage-bird in this country as *Palæornis fasciata*.

BLYTH'S NICOBAR PARRAKEET.

Palæornis caniceps (Blyth).

This large Parrakeet is practically unknown in captivity in this country. Two specimens were received by the Zoological Society on deposit, on June 7 last (1902), one of which soon died. I have much pleasure in presenting an admirable drawing of this fine species, by Mr. Grönvold, which shows at once the difference between this and the better-known *P. nicobarica*.

Blyth's Nicobar Parrakeet is confined to the Nicobar Islands. Mr. Davison tells us that it does not associate in flocks like other members of the genus, but is found singly or in pairs, occasionally in small parties of five or six. Its note is said to be a loud screech, and to be continually uttered, both when flying and settled, and its food to consist, to a large extent, of the ripe fruit of the pandanus.

"We had very few opportunities of *observing* it," writes Mr. Hume; "its flight is much like that of *sivalensis** and *magnirostris*, but more rapid; it is a noisy bird, and its call can be heard a long way off. We saw numbers, but mostly only for a moment as they dashed past through the trees at heights of from fifty to seventy yards above our heads; their cries just gave one time to get the gun to one's shoulder, and in less than half a minute from their first becoming visible, they were either falling to the shot, or out of sight." (*Stray Feathers*, vol. ii., p. 180.)

Prevailing colour of the male green, brighter on the rump; head grey; a broad black band from the forehead to the eyes; broad black stripes from the lower mandible passing to the side of the neck; primaries blackish; middle tail-feathers greyish

---

* *P. nepalensis*.

towards the tips; upper mandible red, lower black. Total length about 22 inches, of which the tail measures 14 inches.

The female has a bluish tinge on the head and nape, and the bill is entirely black.

THE LUCIAN PARRAKEET.

Palæornis modesta, Fraser.

Single specimens of this beautiful Parrakeet *very occasionally* reach this country; the birds sometimes advertised by bird-dealers as "Lucians" almost invariably proving to belong to a nearly allied species—

Palæornis modesta.

generally *P. longicauda.* For a long time the habitat of this Parrot was unknown, but there appears now to be little doubt that it is confined to the island of Engano, off the coast of Sumatra. Nothing appears to be known of its wild life, though its habits, in all probability, do not differ from those of its congeners. In captivity it becomes very tame, but, like many of the other members of the genus, it is a dull and stupid cage-bird. The prevailing colour is green. The male has the forehead dark bluish green; crown dull reddish with a greenish tinge; nape brighter reddish; black lines on the forehead and from lower mandible; cheeks bright brick-red; back tinged with bluish; breast pale yellowish green; under wing-coverts blackish; tail green, with central feathers bluish. Total length about 16 inches, tail 9 inches. The female has the top of the head greenish brown; the stripes, which are black in the male, are dark bluish green, almost black, in the female; cheeks and ear-coverts reddish, the latter edged behind with a bluish band.

THE NICOBAR PARRAKEET.

Palæornis nicobarica, Gould.

This species, as its name implies, inhabits the Nicobar Islands, and is not often imported alive into this country. Davison, quoted by Mr. Hume, writes: " This species is exceedingly abundant on all the islands of the Nicobar group. They wander about . . . . frequenting alike the forest, gardens, and the mangrove swamps. They are generally found in small flocks, but I have occasionally found them singly, more often in pairs, or small parties of four or five, but then it has generally been in gardens when they were feeding. They feed largely on the papaya (*Carica papaya*) and on the ripe pandanus fruit, and I have seen them eating the ripe outer covering of the betel-nut (*Areca catechu*), which is so very abundant on some of the Nicobar Islands; but this is evidently not a favourite food with them, and they apparently never touch it when they can obtain better food, as on Camorta.

They are easily reared in captivity, even when taken from the nest very young. One of my men reared successfully two young ones which I took from a nest in Trinkut Island, although one was so young that it had both its eyes closed, and had not a trace of feathers on it beyond a few stumps on its tail and along the wings. The way he managed it was this—he got a small whelk shell and inserted the narrow end between the mandibles of the bird, so as to form a small channel into its mouth, and down this he used to pour small quantities of milk; this he continued to do till the bird could take more substantial food, and he then fed it on bread and milk, or boiled rice and milk, and for this it would readily open its mouth; it very soon learned to feed itself. I have often seen this bird in the houses of the Nicobarese fastened to a perch made of cane, by a ring of cocoanut shell." (*Stray Feathers*, vol. ii., p. 182.)

The male is green; lores bluish-black; cheeks and ear-coverts brick-red; black stripes from the lower mandible as in other species; nape yellowish-green; a bluish tinge on the upper back; breast yellowish-green; quills mostly blue; primary-coverts blue; central tail-feathers blue; underside of tail golden-yellow; upper mandible red, becoming yellowish at the tip; lower mandible generally black, but sometimes reddish.

The female has both mandibles blackish, and the red colour of the cheeks duller.

According to Hume the young of both sexes have both mandibles dull red.

The illustration is drawn from skins in the British Museum.

THE ANDAMAN PARRAKEET.

Palæornis tytleri, Hume.

This species, which is confined to the Andaman Islands, is slightly smaller than the preceding, but in other respects resembles it very closely. Concerning its wild life, Mr. Hume tells us that its habits are identical with those of *P. nicobarica;* "they abound everywhere," he writes, "land where you will, throughout the group, their screeching note is sure to greet you. On Mount Harriet they swarm to a degree scarcely to be credited, and in Macpherson's Straits, as you thread your way through the narrow channels that divide the islets there clustered, small flocks pass overhead every five minutes, flitting from isle to isle, and screaming *à qui mieux, mieux,* as they fly. They are permanent residents ; we secured them from December to April and received specimens killed in every month from May to September." (*Stray Feathers*, vol. ii., p. 184.)

Palæornis tytleri is not included in the Zoological Society's List, either under the synonym here adopted, or that of *affinis* (Tytler). I think, however, it is most probable that the species has been imported alive, very possibly on several occasions, but it has in all probability been mistaken for its congener from the Nicobar Islands, which, as previously stated, it closely resembles.

Mr. Hume has set forth the difference between the present and preceding species so clearly, that I cannot do better than quote his words ; he writes : "In the Nicobar females, the mandibular stripe is black, except just at the end where it becomes greenish. In the Andaman females, the entire stripe is a deep green, becoming paler, and brighter towards the tip. In the males, the difference is even more strongly marked, but is less easy to express in words. The nape and back are much more strongly suffused in the Andaman bird, with a lilac and glaucous tinge, and the breasts again in the Nicobar birds are a yellowish green, but in the Andaman specimens are suffused with a lighter shade of the back tinge. In other respects the birds are similar, but anyone can separate at a glance the birds of either sex belonging to the two groups of islands." (*Stray Feathers*, vol. ii., p. 24.)

P. tytleri is from 15½ to 18 inches in total length.

THE LONG-TAILED PARRAKEET.

Palæornis longicauda (Bodd).

This species, also known as the Malaccan Parrakeet, inhabits the Malayan Peninsula, Sumatra, Borneo, Nias and Billiton Islands. It is not a particularly rare importation into this country, almost always arriving singly ; and it makes a very beautiful, but intensely apathetic cage-bird. A specimen that lived in my possession for some time became exceedingly tame, but was exceedingly lazy, sitting for hours on its perch without moving. If a true pair of these Parrakeets could be allowed the run of a large garden aviary during the summer months, they would probably prove as interesting as they are beautiful, but they are, like many members of this group, most uninteresting when imprisoned in cages.

The adult male may be thus described : Prevailing colour green, becoming yellowish on the underparts ; cheeks, and a broad collar round the nape vinous red ; broad black stripes from the lower mandible ; upper back yellowish tinged with blue ; rump pale blue ; quills mostly blue ; under wing-coverts yellow ; central tail-feathers blue, the others green; *upper mandible red*, lower brown. Total length about 16½ inches, of which the tail measures 9 inches.

The female differs in having dark green, instead of black mandibular stripes, and in having both mandibles horny brown.

Genus POLYTELIS, Wagl.

The members of this genus resemble those of the genus *Palæornis* in the possession of a very long tapering tail. The bill is, however, very much weaker than in the last genus, and the upper mandible is not notched. Mr. North has removed the species hitherto known as *Polytelis alexandræ* from this genus for reasons which will be stated further on, so that the genus now contains but two species, both of which are well known to English aviculturists, and are easily kept in health in captivity.

BARRABAND'S PARRAKEET.

Polytelis barrabandi (Swains.).

This very beautiful Parrakeet, known to the Australian colonists as the "Green Leek," inhabits the south and south-east of Australia. Mr. Campbell tells us that it is a somewhat scarce species, being limited to isolated localities inland, and that it nests in a hole in a tree, usually by a stream. It is a somewhat rare bird in captivity in this country, but a most desirable species from an aviculturist's point of view. I have at various times possessed no less than six specimens of this lovely Parrakeet, and have found them perfectly hardy when once thoroughly acclimatised. They are generally very shy and wild when first brought over, but very soon get to know their owner and to become tame. Mine have been kept in a fair-sized outdoor aviary, with various small birds, but I have never known them to hurt anything, and can recommend them as being perfectly harmless to the most defenceless birds.

As to the correct diet for Barraband's Parrakeet, some writers have advised the same treatment as has been found necessary for Lorikeets, and one writer considers them more difficult to keep in health than the latter birds. I have found a diet of hemp and canary-seed, with the addition of a few boiled maize and some ripe fruit daily, suits these Parrakeets admirably. The Rev. C. D. Farrar, who succeeded in inducing a pair of Barrabands to breed successfully in his aviary at Micklefield, near Leeds, in 1900, fed his birds on hemp and canary-seed entirely.

Mr. Farrar tells us that the cock commenced to enter the nest to feed the young when the latter were about ten days old, and at night he slept in the nest and assisted in brooding them. The first young bird left the nest three days before the second, and that some days before the third. (*Cf. Avic. Mag.*, vol. vi., p. 219.)

The male is brilliant, shining green, lighter on the under-parts; the forehead, cheeks and throat rich canary-yellow; lower throat bright scarlet; top of the head bluish; lores, and region round the eye green; primary wing-coverts bluish-green; thighs with some scarlet feathers, except in very old examples in which they are green; under-side of tail black; bill red. Total length 16 inches, of which the tail occupies 9 inches.

The female is much duller green; the throat and upper breast greyish-rose; thighs scarlet; inner webs of tail-feathers rose-pink.

The young male is like the adult female.

The illustration is from a living specimen in the Zoological Gardens, and skins in the author's possession.

THE BLACK-TAILED PARRAKEET.

Polytelis melanura (Vig.).

Coloured figure, GREENE'S *Parrots in Captivity*, Vol. III.

This elegant Parrakeet, which is also known as the Rock Pepler, or Rock Pebbler, inhabits the south and west of Australia, frequenting flats in the vicinity of water. Mr. A. J. Campbell writes: "On the Wimmera, north of Lake Albacutya, Dr. Chas. Ryan and party found the beautiful Black-tailed Parrakeets breeding about the first week of October, 1898, when all the clutches were almost incubated. One nest contained a pair of young and four addled eggs.

"The late Captain F. C. Hansen (of the Murray steamer 'Maggie') informed me that he has found the Black-tailed Parrakeet nesting in the Broken Bend cliffs (mallee cliffs) of the River Murray, near Wentworth, also in the cliffs lower down, between Morgan, South Australia, and the border of Victoria. Captain Hansen also states that generally only a pair of young is hatched out of a clutch of four eggs, and that a pair of old birds rears two broods a season in the same nest.

"Mr. W. White, Reedbeds (South Australia), whose roomy aviary contains many beautiful Parrots, has a handsome Black-tailed Parrakeet which has reared several clutches of young Cockatoo Parrakeets [= Cockatiels]. As soon as they were hatched by their proper parents they were handed over (evidently by mutual consent) to the Polytelis." (*Nests and Eggs of Australian Birds*, p. 625.)

The Black-tailed Parrakeet is not very frequently seen in living collections in this country. It is often in very bad condition when it arrives, and so does not live very long. But when properly established it is as hardy as most Australian Parrakeets. I have never heard of these birds breeding in confinement in this country, although probably it would do so if a pair were suitably housed in a large outdoor aviary.

The same diet as I have recommended for *P. barrabandi* is suitable for the present species. The male Black-tailed Parrakeet may be described as follows:—Head, neck, rump, and whole of under-parts yellow, the back of the head being tinged with olive; upper back olive; scapulars, quills, and tail black, the latter having a purple-blue tinge above; some red on the innermost greater wing-coverts and secondaries; bill red. Total length about 16 inches, of which the tail measures $8\frac{1}{2}$ inches.

The female is dull olive-green, darker on the back; rump, breast and abdomen olive, with a yellowish tinge; a greenish-yellow patch on the wing-coverts; quills deep blue; some red on the secondaries and greater wing-coverts; tail-feathers bluish-green, the lateral ones margined on the inner webs, and tipped with rose.

Genus SPATHOPTERUS, North.

(*Cf. Ibis*, 1895, p. 339).

Very closely allied to *Polytelis*, from which it differs in the males having the end of the third primary of each wing singularly elongated and terminating in a spatule. (*North.*)

Only one species is known.

THE ALEXANDRA PARRAKEET.

Spathopterus alexandræ (Gould).

Coloured figures, GOULD'S *Birds of Australia*, Supp. Vol. : *Avicultural Magazine*, Vol. V., p. 168.

This is one of the rarest, and at the same time the most beautiful of the Australian Parrakeets. It inhabits Central and Western Australia and is *very* rarely brought alive into civilization. The species was first discovered during the Stuart Expedition into the interior of Australia in 1862, and the first specimens secured, being forwarded to the late John Gould, were named by him after our present beloved Queen Alexandra. "I feel assured," writes Gould, "that the discovery of an additional species of the lovely genus *Polytelis* will be hailed with pleasure by all ornithologists, and that they will assert to its bearing the specific name of *alexandræ*, in honour of that Princess who, we may reasonably hope, is destined at some future to be the Queen of these realms and their dependencies, of which Australia is by no means the most inconspicuous."

In the *Ibis* for 1895, Mr. Alfred J. North, of the Australian Museum, Sydney, pointed out a hitherto unnoticed feature, which serves at once to separate this species from the genus *Polytelis*, to which it had hitherto been thought to belong, namely, the curious shape of the third primary feather in each wing in the male, which is clearly shown in the annexed cut.

The Alexandra Parrakeet was met with during the Horn Expedition to Central Australia in 1894, and Mr. Keartland, who accompanied the Expedition, writes as follows regarding the species : " The advance party had halted for lunch, and on my arrival Professor Tate said he had seen a strange-looking Parrot in the oaks near at hand. I started off in the direction indicated, and after going about two hundred yards saw what at first appeared to be a Cockatoo-parrot flying towards me. Having carefully noted the branch on which it perched, I hurried forward, but, notwithstanding the sparse foliage of the tree, I had to look carefully for some minutes before I found it. Immediately the shot was fired a number of these beautiful birds flew out of the trees in all directions, in twos, threes, and fours. Five birds flew into one tree, but I had to walk round three times before I could see them. At last four heads were visible, just raised from a thick limb, the bodies and tails lying horizontally along the timber.

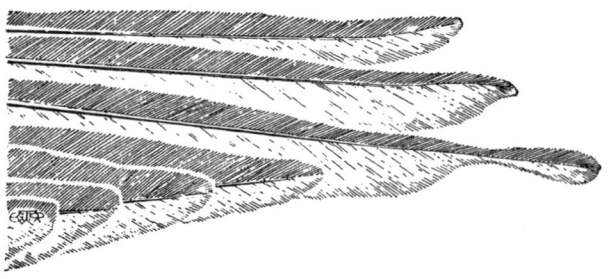

From *The Ibis*, 1895, *by kind permission of the Editors.*
WING OF *Spathopterus alexandræ.*

"I have since heard that one of their breeding places has been discovered on the Hale river. Mr. Charles Pritchard, who accompanied the party as prospector for gold, and assisted me in obtaining my birds, has forwarded to me three eggs out of a clutch of five, which is the usual number. They closely resemble those of the *Platycercus eximius* in shape and size, but have a smooth and glossy surface, more like a pigeon's egg. I have since compared them with one laid by Mr. Magarey's bird in captivity, and find they exactly correspond.

"Writing under date 15th November, 1894, Mr.

Pritchard says:—' Re their appearance here. This is the first time on record that they have made this their breeding ground, but I do not think they have come to stay, and perhaps in a year or so they may be as rare as ever. These birds travel in lots from one pair up to nearly any number, are very tame, feeding about in the grass near the camp, and seem in no way afraid of people, cattle, or horses. They breed in hollow trees, laying five eggs in a clutch, and several pairs of birds occupy holes in the same tree. They are nesting now in the eucalypts on the banks of the Hale river, and other large watercourses. They do not always lie along the limbs as you found them at Glen Edith, but perch as other Parrots. I have a number in captivity, amongst them being an old male bird with a tail seventeen inches long.'"

Writing to Mr. North, under date of April 28, 1895, Mr. Keartland remarks:—" Mr. Winnecke, one of the members of our late Expedition, has sent me a pair of live *Polytelis alexandræ*. I never saw Parrots so tame and gentle. They will fly off the top perch in the aviary on to my arm and eat seed out of my hand, and allow me to stroke them. Mr. Winnecke was informed that when the young nestlings were in boxes at the camp of the men who took them, the old birds came and fed them for days, and were as tame as domestic pigeons." (*Report of the Horn Expedition to Central Australia*, pp. 61, 62.)

It is probable that not more than four or five of these lovely Parrakeets have ever reached this country alive. Mr. H. J. Fulljames obtained a pair in 1899, which were figured by Mr. P. Smit in the *Avicultural Magazine* for September in that year, though the illustration does not nearly do justice to the birds. Mr. Fulljames writes of this species in captivity:—
" Of all the Parrakeets it is the rarest, the most elegant in shape, the most beautiful and, at the same

time, the most delicate in colouring, the tamest, the most desirable as a pet, and the least objectionable in 'song.' I had almost written that it was absolutely without objection in regard to screaming, which is such a drawback to the keeping of Parrots; but when it likes the Princess of Wales's Parrakeet has a very shrill whistle which is somewhat trying to the human ear. This, fortunately, is only resorted to occasionally, and then only when it is protesting against attentions being bestowed upon other inmates of the bird-room." Mr. Fulljames found his specimens decidedly delicate; "Many times," he writes of the female, "her life has not seemed worth a day's purchase. For a long time she refused seed altogether, and was kept alive entirely on fruit and sponge-cake, with port wine and beaten egg in the place of water for drinking." Let us hope that all examples are not so delicate as were Mr. Fulljames', for the Alexandra Parrakeet appears to be one of the most charming of all the numerous Parrot tribe.

Mr. A. J. Campbell informs us that "Mr. A. Zeitz, Assistant Curator of the Adelaide Museum, was successful in getting the Alexandra Parrakeets to breed in captivity. The female alone rears the young." (*Nests and Eggs of Australian Birds.*)

The Alexandra Parrakeet may be described as follows: Top of head pale blue; throat and lower part of cheeks, rosy pink; nape, scapulars and back olive-green; a pale yellowish green patch on the shoulders; breast and abdomen olive-grey; primaries bluish; thighs red; rump olive, with a bluish tinge; tail above olive-green tinged with blue; the inner webs of the outer tail-feathers rosy pink; bill rosy red.

The male only differs from the female in his slightly larger size and brighter colours, and in the possession of "spatules' to the third primary, which she lacks.

Genus **PTISTES**, Gould.

Three species only are known to belong to this genus, which is characterised by the tail-feathers being broad and almost of equal length. It is confined to Australia and the Timor group of Islands.

THE CRIMSON-WINGED PARRAKEET.

Ptistes erythropterus (Gm.).

Coloured Figure, GOULD'S *Birds of Australia*, Vol. V., pl. 18.

This well-known and strikingly handsome species, also known as the Red-winged, or Blood-winged Parrakeet, is an inhabitant of Northern and Eastern Australia, the Northern birds being, as a rule, smaller than those from the Eastern parts of the Continent. Gould separated the smaller race as *P. coccineopterus*, but Count Salvadori finds that some Northern specimens are quite as large as the Eastern ones, and so unites the two forms.

In Australia this bird is known as the Red-winged Lory, an unfortunate appellation for a species which is entirely distinct from the *Loriidæ*.

"It is beyond my powers to describe the extreme beauty of the appearance of the Red-Winged Lory when seen among the silvery branches of the Acacia," writes Gould, "particularly when the flocks comprise a large number of adult males, the gorgeous scarlet of whose shoulders offers so striking a contrast to the surrounding objects. . . . Its flight is performed with a motion of the wings totally different from that of any other member of the *Psittacidæ* I have seen, and has frequently reminded me of the heavy flapping manner of the Pewit, except that the motion was even slower and more laboured. While on the wing, it frequently utters a loud screeching cry.

"Its food," continues the same author, "consists of berries, the fruit of a species of *Loranthus*, and the pollen of flowers, to which is added a species of scaly bug-like insect that infests the branches of its favourite trees; and in all probability small caterpillars, for I have found them in the crops of several of the *Platycerci*. It breeds in the holes of the large eucalypti growing on the banks of rivers; the eggs, which are white, being four or five in number, about an inch and an eighth long by seven-eighths broad."

The Crimson-winged Parrakeet is frequently kept by aviculturists in this country, and it is a delightful and desirable species. Some give it an exemplary character, but I have not found it quite a safe companion for small foreign finches; it will occasionally sidle up to a bird and suddenly make a grab with its bill at any part it can get hold of, generally the leg, with disastrous results.

This species has reproduced its kind in captivity in this country, and the young have been successfully reared. Lady Morshead records the successful rearing of three young birds during the summer of 1901 (*Avic. Mag.*, vol. viii., p. 34), and the Rev. C. D. Farrar had three young hatched in his aviary in Yorkshire in 1899, and again in 1901, but in neither case were they reared (*Avic. Mag.*, vol. v., p. 193, and vol. viii., p. 13.)

Crimson-wings become very tame after a time; a female in my possession would always take food readily from my hand, although her brilliantly dressed husband never became quite tame enough to do likewise.

The diet of these Parrakeets in captivity should be

generous and varied; plain canary-seed is not enough. My own birds were fed on canary-seed, hemp, oats, sunflower-seed, boiled maize, and ripe fruit, especially apples, of which they were very fond. On this diet this lovely Parrakeet—one of the most beautiful of the brilliant family to which it belongs—will live and flourish for years. It is a moderately hardy species when acclimatised, although of course it needs some warmth during the winter months in this country. Some people boast of keeping birds which hail from hot climates, in outdoor, exposed aviaries during the winter months; but although many birds will exist under such conditions, they feel the cold keenly, and the practice is little short of cruelty.

The adult male is bright green on the head, neck, tail and underparts, the latter being lighter yellowish-green; upper back and scapulars black; rump blue; upper tail-coverts yellowish-green; upper wing-coverts bright crimson; primaries dark green; bill orange-scarlet.

The adult female is dull green, more yellowish below; rump blue; some of the upper wing-coverts tipped with red; the lateral tail-feathers edged with pink on the inner webs. Total length of specimens from the East of Australia about $13\frac{1}{2}$ inches; those from the North about $12\frac{1}{2}$ inches.

The adult plumage is attained at the commencement of the third year, before which the sexes are alike.

Genus APROSMICTUS, Gould.

This genus contains some nine species, inhabiting Australia and the Austro-Malayan subregion; one species only, however, appears to have been brought alive to this country.

The genus differs from *Ptistes* by the longer and much graduated tail.

THE KING PARRAKEET.

Aprosmictus cyanopygius (Vieill.).
Coloured Figure, GOULD'S *Birds of Australia*, Vol. V., pl. 17.

This grand Parrakeet is indigenous to the Southern and Eastern parts of Australia, where it is known to the colonists by the inappropriate name of King Lory. It is very well known to aviculturists in this country, although the female, which is popularly termed the Queen Parrakeet, is not so often seen as the more brilliantly dressed male.

Gould informs us that "all the brushes stretching along the southern and eastern coasts appear to be equally favoured with its presence, as it there finds a plentiful supply of food, consisting of seeds and berries. At the period when the Indian corn is becoming ripe it leaves its umbrageous abode and sallies forth in vast flocks, which commit great devastation on the ripening grain. It is rather a dull and inactive species compared with the members of the restricted genus *Platycercus*; it flies much more heavily, and is very different in its disposition, for although it soon becomes habituated to confinement, it is less easily tamed and much less confiding and familiar; the great beauty of the male, however, somewhat compensates for this unpleasant trait, and consequently it is highly prized as a cage-bird."

Mr. Campbell tells us that it nests within the hollow limb or trunk of a giant-tree (eucalypt), sometimes as far down as the base, in heavy forest country, and that the eggs number from four to six to the clutch.

In captivity I have found the King Parrakeet a

somewhat lazy and uninteresting bird, in fact a pair that I once possessed, which had been kept in a cage for some time, were, when put into an outdoor aviary, too lazy to descend from the perch to feed, expecting to be fed by hand, or to have the food always placed within reach of their favourite perch.

The King Parrakeet requires a liberal and varied diet in captivity; canary-seed, hemp, oats, millet, sunflower-seed and boiled maize being the most suitable staple food, to which should be added ripe fruit, such as apple, pear, grapes or banana, and green food, such as chickweed and groundsel.

Young have been reared by these birds in captivity on several occasions, and their breeding in captivity would doubtless be considerably more frequent if the females were as often imported as the males. One instance of a young bird being reared is recorded in *Notes on Cage Birds* (second series, p. 176), where a correspondent who signs himself " M." writes : " I have succeeded in breeding a young King Parrot, and it is now nearly as big as the old ones. I think it must be a 'Queen,' as the markings are similar; but I fancy you cannot tell when the bird is so young. It is a nice strong bird and very tame."

In the *Field* of August 30, 1902, a correspondent records the successful breeding of a pair of " Australian Parrots," and on inquiry I found that the species referred to was the one now under consideration.

The adult male has the whole of the head, neck, breast and underparts bright scarlet; back and wings dark green; a band of pale green on the upper wing-coverts; rump, and a narrow band separating the scarlet on the nape from the green back, blue; upper tail-coverts and tail black with an olive tinge; bill red. Total length about 17 inches.

The adult female has the head, back, wings, and tail dark green; throat and chest duller green with a vinous tinge; abdomen and flanks scarlet; bill blackish.

The young birds, which do not attain their full plumage until the third year, resemble the female, except that the lateral tail-feathers are tipped with rose colour.

Genus **PYRRHULOPSIS**, Reichenb.

Five species are known belonging to this genus, which inhabits the Fijian Islands, and has probably been introduced into the Tonga Islands. The members of this genus may well be termed the Shining Parrakeets, the excessive brilliancy of their plumage being unsurpassed by any other member of the *Psittacidæ*.

In the *Ibis* for 1876 (p. 143) Mr. E. L. Layard remarks concerning these birds: "They frequent the forest, feeding on various fruits and berries as they come into season, and making descents on the planters' Indian corn crops, where their depredations are very serious. They are very shy and wary, planting sentinels, who with harsh cries warn the flock of approaching danger, when off they all troop to the forest, and hide silently in the dense crowns of the broadest-leafed trees. If they find themselves discovered they utter loud cries, swaying themselves to and fro on their perches, and holding themselves ready for flight in a moment." The same author tells us that these birds can be tamed to any extent, and a lady of his acquaintance, living in the Fijian Islands, had several pairs that used to fly about the woods unrestrained, returning to their cages at night.

"When she walks out," he writes, "they fly to her and perch on her head or shoulder; and the last sight I had of my fair friend was to see her standing on the high banks overlooking the river where her house was situated, with a pair of *P. personatus* on one shoulder, and a pair of *P. splendens* on the other."

Three species only appear to have been imported alive into this country.

THE RED SHINING PARRAKEET.

Pyrrhulopsis splendens (Peale).

Coloured Figure, GREENE'S *Parrots in Captivity*, Vol. III.

This splendid Parrakeet is but little known in this country, where single specimens may occasionally be seen at the Zoological Gardens, or at one of the large bird shows at the Crystal Palace. It inhabits the islands of Viti Levu and Kandavu, in the Fijian group, where the natives rear the young birds and sell them to travellers. The inhabitants of the Samoan Islands are said to be very fond of these Parrots, and to purchase them from the Fijians at high prices. (*Cf. Ibis*, 1875, p. 437.)

In captivity these Parrakeets should be fed as recommended for the King Parrakeet of Australia.

The sexes of the Red Shining Parrrakeet are alike in plumage, but the female is slightly smaller than the male. The colouring is as follows: head and underparts bright crimson; a blue band across the nape; back, rump, and wings green; primaries and primary coverts blue; tail blue, shading into greenish at the base; irides orange; bill black. Total length about 18 inches, of which the tail measures about $8\frac{1}{2}$ inches.

THE TABUAN PARRAKEET.

Pyrrhulopsis tabuensis (Gm.).

The Tabuan Parrakeet is also a very rare species in this country. It inhabits the Island of Vanna Levu in the Fiji group, and also Tongatabu and Eua, where it has probably been introduced from Fiji.

I once saw a Tabuan Parrakeet at a Crystal Palace bird-show which uttered several words very distinctly.

This species very closely resembles *P. splendens*, from which it differs in the red parts being *dark cherry-red* instead of crimson. Total length about 17 inches. The sexes are similar in colouring, but the male is slightly the larger bird.

THE MASKED PARRAKEET.

Pyrrhulopsis personata (Gray).

Coloured Figure, GREENE'S *Parrots in Captivity*, Vol. III.

This, although a decidedly rare species, is the most frequently imported of the genus. It is the only species that is almost entirely green, the predominant colour of the other four being red.

The Masked Parrakeet inhabits the western group of the Fijian Islands, of which Viti Levu and Kandavu are the chief.

In captivity it readily becomes tame, and will soon learn to repeat words, or even short sentences, but most people who have kept it consider it a dull, quiet bird in a cage.

Miss R. Alderson has kindly supplied me with the following account of two specimens in her possession: " One is named ' Dick Turpin,' and he is the sweetest tempered and brightest Parrakeet I have ever kept.

He loves to sit on my hand, and when he wishes to be petted always fluffs out his feathers and makes odd little noises to show his joy. He will let me stroke him all over, under his wings and all round his neck, face and breast, and will let me take hold of either feet, or put both my hands under him and pick him up. 'Dick' quite enters into the fun of a game of play, and has a funny way of trotting round and round in a circle with his head on one side, looking up at me

Pyrrhulopsis personata.

with one eye when he wants to begin. 'Jack,' my other specimen, is a nice bird, but not nearly so bright and active as 'Dick,' and, it must be confessed, not nearly so amiable. 'Jack' has a larger head, and is much more hawk-like in appearance. He will sit on my hand or shoulder, but does not care for being stroked, I think partly from nervousness. He used to gnaw his feathers, but sunflower-seed was found to be the cause, and since this was stopped 'Jack' has ceased his bad habit. He and Dick do not agree well; I fear the latter is rather jealous, and looks on me as his entire property."

This fine Parrakeet is bright, shining green, with a black face, and a yellow patch on the breast, running into orange on the abdomen. The primaries and primary-coverts are blue; quills and underside of tail black; bill black; irides yellow. Total length about 18 inches, of which the tail occupies $8\frac{1}{2}$ inches.

The female is similar to the male in colouring, but somewhat less in size; and the immature birds are said to be like the adults, but less brilliant.

Genus PSITTINUS.

THE BLUE-RUMPED PARRAKEET.

Psittinus incertus (Shaw).

This rare Parrakeet inhabits Tenasserim, the Malayan Peninsula, Sumatra, Borneo and Banka, and is the only representative of its genus. The Zoological Society has possessed examples at various times, but it is practically unknown to aviculturists. Mr. W. Davison writes of this species:—

"It frequents principally old tounyahs and other places where there is a dense growth of secondary scrub. It feeds chiefly on the small gummy flowers of a plant that always springs up where forest has been felled and burnt. It goes about in small flocks of fifteen or more, and is not at all shy or wild.

"It is migratory in Tenasserim, coming in just before the setting in of the rains, about April and May, though a very few do arrive earlier, about the last week in March. In June and July, I am told, they are very common about Malewoon.

"They have nothing of the harsh screaming notes of the Parroquets, their usual note being a sharp whistle not unlike that of *Calornis;* they have also a series of pleasant notes, a warble in fact, which they chiefly give utterance to when seated.

" It has a rapid flight, and you often see small parties of them (like *Loriculus*) flying about round and round over the tops of the trees apparently for fun or exercise, now settling for a moment, then off again, whirling round and round, and all the time whistling at the top of their voices." (*Stray Feathers,* vol. vi., p. 120.)

The adult male has the head and neck grey, with a bluish tinge; upper back and scapulars blackish, tinged with olive; lower back, rump and upper tail-coverts blue; underparts olive-green tinged with bluish; under tail-coverts greenish-yellow edged with blue; wings green, with a red patch on the minor coverts; primary coverts blue; under wing-coverts red; centre of tail green, the lateral feathers greenish-yellow; underside of tail yellow; upper mandible red, lower brownish-red.

The female has the head and nape reddish-brown, the sides of the head with a yellowish tinge, the shafts being dusky; back and upper tail-coverts green; a small patch of blue on the lower back; the underparts yellowish-green, the breast-feathers being darker in the centre, producing a scaly appearance; bill whitish. Total length about $7\frac{1}{2}$ inches.

Genus **AGAPORNIS**, Selby.

Nine species are known in this genus, which is confined to the Ethiopian region, and which may be distinguished by the short, rounded tail, crossed by a sub-terminal band of black, and by the absence of any distinct ridge along the middle of the gonys, or underside of the lower mandible. Apparently three species only have been represented by living examples in this country.

The present genus is a singularly interesting one, not only from the fact that its members differ from almost every other genus of Parrots in being skilful nest-builders, but also from the unique manner in which the nesting material is conveyed to the selected site. Parrots, with very few exceptions, select a hole in some tree-trunk or limb, which has been formed by the decay of the inner part of the wood, in which to rear their brood, the great majority making no nest whatever, but merely laying their eggs on the bare decaying wood. The true Lovebirds, however, which constitute the present genus, are not content with so rude a bed for their offspring, but carefully construct a soft, warm nest, with fine strips of the pliant green bark of trees, which is peeled off by the female by a succession of nips as she passes her beak along sideways. Having secured a strip of about three inches in length, she gives it one nip in the centre to bend it into a V-shape, and turning her head and bending over her back, she tucks it away under her somewhat lengthy upper tail-coverts. This process, of which the present writer has frequently been an eye-witness in the case of *A. roseicollis* in captivity, is continued until a considerable quantity of material has been collected, when the bird flies off, looking like an animated ball of hay, to her nesting hole, into which she climbs by the aid of her bill and feet. The site selected for the nest is generally the hollow of a tree, as in the case of other Parrots, but according to Andersson, one species sometimes takes possession of the large nests formed by the Social Weaver-birds, in which it doubtless forms its own nest.

The reason for the adoption of the remarkable method above described of conveying the material to the desired spot is not far to seek. Parrots of all kinds use the bill nearly as much as the feet in climbing, and if this is occupied in carrying a quantity of material, the bird would have great difficulty in climbing into the nest, which is generally situated where it would be impossible for the bird to reach it without the use of the bill as well as the feet,

In captivity a box, say 6 or 8 inches square, with an entrance-hole from 1½ to 2 inches in diameter, answers well as a receptacle for the nest. It should be hung in some partially hidden corner of the aviary, at a considerable height from the ground. Green branches of willow or poplar should be supplied, the bark of which will be stripped off to form the nest; otherwise the woodwork of the aviary itself will be attacked.

The Lovebirds are simple feeders; canary seed, millet, hemp and oats should be supplied, as well as groundsel, chickweed, flowering-grass and such like, when obtainable. Fruit does not seem to be much appreciated by these birds.

THE MADAGASCAR LOVEBIRD.

Agapornis cana (Gm.).
Coloured Figure, GREENE'S *Parrots in Captivity*, Vol. I.

The present species, which is also known as the Grey-headed Lovebird, is frequently imported in large numbers to this country. As its name implies, its home is Madagascar, but it is also found in Reunion, Mauritius, Rodriguez, Anjuan and the Seychelles, where it has undoubtedly been introduced. The Rev. J. Sibree, jun., writing on the birds of Madagascar, tells us that this species "is found in considerable numbers in the outskirts of the woods, and near the cultivated districts, all over the island. They go in large flocks, often of as many as a hundred together, and sometimes do considerable damage to the rice-crops." The same

From *The Royal Natural History.*
MADAGASCAR LOVEBIRDS, *Agapornis cana.*

author proceeds: "One of the native names of this Parrakeet, *Karaska*, is probably descriptive of its cry; while another, *Masèsy* means 'degenerated,' or 'become small'" (*Ibis*, 1891, p. 217).

The Madagascar Lovebird will breed readily in a large, quiet aviary, selecting a hollow log or box for the nesting site, and carrying strips of green

1. MUSKY LORIKEET, *Glossopsittacus concinnus* (now known as MUSK LORIKEET, *Glossopsitta concinna*); text page 17.
2. PERFECT LORIKEET, *Psitteules euteles* (now known as PERFECT LORIKEET, *Trichoglossus euteles*); text page 13.

MANY-COLORED PARRAKEET, *Psephotus multicolor* (now known as MULGA PARROT, *Psephotus varius*); text pages 206, 260.

BROWN'S PARRAKEET, *Platycercus browni* (now known as NORTHERN ROSELLA, *Platycercus venustus*); text page 168.

1. WHITE-EARED CONURE, *Pyrrhura leucotis* (now known as WHITE-EARED CONURE, *Pyrrhura leucotis*); text page 61.
2. PEARLY CONURE, *Pyrrhura perlata* (now known as PEARLY CONURE, *Pyrrhura perlata*); text page 62.

1. RED-COLLARED LORIKEET, *Trichoglossus rubritorques* (now known as RED-COLLARED LORIKEET, or RAINBOW LORY, *Trichoglossus haematodus rubritorquis*); text page 10.
2. FORSTEN'S LORIKEET, *Trichoglossus forsteni* (now known as FORSTEN'S LORIKEET, *Trichoglossus haematodus forsteni*); text page 4.

1. BLYTH'S NICOBAR PARRAKEET, *Palaeornis caniceps* (now known as BLYTH'S PARAKEET, *Psittacula caniceps*); text page 115.
2. NICOBAR PARRAKEET, *Palaeornis nicobarica* (now known as LONG-TAILED PARAKEET, *Psittacula longicauda nicobarica*); text page 117.

1. YELLOW-VENTED BLUE-BONNET, *Psephotus xanthorrhous* (now known as BLUE BONNET, *Psephotus haematogaster*); text page 193.
2. RED-VENTED BLUE-BONNET, *Psephotus haematorrhous* (now known as BLUE-BONNET, *Psephotus haematogaster haematorrhous*); text page 191.

1. RED-HEADED CONURE, *Conurus rubrolarvatus* (now known as RED-MASKED CONURE, *Aratinga erythrogenys*); text pages 37, 267.
2. BLACK-HEADED CONURE, *Conurus nenday* (now known as NANDAY CONURE, *Nandayus nenday*); text page 36.

1. BROWN-THROATED CONURE, *Conurus aeruginosus* (now known as BROWN-THROATED CONURE, *Aratinga pertinax*); text page 44.
2. CACTUS CONURE, *Conurus cactorum* (now known as CACTUS CONURE, *Aratinga cactorum*); text page 115.

GOLDEN-FRONTED NEW ZEALAND PARRAKEET, *Cyanorhamphus auriceps* (now known as YELLOW-FRONTED PARAKEET, *Cyanorhamphus auriceps*); text page 234.

1. BARNARD'S PARRAKEET, *Barnardius barnardi* (now known as MALLEE RINGNECK PARROT, *Barnardius barnardi*); text pages 183, 260.
2. BAUER'S PARRAKEET, *Barnardius zonarius* (now known as PORT LINCOLN PARROT, *Barnardius zonarius*); text page 189.

ORNATE LORIKEET, *Trichoglossus ornatus* (now known as ORNATE LORY, *Trichoglossus ornatus*); text page 11.

1. SPLENDID PARRAKEET, *Neophema splendida* (now known as SCARLET-CHESTED PARROT, *Neophema splendida*); text page 226.
2. TURQUOISINE PARRAKEET, *Neophema pulchella* (now known as TURQUOISE PARROT, *Neophema pulchella*); text page 223.

THE VARIED LORIKEET, *Ptilosclera versicolor* (now known as VARIED LORIKEET, *Trichoglossus versicolor*); text page 255.

1. PENNANT'S PARRAKEET, *Platycercus elegans* (now known as CRIMSON ROSELLA, *Platycercus elegans*); text page 157.
2. YELLOW-RUMPED PARRAKEET, *Platycercus flaveolus*, (now known as YELLOW ROSELLA, *Platycercus flaveolus*); text pages 163, 259.

BARRABAND'S PARRAKEET, *Polytelis barrabandi* (now known as BARRABAND'S PARROT, or SUPERB PARROT, *Polytelis swainsonni*); text page 121.

bark or splinters from the framework of the aviary to form the nest. If kept in a small and overcrowded aviary, these birds will seldom do more than play at nesting, often carrying bits of string or pieces of paper up to the nest, sometimes in their beaks, a mode of conveyance that is probably never adopted in a natural state, in which the material, consisting of pliant strips of green bark, is carried under the feathers of the lower back.

As an aviary-bird, the present species has not much to recommend it, being as a rule wild, and, especially when nesting, very spiteful.

The adult male is green, brighter on the rump and upper tail-coverts, and yellowish-green on the underparts; the whole of the head, neck and upper breast pearly-grey; *under wing-coverts black;* tail with a broad sub-terminal black band; bill and feet grey. Total length about 5½ inches.

The female differs from the male in having the head and *under wing-coverts green.*

THE RED-FACED LOVEBIRD.

Agapornis pullaria (Linn.).
Coloured Figure, GREENE'S *Parrots in Captivity*, Vol. I.

This very well-known species inhabits West Africa, from the Gold Coast to the Congo, and eastwards to Niam Niam. It is sometimes brought to Europe in large numbers, and is consequently a common cage-bird in this country and on the Continent. It occurs in flocks in its native country, but on account of so very many being caught for sale to the passing steamers, its numbers are said to be decreasing. As long ago as 1874 Mr. H. T. Ussher wrote as follows in the *Ibis* : "This little bird existed some years since in considerable numbers near Accra and Cape Coast, and might have been seen at any time in little flocks of from eight to ten in the bushes and low vegetation. Now, however, in consequence of the persecution it suffers for the sake of profit by sale to the mail-steamers, it is becoming scarce in the vicinity of the settlements."

Although so common a cage-bird in this country, I have been quite unable to find any record of young having been reared, or even hatched in captivity, although eggs have been laid both here and in Germany.

When first imported, the Red-faced Lovebird is a delicate bird, and, unfortunately, on arrival it is almost invariably crippled by having the flight feathers of its wings cut, a cruel and useless practice, for which there is no excuse whatever. The result of this barbarous proceeding is that in the effort to shed the stumps and produce the new flight feathers the bird's constitution is weakened, and but a small percentage of those which arrive on our shores live to attain their full powers of flight.

There would seem to be no reason why an established pair of these birds, with full powers of flight, should not succeed in rearing young in our aviaries, but it is rare even to hear of eggs being laid in captivity, though two cases occurred in 1902, one in an aviary at Cambridge (*cf. Bird Notes*, vol. i., p. 265) and the other in Mr. Phillipps' aviary in London. Mr. Phillipps informs me that the birds laid in a box in his bird-room in the autumn, but made no nest, which is doubtless to be accounted for by the unnatural conditions under which they attempted to breed. There can be little doubt that this species when wild, builds a nest in a hole in a tree in the same way, and with the same material as do its congeners.

Agapornis pullaria is not nearly so noisy nor so spiteful towards other birds as *A. roseicollis*, though it is hardly a safe companion for small passerine birds.

The popular notion that if one of a pair of Lovebirds dies, the other will immediately pine away and follow suit, has on many occasions been proved to be a fallacy.

The prevailing colour of this species is green, the underparts having a yellowish tinge : whole of face bright brick-red ; rump blue ; central tail-feathers green, the others yellowish-green at the base, then red, then black and green at the tips, these colours forming bands, broken only by the central feathers. Under wing-coverts *black in the male* and *green in the female*. The female may also be distinguished by the paler colour of her face and rump. The bill is red in both sexes, but brighter in the male. Total length about 6 inches.

The young birds are like the female, but with yellow foreheads.

THE ROSY-FACED LOVEBIRD.

Agapornis roseicollis (Vieill.).

Coloured Figure, GREENE'S *Parrots in Captivity*, Vol. I.

This, the largest and handsomest of the three important species of this genus, inhabits Benguela, Damaraland and Ovampoland in South-West Africa, and according to Layard, it is also found on the Limpopo River in the South-East.

Andersson gives the following account of this Lovebird in his *Birds of Damaraland :*—

" This pretty little species is very generally distributed over Damara and Great Namaqualand, and is also found on the Okavango and at Lake

Ngami. It is always observed in small flocks, and seldom far from water, to which it resorts at least once in the day, and is consequently not a bad guide

From The Royal Natural History.
ROSY-FACED LOVE-BIRDS. *Agapornis roseicollis.*

to a thirsty traveller, though if he be inexperienced it would hardly avail him much, as it frequently happens that the drinking-places resorted to by this and other water-loving birds are of but small compass and strangely situated.

"This species is very swift of flight, and the little flocks in which it is observed seem to flash upon the sight as they change their feeding-grounds or pass to or from their drinking-places; their flight, however, is only for a comparatively short distance at a time. They utter rapid and shrill notes when on the wing, or when suddenly disturbed or alarmed. Their food consists of berries and large berry-like seeds."

The same author goes on to make the following almost incredible statement; he writes: "This bird does not make any nest of its own, but takes possession of nests belonging to other birds, especially *Philetærus socius* and *Plocepasser mahali*. I cannot say whether it forcibly ejects the rightful owners of these nests, or merely occupies such as they have abandoned; but in the case of the first-named species, I have seen the Parrots and the Grosbeaks incubating in about equal numbers under the shelter of the same friendly roof."

Although we cannot doubt Andersson's statement that the huge nests of the Social and White-browed Weaver-birds are often used by *Agapornis roseicollis* as nesting places, his contention that this species builds no nest of its own cannot be accepted by those who have known the bird under more or less natural conditions in large aviaries in this country and on the Continent.

My friend, Mr. Reginald Phillipps, has given a full and most interesting account of the nesting of this species in his garden-aviary in the *Avicultural Magazine* of 1896 (vol. ii., p. 128), and the present writer has watched the process of nest-building by these birds in his own aviary. There is little doubt that the enormous umbrella-shaped nests of the

Weaver-birds, which are described as consisting of "whole cartloads of grass," are used merely as receptacles for the nests of the Lovebirds, possibly in districts where large trees, containing suitable holes and crevices for nests, are scarce.

Mr. Phillipps' account, above-mentioned, of the nesting of this species is so very interesting that I cannot do better than give my readers a part of it here. He writes: "Neither in bird-room nor garden did the Rosy-faces associate with any of the other birds, but kept to themselves, and seemed supremely happy in their own company. The female, at any rate, in season and out of season, seemed to be filled with but one thought—how best to increase and multiply the species; and she pursued her self-appointed task with so much zeal and perseverance that if she had had a proper mate my aviary would have been well-nigh filled with Rosy-faces. She never now carried nesting materials in her beak or amidst the feathers of the thigh; she never made use of any material for her nest but the bark of living trees so long as she had the run of the wilderness; and when shut off from her chosen trees she fell upon those in the other aviary as far as they would go, occasionally taking tiny strips from the perches, but never touching hay or straw, nor picking up any stuff of any kind from the ground. Artificial nesting-places of every kind—logs, barrels, cocoa-nut husks—all were ignored; and for many a day did the pair pursue their hunt for a suitable spot in which to build, evidently attaching the greatest importance to this point. The cracks and crevices they squeezed themselves into and explored were marvellous; for a time a chink between two cages in the bird-room, where a slight ledge afforded walking space for a mouse, seemed to be the nearest approach to what they desired, but as there was not anything to lay the eggs upon, just a clear drop of some three feet to the floor, the place was reluctantly abandoned ; but not until after the happy pair had passed several very uncomfortable nights hanging on by their eyelids, did they wholly desert it. Eventually they found a spot in the garden, which in some respects evidently pleased them.

" Between the ceiling and roof of one of the sheds there was an empty space several feet in length and breadth, and some three or four inches high along the highest part. Into this they managed to force an entrance through a hole barely large enough to admit a mouse or a Blue Tit, and there during the summer the busy little lady gathered together a large mass of prepared bark. During the colder months, when confined to the house at night, they found a very similar place in the bird-room, with an entrance hole no other bird could make use of, and there also the lady piled up a marvellous stock of material, for on most days in the autumn and spring they were let out into the garden for a fly, and also during the winter on mild days ; but of course this second and more permanent nesting-place had not been sought out and adopted until after I had closed up the entrance to the first. They seemed to have a decided predilection in favour of making use of the same nest time after time ; but as the female practically never ceased working, even when sitting rarely failing to carry home a load when returning from a fly, the size of the nest was ever on the increase."

The Rosy- or Peach-faced Lovebird has reared young successfully on several occasions in this country and on the Continent. It is a pretty and interesting species, and would be a nice aviary bird but for two serious drawbacks which it possesses, namely, its spitefulness towards other birds, and its intolerable, oft-repeated shriek, which one writer has compared to the sound produced by an unlubricated train-wheel.

The prevailing colour of this species is green, with a yellowish tinge on the underparts; forehead bright crimson; lores, cheeks, throat, and in the male the chest, rosy-pink; rump and upper tail-coverts bright cobalt-blue; quills mostly dusky; central tail-feathers blue, the rest red at the base, then green, then black and tipped with blue; bill horn-colour with a greenish tinge. Total length about 6 inches.

The sexes are practically similar in plumage, the only difference being that the rosy colour extends farther towards the breast in the male than in the female.

The young birds have no red on the forehead, which is yellowish, and the rosy colour of the cheeks very pale.

Genus LORICULUS, Blyth.

This genus comprises a group of small Parrots in which the bill is thin, and the upper mandible very little curved. In some ways these birds closely resemble the *Loriidæ*, though they do not possess the filamented tongue which characterises that family. They feed on honey and fruit, like the Lories, and require the same treatment in captivity as those birds; like the Lories also, they are extremely dirty in their habits, and require a very large cage or aviary. They possess, however, one curious habit which at once distinguishes them from all other Parrots, namely, that of suspending themselves head-downwards from a branch, or the roof of their cage when sleeping, on account of which the popular name of "Hanging

Parrakeets" has been bestowed upon them. Twenty-four species are known, ranging from India eastward, to the Philippines and the Papuan sub-region.

THE VERNAL HANGING-PARRAKEET.

Loriculus vernalis (Sparrm.).

This beautiful little Parrakeet has a wide range, extending through Southern India, the Eastern Himalayas, Assam, Burma, the Malayan Peninsula and the Andaman Islands. It is a rather rarely imported species.

Jerdon informs us that "it is found in small flocks, and keeps up a continual chirping when feeding, which it does on fruit and flower-buds, partly probably for the nectar contained in the latter. It is said to be fond of the toddy of the cocoanut palm, and to be sometimes taken stupefied at the toddy pots."

Oates, in his *Birds of British Burma*, writes: " This pretty Loriquet is a forest-loving bird, seldom being found in the open, except in thick groves and orchards. It associates in small flocks, and is remarkable for its rapid flight. It feeds on small fruits and flower buds, and probably on grain, but I have never detected them in paddy fields. They bear confinement well, and are more frequently caged than any other species of Parrot. When sleeping, they hang from their perch head downwards. The eggs, usually three to five in number, are deposited in the hole of a tree or of a branch at a considerable height from the ground. Capt. Bingham found the nest in Tenasserim in February."

Davison, quoted by Hume in *Stray Feathers* (vol. ii.), remarks of this species : " I have always found it in pairs, never singly or in parties ; it is a very lively bird, flying from tree to tree, uttering quickly its sharp shrill note. It is amusing to watch a number of these birds in a cage; they start from the bottom of the cage, climb up the side, then along the top till they get to about the centre of the roof, where they hang head downwards for a second or two, then fly down on to the perch, or the bottom of the cage, and recommence the ascent; this they will continue for an hour at a time. Like all the Lorikets* they sleep hanging head downwards and usually with their heads tucked under their wings. Numbers are caught by the native convicts, and any number of live birds can generally be obtained in the bazaar at Ross Island. The natives catch them by putting one into a small cage, which is fastened to a long thin bamboo, the cage is covered over with small green branches, and from the top of the cage projects a small dry branch, or blackened stick with another piece of stick tied across it at right angles, cross fashion. This twig or stick is then covered with bird-lime, and the bamboo is stuck upright in the ground. The call of the caged bird soon attracts some other, which, flying to the spot, invariably settles on the exposed limed branch and is of course caught.

"The birds were breeding before I left the Andamans. On April 19, while returning to Ross from Port Monat, a Burman convict who was with me saw a bird of this species fly into a hole in the branch of a forest tree growing by the roadside. He called my attention to this and I sent him up the tree. On his climbing up he found the bird (which he caught and brought down with him) sitting on three round white eggs. The hole was about 20 feet from the ground, and contained no lining or attempt at a nest,

---

* *Loriculus.*

the eggs being laid on some soft black earthy-looking powder that lay at the bottom of the hole and which had evidently fallen from the top and sides of the hole. The hole, which was a natural one, not excavated by the bird, was moderately large, but not quite large enough to admit the convict's hand without a little cutting away at its lower edge."

The adult male is green, brighter on the head, the underside paler, and a tinge of orange on the interscapular region; rump and upper tail-coverts bright red; throat with a blue spot; breast tinged with yellowish; quills blue; under tail-coverts blue: iris pale yellowish; bill red.

In the female the green colour is rather more yellowish, and the head less brilliant green; blue of the throat almost or entirely absent. Total length $5\frac{1}{2}$ inches.

THE GOLDEN-BACKED HANGING PARRAKEET.

Loriculus chrysonotus, Scl.

This rare species inhabits the island of Cebu, in the Philippine group. Nothing seems to be known of its habits in a wild state.

A living pair of this beautiful form were purchased by the Zoological Society in March, 1871, from which Dr. Sclater named the species, and this pair appear to have bred in the gardens, as the eighth edition of the *List of Animals* in the Society's Gardens contains a record of a young bird of this species being hatched on August 23, 1871.

The coloured plate here given has been drawn from the type specimen in the British Museum.

The male has the greater part of the plumage green, becoming more yellowish on the underparts;

forehead, rump and upper tail-coverts red; top of the head, occiput, nape and back golden, an orange-red patch on the throat; upper side of tail dark green; under side blue. Total length about $6\frac{1}{4}$ inches.

The female has the cheeks and throat tinged with blue; throat with *no red patch;* back green, washed with golden; the golden colour on the head and nape less bright than in the male.

THE CEYLONESE HANGING PARRAKEET.

Loriculus indicus (Gm.).

Coloured Figure, LEGGE'S *Birds of Ceylon*, Pls. VI. and XI.

As its popular name implies, this little species inhabits the island of Ceylon. None of this genus can be considered common cage-birds in this country, but this is one of the better known forms, so far as aviculturists are concerned.

Colonel Legge gives the following full account of the wild life of this species in his *Birds of Ceylon* :—

"The Ceylon Lorikeet frequents woods, detached groves of trees, compounds, native gardens, patnas dotted with timber, and in fact, any locality which is clothed with fruit-bearing trees or those whose flowers afford it its favourite saccharine food. It is a most gluttonous little bird, constantly on the wing in active search for its food, darting with a very swift flight through the woods, uttering its sibilant little scream, its bright plumage flashing in the rays of the tropical sun. When it reaches a tree which attracts its attention it instantly checks its headlong progress, and alighting on the top, actively climbs to the fruit which it has espied, or should the tree prove barren, after giving out its call-note for a short time, darts off, perhaps in the opposite direction from which it came.

It is exceedingly fond of 'toddy,' or juice which exists in the kitool or sugar-palm (*Caryota urens*), and feeds on it to such an extent that it becomes stupefied and falls an easy captive to the natives, who cage it in large numbers for sale at Port de Galle. "While in a state of captivity they are fed on sugar-cane, of which they are very fond, but they do not live for any length of time should the supply of cane come to an end. It feeds so gluttonously on the beautiful fruit of the Jambu-tree that I have seen bird after bird shot out of one tree without their companions taking the slightest notice of the gun or the death of so many of their little flock. When held up by the legs after being shot, the juice of this fruit pours from their mouths and nostrils. The flowers of the cocoanut-tree come in for a large share of its patronage, as do also those of other trees, on the 'cups' or calyces of which it subsists, biting them off in a pendant attitude."

The sexes of *L. indicus* are alike in plumage, and may be described as follows :—

Prevailing colour green, paler below than above; top of the head, rump and upper tail-coverts bright red; the back tinged with orange; a bluish tinge on the face; under side of tail blue; legs and feet yellowish. Total length about $5\frac{3}{4}$ inches.

THE BLUE-CROWNED HANGING PARRAKEET.

Loriculus galgulus (Linn.).

This is one of the prettiest of the genus, and is comparatively well-known to aviculturists. It inhabits the Malayan Peninsula, Sumatra, Banka, Borneo and Nias.

Lieut. Kelham, writing on Malayan Ornithology,

remarks: "A common cage-bird in all the settlements, prized on account of its gaudy colours and the ridiculous way it climbs about the wires of its cage, often hanging head downwards. During December I came across a small party of them on Pulo Battam,

BLUE-CROWNED HANGING PARRAKEETS. *Loriculus galgulus.*
From *The Royal Natural History.*

a large thickly-wooded island near Singapore." (*Ibis*, 1881, p. 387.)

The Blue-crowned Hanging Parrakeet does not differ in its habits in captivity from the other members of the genus.

The male is bright green; top of the head with a deep blue spot; a yellow spot on the upper back; a bright yellow bar across the lower back; a red spot on the throat; rump and upper tail-coverts red; the tail-feathers with yellowish tips; underside of both tail and wings blue. Total length about $5\frac{1}{4}$ inches.

The female lacks the red patch on the throat, and the yellow band across the lower back, and is much duller than the male.

SCLATER'S HANGING PARRAKEET.

Loriculus sclateri, Wall.

This very rare Parrakeet is indigenous to the Sula Islands, and may be said to be unknown to present day aviculturists.

Dr. A. R. Wallace named it in 1862, in honour of Dr. P. Lutley Sclater. A specimen was exhibited at the Zoological Gardens in 1865.

The sexes are alike in plumage. Prevailing colour green, tail and quills being a darker shade; back golden-orange, deepening to orange-red in the centre; rump and upper tail-coverts bright red; a red stripe on the throat; underside of tail blue; bill black.

Sub-family PLATYCERCINÆ.

This sub-family, which is confined to Australasia, comprises some eleven genera, in which the bill is generally short and thick, and the lower mandible more or less hidden by the cheek feathers. It seems strange to students of living birds that the brush-tongued *Nanodes*, whose habits resemble the *Loriidæ*, should be placed by Count Salvadori in this sub-family, the other members of which have no filament to the tongue, and feed mainly on seed.

Genus PLATYCERCUS, Vig.

In this genus the tail is broad, the back has a scale-like appearance, each feather being black with a broad border of some other colour, and the bill has a distinct notch. There are some fifteen or sixteen known species, all inhabiting the Australian Continent, and eleven or twelve of these have been represented by living examples in this country. The Broad-tailed Parrakeets are, as a rule, extremely hardy and will live for many years in this country under suitable treatment. Their food in captivity should consist of canary seed, hemp, oats and dari, pea-nuts, and fruit, or green food such as chickweed, groundsel, or flowering grass. Some are fond of insects, and mealworms may be given occasionally, especially towards the nesting season. The commoner species breed more or less freely under suitable conditions in captivity, and there is little doubt that the rarer kinds would do so also. The sexes are superficially alike.

MASTERS'S PARRAKEET.

Platycercus mastersianus, Ramsay.
Coloured Figure, P. Z. S., 1902, Vol. I., Pl. XIX.

This very rare Broad-tail was named by Dr. Ramsay, in honour of Mr. George Masters, who drew his attention to a specimen in the Sydney Museum as being a new species. It was unknown to Count Salvadori when he wrote the Parrot volume of the *British Museum Catalogue of Birds* in 1891, but he copied Dr. Ramsay's original description in a footnote. Subsequently Mr. Rothschild procured a living example which was deposited in the Zoological Society's Gardens on October 29, 1897; and this bird was the subject of a coloured illustration in the *Proceedings of the Zoological Society* for 1902.

P. mastersianus is closely allied to *P. elegans*, from which it differs in having the centre part of the tail-feathers nearly white, the underparts bluish-green, and the back and upper wing-coverts mostly blue.

According to Dr. Ramsay, Masters's Parrakeet inhabits the interior of New South Wales.

PENNANT'S PARRAKEET.

Platycercus elegans (Gm.).
Coloured Figure, GOULD'S *Birds of Australia*, Vol. V., Pl. XXIII.

This magnificent Parrakeet is one of the most gorgeous, and at the same time one of the most frequently imported of the genus. It inhabits the eastern and southern parts of the Continent, but is especially abundant in New South Wales. The birds found in Northern Queensland appear to be smaller, with the interscapular region blacker, and to possess a different voice.* (*Cf.* Campbell's *Nests and Eggs*, p. 630.) Gould writes of this species: "This beautiful bird is very generally dispersed over New South Wales, where it frequents grassy hills and brushes, particularly those of the Liverpool range and all similar districts; it also inhabits Kangaroo Island, but I never met with it in the belts of the Murray, or in any of the forests round Adelaide, in which part of the country the *Platycercus adelaidensis* occurs abundantly. Its food consists of berries and

---

* *P. elegans* var. *nigrescens*, Ramsay.

the seeds of various grasses, to which insects and caterpillars are occasionally added, and to obtain which it descends to the bases of the hills and to open glades in the forests; I have often flushed it from such situations, and when six or eight rose together with outspread tails of beautiful pale blue, offering a decided contrast to the rich scarlet livery of the body, I never failed to pause and admire the splendour of their appearance, of which no description can give an adequate idea; the *Platycerci* must, in fact, be seen in their native wilds before their beautiful appearance can be appreciated, or the interesting nature of their habits at all understood. Like the other members of the genus, the *Platycercus pennantii* runs rapidly over the ground, but its flight is not enduring. . . .

"It breeds in the holes of large gum trees, generally selecting those on the hill-sides within the brushes, of which situations the cedar brushes of the Liverpool range appear to be a favourite. The months of September, October, and November constitute the breeding-season. The eggs, which are white, about an inch and two lines long, eleven and a half lines broad, and from four to seven in number, are deposited on the rotten wood at the bottom of the hole."

Mr. A. J. Campbell, in his admirable work on the *Nests and Eggs of Australian Birds*, remarks: "When a flock is seen passing through the forest they describe as it were so many streaks of the richest crimson colouring. . . .

"I have noticed the birds nesting in the foot-hills of the Pyrenees, and afterwards in the Upper Werribee district, where in conjunction with Messrs. Brittlebank, several nests were found. One in particular was interesting, from the fact that one of the birds (apparently the female) belonging to the nest had the mottled greenish dress, and was not in full plumage.

"The nest was in a stringy-bark tree that grew in a deep secluded gully. The nesting hole was ten or twelve feet from the ground, in a barrel near the junction of a projecting limb. The eggs, seven, slightly incubated, were within arm's length of the entrance."

Platycercus elegans is one of the hardiest of Parrakeets, and when once established and acclimatised in an English aviary will withstand the rigours of our severest winters without taking any harm, or appearing to mind the cold in the least. Its diet should consist of the usual seeds, canary, hemp, oats, dari, and sunflower, nuts, and plenty of green food, and a few meal-worms, especially when breeding.

Each pair should have an aviary to themselves if they are expected to breed, and be provided with two or three nest-boxes or large hollow logs.

They have bred in captivity in this country and on the Continent several times.* The female alone incubates, and the sound of the young in the nest is stated by the Rev. C. D. Farrar to resemble at first "the barking in miniature of a pack of hounds," and to gradually change to the whistle of the adults, "and then to a hoarse grumbling noise."

The following is a description of *Platycercus elegans:* Prevailing colour bright crimson; cheeks violet-blue; feathers of the back black, edged with crimson; a black bar on the upper wing-coverts; secondaries blue; under wing-coverts blue; tail blue, presenting a green tinge in some lights. The sexes are practically alike in plumage, but the male is, as a rule, slightly larger and more brightly coloured than the female. The length of a full-grown male

---

* *Cf. Avicultural Magazine*, vol. v., p. 190.

is about 14 inches. The young are olive-green with the cheeks and wing-coverts blue; the red generally appears first on the crown, throat, and upper tail-coverts, gradually extending over the whole body.

THE ADELAIDE PARRAKEET.

Platycercus adelaidæ, Gould.

This species inhabits South Australia and the Interior, where it takes the place of its very near ally *P. elegans*. Gould informs us that he was induced to give it the specific name of *adelaidensis*, from the fact of his having procured some of his first specimens in the very streets of Adelaide. "When I visited the interior of South Australia, in the winter of 1838," writes the above-named author, "I found the adults associated in small groups of from six to twenty in number; while near the coast, between Holdfast Bay and the Port of Adelaide, the young in the green dress were assembled in flocks of hundreds; they were generally on the ground in search of grass-seeds, and when so occupied would admit of a near approach; when flushed they merely flew up to the branches of the nearest tree. It is impossible to conceive anything more beautiful than the rising of a flock of newly moulted adults of this species, for their beautiful broad tails and wings glittering in the sun present a really magnificent spectacle."

Mr. Campbell tells us that Mr. White, of Reedbeds, had young of this species hatched in his aviary, and that the South Australians call this the Pheasant Parrakeet.

The Adelaide Parrakeet so closely resembles Pennant's Parrakeet, that some authorities have believed it to be a hybrid between the last-named and either the Yellow-rumped (*P. flaveolus*) or the Pale-headed (*P. pallidiceps*) Parrakeets, but there is not the slightest doubt that it is a good species. It is, unfortunately, but seldom imported into this country.

P. adelaidæ may be described as possessing the same markings as *P. elegans*, but the red colour is much paler and more yellowish, many of the feathers possessing yellowish edges. The female is similar in colour to the male, and the young are much more greenish. Total length about 14 inches.

THE YELLOW-RUMPED PARRAKEET.
Platycercus flaveolus, Gould.

A glance at the accompanying coloured plate will show how very closely this species resembles Pennant's Parrakeet in all but its colour, which, instead of being crimson, is yellow. An individual of this species might well be mistaken for a yellow variety of *P. elegans*.

Platycercus flaveolus inhabits the district from Victoria to New South Wales and the interior of Australia, and is but seldom brought alive to this country. I noticed a very fine pair in Mr. W. Fasey's collection at Snaresbrook, in the spring of 1902, but have never heard of young having been reared in captivity. The eggs were first described in Australia by Mr. A. J. Campbell, from a clutch of four obtained by Mr. W. White, on September 20, 1894, from a hole in a eucalyptus tree in the Warrabra Forest, some 200 miles north of Adelaide.

Mr. Campbell writes in his *Nests and Eggs of Australian Birds:* "I have noticed the Yellow Parrakeet as far south as the Pyramid Hill and Echuca districts, Victoria. At the latter place, one dewy morning in early spring, I came upon a flock of about thirty or forty, feeding upon the surface of a sand rise. While placing myself under a clump of silver wattles, all abloom, to make observations upon this unusually large congregation of Parrots, a pair of vagrant dogs, that had been rabbiting on their own account close by, crossed the rise, and dispersed my feathered friends. On another occasion I watched a pair of these birds feeding on 'Bathurst' burrs, by a dead log, a few paces from me. The male appeared to be the larger and brighter coloured bird."

The prevailing colour of this Parrakeet is pale yellow; forehead red; throat and lores splashed with red; cheeks blue; feathers of the back black, bordered with yellow; a black patch on the upper wing-coverts; wings and tail blue, the outer tail feathers being tipped with white. Total length about 14 inches.

The young are much more greenish than the adults.

THE YELLOW-BELLIED PARRAKEET.

Platycercus flaviventris (Temm).

Coloured Figure, GOULD'S *Birds of Australia*, Vol. V., Pl. XXIV.

I have never known the Yellow-bellied or Green Parrakeet offered for sale in this country, but it has been represented in the Zoological Society's collection. It inhabits Tasmania, Southern Australia, and the Islands of Bass Strait. Gould found it abundant on the banks of the Tamar, and on one occasion saw hundreds feeding amongst some newly thrashed straw at a barn door. "Besides grass-seeds," he writes, "the flowers of the *Eucalypti* with insects and their larvæ constitute a considerable portion of its food, and it may be often seen very busily engaged about the branches loaded with flowers in the depths of the forest far away from any cleared lands."

Mr. A. J. Campbell writes: "The large Yellow-bellied or Green Parrot is peculiar to Tasmania and the larger islands of Bass Strait. Odd examples may have been found on the mainland opposite, because, in the excursion of the Field Naturalists' Club of Victoria, the Parrots were found on Kent Group, not more than sixty miles from the nearest Victorian Coast. In all examples seen in the Strait we noticed none so highly coloured as the figure shown in Gould's plate, possibly they had not reached perfection, because, like the Crimson (Pennant) Parrakeet, the full adult plumage is the progress of seasons."

The nest is said to be in a hole in a tall Eucalyptus tree.

P. flaviventris has the head and underparts yellow, each feather on the head slightly margined with brown; forehead, lores, and space under the eye crimson; cheeks blue; back and scapulars greenish-black, each feather having a green margin; wings mostly blue; rump and upper tail-coverts green; central tail-feathers green, the others blue, tipped with white. The female is smaller and duller in colour than the male. The young are much greener than the adults.

THE PALE-HEADED ROSELLA.

Platycercus pallidiceps, Vig.

Coloured Figure, GOULD'S *Birds of Australia*, Vol. V., Pl. XXVI.

The Pale-headed, Mealy, or Moreton Bay Rosella is an inhabitant of Eastern Australia, and also the Interior. It is well known to aviculturists in this country, although not nearly so often to be obtained as its commoner relative *P. eximius*. The

Mealy Rosella is a hardy and easily kept species, and although not nearly so ready to reproduce its kind in captivity as the better known species, has been bred on several occasions in this country; and hybrids have been produced between this Parrakeet and *P. eximius*. In *Notes on Cage Birds* (sec. series, p. 185), Mr. C. P. Arthur gives the following interesting account of the successful rearing of two young Pale-headed Rosellas. He writes—

"The hen laid four eggs (the first two of which got broken in an unaccountable manner) in a box with sawdust, and the remains of a cocoa-nut husk left there by the Golden-headed Parrakeets. The eggs were about the size of a Cockatiel's, but rather more stunted in shape and of a pinkish-white colour. She commenced sitting with the first egg. The third egg was hatched on the twenty-first day after it was laid, and the fourth two days later, so it is evident that these birds hatch on alternate days, the same as the eggs are laid.

"The first young one left the nest on July 11, being five weeks and two days old; the other one day later. They both returned to the nest the first night, but not afterwards. The hen sat very close the whole of the time, only leaving the nest to be fed by her mate, which never entered the box to my knowledge until the first young one was hatched, when he was in the nest all day, and spent the greater part of his time in with the young ones until they were fourteen days old. During incubation, if any one approached the aviary while the hen was out of her nest, she would make a rush to her nest box and tumble in, like a rat into his hole. After the young were about fourteen days old it was a rare thing to see the parents go near their nest, for although very tame themselves, they were very shy with regard to their young, so much so that on two or three occasions I thought they had forsaken them. On examining the young, however, I found their crops to be full of food. The young of the Mealy Rosella are very quiet in the nest, unlike a nest of eight young Red Rosellas I had at the same time, which were as noisy as a lot of young starlings.

"There is even more difference in the colouring of the two young ones than in their parents, and they are no doubt a pair, so that it will not be difficult to distinguish the sexes in future when they leave the nest, after I have found which of these turn out to be male, and which female, as one of them has scarlet under-tail coverts, and the other very faint orange."

A pair of Mealy Rosellas, which lived for some time in the writer's possession, showed the greatest antipathy to a pair of Blue-bonnet Parrakeets (*Psephotus xanthorrhous*) which occupied the next aviary to theirs, although they took no notice whatever of a pair of Many-coloured Parrakeets (*Psephotus multicolor*) which shared their own aviary. So savagely did the male Pale-head fight with the Blue-bonnets through the wires, sometimes biting their toes so that they bled freely, that I was obliged to part with them, which I was very sorry to do, as they are some of the most beautiful of the *Platycerci*.

This species has the top of the head, nape, and borders of black feathers of the back and scapulars, pale yellow ; cheeks white, with a blue border below (except in some specimens where this is absent) ; wings blue ; rump, upper tail-coverts, and under-parts pale blue, each feather being fringed with black ; centre tail-feathers blue, with a green tinge towards the base ; the lateral ones blue, tipped with white.

Some specimens have the head and other parts of the body splashed with red, which may be due to hybridisation.

THE BLUE-CHEEKED PARRAKEET.
Platycercus amathusia, Bp.
Coloured Figure, GOULD'S *Birds of Australia*, Supp. Vol., Pl. LXIII.

This rare Broadtail may be considered as the Northern form of *P. pallidiceps*, being found only in the north of Australia, from Port Darwin to Rockingham Bay, and differing but slightly in plumage from the last species described. It was first represented in the living collection of the Zoological Society of London in 1887, and again in the following year.

The nest and eggs, according to Mr. Campbell, are undescribed. *Platycercus amathusia* differs from *P. pallidiceps* in the cheeks being almost entirely blue, in the paler edges to the feathers of the back, in the yellower tinge of the feathers of the rump and breast, and in the much greener tinge of the blue feathers of the underparts and base of tail-feathers. Total length about $12\frac{1}{2}$ inches.

BROWN'S PARRAKEET.
Platycercus browni (Temm.).

Although a well-known species, it is only within the last few years that the "Smutty" Parrakeet of the Australian Colonists has been imported alive to Europe. Mr. H. J. Fulljames exhibited a pair at a bird-show at Balham, in November, 1899, which were the first living specimens I had ever seen, and probably the first ever owned by a private individual in this country. Four specimens were deposited in the Zoological Gardens on October 20 in the following year, and in the year 1901 a few more were brought to this country, and a pair came into the present writer's possession in October of that year.

Brown's Parrakeet inhabits the north of Australia, from Port Darwin to Port Essington, where, Gould informs us, it is an abundant species, inhabiting grassy meadow-like land and the edges of swamps, and feeding upon the seeds of grasses and other plants. "Sometimes it is seen in pairs," he writes, "but more frequently in families of from ten to twenty in number. It frequently utters a rapid succession of double notes resembling '*trin-se, trin-se.*' Its flight is low, somewhat rapid and zigzag, seldom farther prolonged than from tree to tree."

Although inhabiting a hot region, *Platycercus browni* seems to be a fairly hardy species. My pair have spent the past winter in an aviary in which one morning at least I found ice on the drinking water. During last summer they occupied an outdoor aviary, but, although the hen seemed anxious to breed, and was often seen examining nest-boxes, no eggs were laid; but we hope for better luck in the coming warm weather. The male is very excited and angry at the sight of other Parrakeets, except Budgerigars, which he ignores. He was particularly anxious to fight a cock Blue-bonnet, which until recently occupied a neighbouring aviary.

The male *browni* has a particularly loud and clear note, which he is very fond of repeating with great rapidity. I consider this species one of the most desirable and beautiful of the genus.

The Rev. C. D. Farrar mentions a pair of Brown's Parrakeets belonging to the Honourable Walter Rothschild, which laid eggs during the summer of 1902. (*Avic. Mag.*, vol. ix., p. 102.)

Crown, lores, ear-coverts and nape black, deeper in the male than in the female; feathers on the back and scapulars black, bordered with pale yellow; rump, upper tail-coverts, breast and abdomen yellow, each feather being narrowly edged with black; cheeks white, with a narrow line of blue below; wings blue; tail blue, with a greenish tinge at the base, and the lateral feathers tipped with white; under tail-coverts red. Total length about 11 inches.

There is considerable individual variation in this species, some specimens having the feathers of the breast and back washed with blue; others have numerous minute red feathers on the crown, and Gould figures a specimen in which the crown is entirely red.

The young birds are similar in colour to the adults, according to Gould, "but have all the markings dull and indistinct; as the individual approaches to maturity the breast becomes ornamented with a number of crescent-shaped markings of black and pale yellow, and as the bird advances in age the yellow increases in extent and the black nearly disappears."

THE RED-MANTLED PARRAKEET.

Platycercus erythropeplus, Salvad.
Coloured Figure, P. Z. S., 1891, Pl. XII.

This fine Parrakeet is exactly intermediate between Pennant's Parrakeet and the common Rosella, and some ornithologists consider it to be merely a hybrid between those two species. It appears to be quite unknown in a wild state, and it seems to me probable that the few specimens that have been seen—all, I believe, in captivity—have been reared on the Continent from the two most commonly imported species. It should not be at all difficult to solve the problem once and for all by any aviculturist who possesses aviary accommodation for experimenting in hybridising Parrakeets. The different species of *Platycercus* are so very closely related to one another that it is probable that almost any two forms would readily interbreed under suitable circumstances, and it seems to the writer most probable that the offspring would be fertile; but this can only be proved by experiment. Whether the Red-mantled Parrakeet is a hybrid or not, there is no doubt about its being perfectly capable of reproduction, since a pair owned by Mr. Le Heup Cocksedge hatched two young ones in 1899, neither of which were reared. (*Cf. Avic. Mag.*, vol. v., p. 190.)

Count Salvadori described this Parrakeet from a pair living in the Zoological Society's Gardens, and he makes the following observations regarding it:—

"The red colour of the head and breast is, like that of *P. eximius*, a little brighter than in *P. elegans*. The feathers of the upper back have broad red edges like *P. elegans*, while the scapulars are edged with pale yellow, as in *P. eximius*, but tipped with red. The predominant red colour of the underparts connects the new species with *P. elegans*, but the yellow bases of the red feathers of the breast and abdomen show a certain affinity to *P. eximius;* the yellow colour on the middle of the abdomen and on the flanks, and the two central tail-feathers being green, passing into bluish at the tip, also betray affinity with *P. eximius*. The red edges of the yellowish feathers of the lower back and rump is a peculiar feature of this bird. The cheeks, blue in the lower part and white near the lower mandible, show more than anything else how truly intermediate this bird is between the blue-cheeked *P. elegans* and the white-cheeked *P. eximius*." (*Cat. B. Brit. Mus.*, vol. xx., p. 155.) The Red-mantled Parrakeet is about $13\frac{1}{2}$ inches in total length.

THE ROSELLA PARRAKEET.

Platycercus eximius (Shaw).
Coloured Figure, GOULD'S *Birds of Australia*, Vol. V., Pl. XXVII.

With the exception of the familiar Budgerigar and the Cockatiel, the common Rosella, or Rose-hill, Parrakeet is by far the most frequently imported of Australian Parrakeets. Were it less common, there is little doubt that it would be very highly prized on account of its showy plumage; but familiarity breeds contempt, and the Rosella is not so popular amongst aviculturists as it deserves to be. Gould writes as follows concerning this species: "Although the Rose-hill Parrakeet is one of the commonest birds of New South Wales and Tasmania, it is very local, a river frequently constituting the boundary of its habitat, over which it so rarely passes, that I never saw the bird on the south side of the Derwent; while in the forests of the opposite shore, not more than a quarter or half a mile distant, it was very numerous. I believe it is never seen in the forests clothing the borders of D'Entrecasteaux' Channel on the south, or of the River Tamar on the north of the island, those districts being inhabited by the *Platycercus flaviventris*, whose greater size and olive-green plumage are in beautiful accordance with those vast and but little explored forests of evergreen Eucalypti. The *Platycercus eximius* resorts to the open parts of the country, undulating grassy hills and plains bordered and studded here and there with large trees or belts of low acacias or banksias, among the branches of which, particularly those of the acacias, this beautiful bird may be seen in small companies, the rich scarlet and yellow of their breasts vieing with the lovely blossoms of the trees; in a word, districts of a sandy nature, small plains, open spots among the hills and thinly timbered country where grass abounds, constitute the peculiar and natural habitat of this bird. Like the Sparrow in England, this beautiful Parrakeet may constantly be seen resorting to the public roads,

From *The Royal Natural History.*

Rosella Parrakeet, *Platycercus eximius.*

and upon being disturbed by the passer-by will merely fly off to the nearest tree, or to the rails of the wayside fences. . . .

"The natural food of this bird consists of seeds of various kinds, particularly those of different grasses, and occasionally of insects and caterpillars.

"Its flight is short and undulating, and is rarely extended to a greater distance than a quarter of a mile, as the bird frequently alights on a leafless branch, always flying a little below it and rising again just before it settles."

The Rosella is an extremely hardy Parrakeet, caring little for the severity of our English winters, providing its aviary is protected from the north and east winds; and it breeds quite freely in captivity. So well does it stand our climate, in fact, that there would seem to be no reason why it should not be successfully naturalised in this country were it not for the fact that any brilliantly-coloured bird that appears is immediately shot. Whether these birds would prove mischievous to the crops I cannot say, but they would most certainly do a deal of good in devouring the seeds of noxious weeds, and they would never have a chance of becoming numerous enough to do much harm. I remember well, some years ago, examining a magnificent specimen that had just been shot in a wood in Sussex, in which it had spent some months of freedom.

Mr. John Sergeant gives the following useful hints on the breeding of Rosellas: "From my experience of the Rosella, I think it is invariably necessary to wait until your birds are about two years old before you can expect them to nest; so that in buying birds it is best to select the largest you can find, and those that are in the most brilliant plumage, as being presumably adults. It is not very difficult in the case of the Rosella to discover the sexes, as the hen is always lighter in colour, smaller and flatter in the head, and has altogether a more feminine look about her. Rosellas are not so intolerant of the presence of other birds as other members of their family, and they can be safely turned into any aviary that is not overstocked with birds. A nesting log (the best are procurable at Abrahams') should be hung up in a well-lit situation, either in the inner aviary, or in a sheltered position in the outer aviary. They generally commence nesting in the early spring months, although some imported birds I have had persisted in nesting in winter with, naturally, no result; but after a time they came to the conclusion that they had better fall in with the vagaries of the new climate, and have since always nested in summer. When after some days you have missed the hen from her usual perch, do not on any account allow your zeal to outrun your discretion by permitting yourself to take the log down to look inside, or you will in all probability make her forsake her eggs.

"During incubation and subsequent rearing of the young, I give an occasional dish of bread sop and a few oats, with plenty of hard fruit, in addition to hemp and canary seed. The hen lays from three to five eggs, and they hatch generally in about twenty-one days, and the young appear in about thirty days. After the young are hatched the cock takes almost sole charge of them, and is most assiduous in feeding them. When the youngsters are once out of the nest they usually thrive apace and grow almost as big as their parents in a surprisingly short space of time." (*Avic. Mag.*, vol. i., p. 96.)

Lady Morshead writes, under date June 30, 1902, that fourteen years ago a hybrid Parrakeet, between a male Barraband (*Polytelis barrabandi*) and a female Rosella was reared in her aviary, where it has lived ever since; and Mr. C. P. Arthur records the fact of a male Rosella having paired with a female Cockatiel (*Colopsittacus*), which laid and hatched four young birds, none of which were, however, reared. (*Avic.*

Mag., vol. iii., p. 60.) This case is particularly interesting, considering that in the case of the Cockatiel both sexes share in the task of incubation, whereas with the Rosella, as with most of the more typical Parrakeets, the female only incubates. How this pair managed is not recorded. A third case of the Rosella breeding with another species is exemplified by a specimen in the British Museum, bred years ago in the Zoological Gardens between this species and the Red-rumped Parrakeet (*Psephotus hæmatonotus*). The Rosella has bred with its congener, the Pale-headed Parrakeet (*P. pallidiceps*); and the so-called Red-mantled Parrakeet (*P. erythropeplus*) is thought by some to be the result of a cross between the Rosella and Pennant's Parrakeet (*P. elegans*).

My friend Mr. A. Savage, of Rouen, writes, under date July 17, 1902: "I have read that Rosellas have one nest a year only, and that the young do not breed the year following the one of their birth; this, as far as my experience goes, is wrong in both instances; also that the number of eggs per clutch (frequently given as five or six) is not always correct either. The pair I had was sold to me as an imported pair. The hen was a prolific one—she never laid less than five or six eggs per clutch, and on several occasions there were nine, ten, and eleven per clutch. One year she laid, to commence with, nine, and hatched most of them, but all the young died at a very early age; she laid almost immediately afterwards the five or six eggs mentioned above, and hatched several, rearing one young bird, thus making two nests (with young in each) the same season. A gentleman in France, to whom I sold a pair of the young, wrote me the following season that they had bred with him, showing that the species is capable of breeding when a year old."

With regard to the distinguishing points in the

sexes of this and other of the *Platycerci*, Mr. Savage points out that the notches in the upper mandible are deeper in the male than in the female, and in France this is considered a sure mark of distinction.

Platycercus eximius has the head and breast bright scarlet; cheeks white; nape yellow; feathers on the back black, bordered with greenish-yellow; rump, upper tail-coverts and underparts yellowish-green; anterior wing-coverts and under wing-coverts violet-blue; centre tail-feathers green, becoming blue at the tip; outer ones green at the base, then blue, becoming lighter and ending in a white tip; under tail-coverts red. Total length about $13\frac{1}{2}$ inches.

THE YELLOW-MANTLED PARRAKEET.

Platycercus splendidus, Gould.

Coloured Figure, GOULD'S *Birds of Australia*, Vol. V., Pl. XXVIII.

This very beautiful Parrakeet was first procured by Gilbert to the north of the Darling Downs in New South Wales. It is very closely allied to the common Rosella, from which it differs in the absence of any greenish tinge in the borders of the back feathers, which are pure gamboge-yellow, the absence of any yellow on the nape, and in the rump, upper tail-coverts and abdomen being pale verditer-green instead of yellowish-green.

P. splendidus is indigenous to Eastern Australia and the interior. It is very rarely imported alive into this country. Mr. Campbell, in his *Nests and Eggs* (1901), informs us that the nest and eggs of this species are undescribed.

THE STANLEY PARRAKEET.

Platycercus icterotis (Kuhl).
Coloured Figure, GOULD'S *Birds of Australia*, Vol. V., Pl. XXIX.

This species, which is also known as the Yellow-cheeked Parrakeet, the Earl of Derby's Parrakeet, and the Western Rosella, inhabits the South-west of Australia. It is a decidedly rare importation, though so beautiful a species is at any time a very welcome addition to our living collections. The species has been represented in the London Zoological Gardens on several occasions, and is not altogether unknown in private living collections.

Mr. A. J. Campbell writes: "I was often charmed with the lovely figures of the Yellow-cheeked Parrakeet, locally called the Rosella, about my hut door at Karridale, or perched upon the garden fence. Fearless of human beings, a pair was breeding in the hollow tree near the house, but to me the eggs were so many sour grapes, for the reason that I could not climb the stiff tree. The birds are particularly partial to the fruit of the Cape Gooseberry, and well they may be, for I know of no preserve more delightful.

"Breeding months October to December. The Western Rosella makes a good cage bird. One bird was apparently happy during twenty-one years of confinement."

The Stanley Parrakeet may be described as follows: Head, neck, chest and underparts scarlet; cheeks yellow; feathers of the back black bordered with greenish-yellow; rump and upper tail-coverts yellowish-green; primaries blackish, with the outer edge blue; a black patch on the upper wing-coverts; anterior wing-coverts from the bend of the wing to the primary coverts blue; flanks yellowish; centre pair of tail-feathers green; next pair green, tinged with blue towards the tips and white at the tips; outer tail-feathers light blue, tipped with white. Total length about $10\tfrac{1}{2}$ inches.

The female is similar to the male, only duller in colour.

The young are said by Gould to be nearly uniform green, becoming parti-coloured as they get older, the scarlet of the crown and underparts and the yellow of the cheeks gradually taking the place of the green colour.

Genus PORPHYROCEPHALUS, Reichenow.

THE PILEATED PARRAKEET.

Porphyrocephalus spurius (Kuhl).
Coloured Figure, GOULD'S *Birds of Australia*, Vol. V., Pl. XXXII.

The Pileated, or Red-capped, Parrakeet, is the sole representative of its genus. It inhabits Western Australia, where it is sometimes known as the "King Parrakeet." Gould tells us that it is generally seen feeding on the ground in small families, and that it selects the hollow dead branch of a gum- or mahogany tree for its nest. The same author further states that "the flight of this species, although swift, is not of long duration, nor is it characterised by those undulating sweeps common to the members of the genus *Platycercus*. Its voice is a sharp clucking note several times repeated, in which respect it also offers a marked difference from those birds."

Mr. A. J. Campbell writes: "I enjoyed many opportunities of observing them in the karri and jarrah forests, where they loved to feed upon the kernel of the native pear (*Xylomelum*), when the fruit opens under the summer sun.

"It was with much satisfaction that I brought home and let loose in my aviary one of these handsome birds."

This very fine species is exceedingly rare in this country, although a very good specimen was exhibited on several occasions at the annual bird-show at the Crystal Palace, and the species has occasionally been represented in the Zoological Gardens. It should be treated in captivity as directed for the King Parrakeet (*Aprosmictus*).

H. Gronvold, del.

Porphyrocephalus spurius.

Dr. Greene gives the following account of a specimen of this very rare Parrot that lived for some time in his possession:—

"It was purchased at a little suburban bird-shop, of which the owner had obtained it from a boy in the neighbourhood to whom it had been made a present by a friend, who was reported to have brought it from Australia.

"It was then adult, and perhaps two years old, in splendid condition, and very tame and gentle. It soon grew reconciled to its new home and surroundings, but after a while, whether it pined for its late ungrateful master, or the change of diet did not agree with it, for the dealer was unable to say to what food the bird had been accustomed before passing into his possession, it grew sick and weak and seemed as if it must certainly die.

"Careful nursing, however, soon brought it round, and in the course of a week or two 'Richard was himself again,' while a sojourn in a large out-door aviary during the summer months so improved its appearance and invigorated its frame, that at the present time it is able to fly a dozen times or more round the room without losing breath. It is rather sensitive to cold and a small eater, preferring canary seed, but taking a little maize and hemp now and then. Of fruit it is extremely fond, but if given a lump of sugar, it proceeds at once to drop it into its water-tin, into which it also dips every piece of crust or biscuit, or even boiled potato, that may be given to it.

"When it perceives anything on the table that it fancies it comes close up to the wires, stretches out its head, and raising its tail to the level of its back, flaps its wings quickly, without, however, opening them out, and emits a series of little calls that sound something like 'chee chu chu' rapidly repeated, but so far, although it answers to its name, 'Pilate,' by the above-described call, it has never attempted to speak, or even to imitate any kind of domestic noise, as most of its congeners are in the habit of doing. It is amazingly fond of whittling, and if not supplied with a log of soft wood on which to exercise its long and sharp upper mandible, soon cuts a perch to pieces, or picks holes in the wall; in default of other material it will even nibble the bars of its cage, but it is always supplied with timber, which it converts into minute chips in a very short space of time. Eating little, and always, or nearly always, dry food, it is a very clean bird, bathes frequently, and takes great care of its beautiful plumage, which is in as perfect a condition as if it enjoyed entire liberty, which it might do but for one objection, namely, the havoc it makes with wood of every description—picture frames, backs of chairs, and especially the top of an over-mantel, of which it seems to be particularly fond; it has quite a passion for over-hauling a desk or box, lifting up the covers of the little receptacles for pens, &c., and pulling out and scattering the contents on all sides. Pencils and penholders it seems to have an extreme liking for, and will even try to pull them from one's fingers, when they are speedily broken, or cut rather, into pieces, if the bird is allowed to have its way." (*Parrots in Captivity*, vol. iii., p. 8.)

The Pileated Parrakeet has the forehead, crown and nape deep maroon-red; cheeks yellowish-green, becoming yellower on the sides of the neck; back, scapulars and upper wing-coverts green; breast and abdomen violet-blue; vent greenish-yellow, tipped with red; thighs red; primary coverts, primaries and under wing-coverts blue; rump and upper tail-coverts greenish-yellow; central tail-feathers green, becoming blue towards the tips; lateral tail-feathers green at the base, passing into black on the inner, and blue on the outer webs, both webs being blue towards the tips, and fading into white at the tips; bill bluish horn-colour. Total length about 15 inches.

The female is like the male but slightly smaller and duller; and "the young during the first year of their existence are of nearly uniform green, at the same time the hues which characterise the adult are perceptible at almost any age." (*Gould.*)

Genus BARNARDIUS, Bp.

This genus contains, as far as is known at present, some five species, very similar to *Platycercus*, but differing in the absence of a notch in the bill, in the possession of a yellow collar round the hind neck, and in the absence of black feathers on the back. The sexes are alike in colour, and in captivity they require the same treatment as the *Platycerci*.

BARNARD'S PARRAKEET.
Barnardius barnardi (Vig. and Horsf.).

This beautiful species inhabits Southern and South-eastern Australia, and also the interior.

"To see Barnard's Parrakeet in perfection," writes Gould, "and to observe its rich plumage in all its glory, the native country of the bird must be visited, its brooks and streamlets traced, for it is principally on the banks of the latter, either among the 'high-flooded gums' or the larger scrub-like trees along the edges of the water that this beautiful species is seen, and where the brilliant hues of its expanded wings and tail show very conspicuously as it passes from tree to tree amidst the dark masses of foliage . . . . It is generally met with in small companies of from five to ten in number, sometimes on the ground among tall grasses, at others among the high trees, particularly the *Eucalypti*."

Barnard's Parrakeet is not particularly rare amongst aviculturists in this country, but I believe it had never been bred here until last year (1902), when Mrs. Johnstone, of Bury St. Edmunds, who is well-known for her success with Parrakeets, succeeded in rearing two young birds of this species in her aviary.

The following account of this success, for which the owner of the birds received the Avicultural Society's medal, was published in the *Avicultural Magazine* (vol. viii., p. 249):—

"It is with much pleasure that I am able to record the nesting of this very beautiful Parrakeet in my aviaries this summer. It was really surprising that they realised the spring had come at all, for it was the coldest and rainiest known on the east coast of England for a great number of years. My Barnard's Parrakeets are a lovely pair, the cock and hen so alike and both so brightly coloured that for some time I feared I had two cocks. The hen I had recently purchased from a well-known member of the Avicultural Society, and had assured her she had sent me a cock bird. This wrong opinion was soon dispelled by the pair taking possession of an old hollow tree, admirably adapted and quite rain-proof. All the holes, with the exception of two small natural holes, being covered over, the said holes being one about 4 feet above the solid part of the tree and the other quite at the top, the whole trunk standing about 8 feet high. It was an old elm, the wood inside being quite soft, large pieces falling in when touched; the most easily removed I thought it safer to take away, as I feared the eggs or young might be smothered with the soft tinder.

"I may here mention that the tree I have attempted to describe is evidently of a very popular description among Parrakeets for nesting purposes. The little hen Many-colour was most envious, but she consoled herself later with an old barrel with some decayed wood at the bottom from the same tree.

"The aviary was shared with the Barnards by a pair of Mealy Rosellas and a pair of Many-coloured Parrakeets. The Barnards commenced house-hunting very early in April, during a week of fine weather, and on April 8 the hen commenced to sit, so they were not long in making up their minds. They were fairly peaceable to the other birds, but constantly chased the cock Mealy Rosella round and round the aviary. This was not surprising, for he was a most interfering bird, and would have undoubtedly spent a large part of his time in investigating the Barnards' new house, and was constantly driven away from the entrance hole by the long-suffering cock Barnard.

"The Many-colours they left alone, and the Mealy Rosella (whose wife by the by had died) persecuted the poor little pair, not by actual pecks or attacks, but by constant worrying, until at last I moved him into another aviary. The hen sat very closely, as nearly as I could judge, three weeks, only coming off in the evenings and early mornings for a little exercise; the cock usually sat just outside the hole and kept off the Mealy Rosella.

"The cock had greatly improved in colouring, or else the hen had become duller during the time she was sitting in the dark tree; there was no doubt now about the sexes, the cock being quite brilliant in comparison to his wife.

"They did not seem to mind the cold and wet at all, and were simply fed on the usual seeds, as much as they liked to take. There was plenty of flowering grass in the aviary, growing, and they seemed to appreciate, with the Many-colours, a plant of flowering mustard, the flowers of which they stripped in pieces and lay about everywhere.

"The morning on which I believe the young hatched (May 7) there was a sharp frost, and ice in the birds' drinking water, storms of hail and sleet, and a N.W. wind.

"On June 19, a fine bright morning, after some wet cold weather, the first young Barnard appeared, he was seen clinging to the top of the wire netting in the aviary, perfectly motionless. As far as I could see from a distance he was a dull edition of the old birds, the ring clearly marked, and the red patch on the forehead, the whole colouring olive-green in different shades, as compared to the beautiful emerald shades in the parent birds, but the tips of the two long feathers in the tail were quite white. The next day another appeared, exactly like the first, perhaps a shade brighter in colouring, and he took up his position next the first, at the top of the aviary, clinging with his beak and quite motionless.

"They soon improved in their flying and perching, and were adopted (when the parents were not looking) by the Mealy Rosella, who fed them industriously. If he was seen he was immediately chased away by the old birds, but at any rate this proved he had no evil intention. They are now (July 8) nearly as big as the old birds, but as dull in colouring as ever, and are very sober editions of their lovely parents. They feed themselves, and the old birds are investigating their old tree-hole again, I hope with further nesting intentions."

Barnard's Parrakeet is perfectly hardy, and Miss Alderson informs me that a hen of this species in her possession passed the bitter winter of 1901-2 in an outdoor aviary, always preferring to sleep in the outer flight rather than the covered shelter. *Barnardius barnardi* is generally known to the colonists of Australia as the "Bulla bulla," a name which is probably also applied to the other members of the genus.

This species has the forehead bright red; the

crown, cheeks, chest, rump and abdomen verditer-green; a broad yellow band across the centre of the abdomen; a bluish tinge on the lower part of the cheeks; a greenish-brown crescent from the occiput to the eyes; a broad collar of bright yellow on the nape; back dark bluish-grey; centre of wing verditer-green; primaries black, with the outer web blue; smaller wing-coverts blue; greater wing-coverts green; under wing-coverts blue with greenish edges; central tail-feathers green, becoming blue at the tips; the outer feathers blue at the base, becoming white towards the tips; bill horn-colour. Total length about 14 inches.

The sexes are alike, but the female is slightly smaller, and as a rule duller than the male.

The young are much paler and duller than the adults.

A very beautiful new form, closely allied to *B. barnardi*, has recently been discovered by Mr. Alexander Sykes Macgillivray in the Cloncurry district of Northern Queensland, and named *B. macgillivrayi* by Mr. A. J. North (*Victorian Naturalist*, vol. xvii., p. 91). A coloured figure of this bird, by Mr. Goodchild, with a description by Dr. Sclater, appeared in the *Ibis* for 1902, p. 610.

THE YELLOW-NAPED PARRAKEET.

Barnardius semitorquatus (Q. and G.)
Coloured Figure, GOULD'S *Birds of Australia*, Vol. V., Pl. XIX.

This very fine species, which is known to the Australian colonists as the "Twenty eight" Parrakeet, from the resemblance of its note to those words, is plentifully distributed through Western and South-western Australia. It is said to inhabit almost every variety of situation, sometimes searching for its food on the ground, at other times on the trees, and feeding on grass-seeds and various hard-stoned fruits.

"While on the wing," observes Gould, "its motions are rapid, and it often utters a note, from which its resemblance to those words has procured for it the appellation of 'twenty eight' Parrakeet from the colonists; the last word or note being sometimes repeated five or six times in succession.

"The *Platycercus semitorquatus* begins breeding in the latter part of September or beginning of October, and deposits its eggs in a hole in either a gum- or mahogany tree, on the soft black dust collected at the bottom; they are from seven to eight in number and of a pure white."

Although well known to aviculturists in this country, the Yellow-naped Parrakeet is not nearly so often to be had as might be wished. Very few aviculturists have made any attempt to breed the species in this country, and I am not aware of any case in which young have been successfully reared, although from the following statement, which appears in *Parrots in Captivity*, it would seem to be no unusual thing to rear any number of these Parrakeets. Dr. Greene writes: "A pair will caress each other incessantly, and under favourable conditions, nest and carefully bring up their young, which so far do not appear to suffer the least deterioration from in-breeding during several generations." This species appears to have been bred on the Continent. It is perfectly hardy.

The Yellow-naped Parrakeet may be described as follows: Prevailing colour green; *a band of crimson on the forehead;* head, blackish-brown; cheeks blue; a broad yellow collar on the nape; upper breast green with a bluish tinge; lower breast, flanks, and under tail-coverts yellowish-green; abdomen bluish-green;

primary coverts and outer webs of primaries blue; centre of tail green; outer tail-feathers green at the base, passing to blue and ending in a whitish-blue tip. Total length about 17 inches.

The sexes are alike, but the female is slightly smaller and duller than the male.

BAUER'S PARRAKEET.

Barnardius zonarius (Shaw).

Bauer's Parrakeet so closely resembles the last described that aviculturists sometimes find it difficult to determine to which species a given bird belongs. *B. zonarius* may, however, be readily distinguished from *B. semitorquatus* by its smaller size (total length about 15 inches), by the absence of a red frontal band, and by the yellow abdomen and lower breast.

This Parrakeet inhabits the south and interior of Australia, and is known to the colonists as the "Port Lincoln Parrakeet." It is not very rare as a cage bird in this country, but I am not aware of any case in which it has bred here. It is a very handsome and desirable species, which would without doubt breed successfully if suitable accommodation were provided for a pair. In the case of all the hardier Parrakeets—and *B. zonarius* is as hardy as any—a large outdoor aviary is essential if the birds are expected to breed, and it is best to let the pair be the sole occupants. Like the majority of its tribe, this species breeds, when wild, in the hollow trunk or limb of a tree; and the nearer the natural nesting site can be imitated in captivity the more likely will the birds be to breed successfully.

In the Report of the Horn Expedition to Central Australia, Mr. Keartland writes: "Some surprise was felt at the wide extent of country over which this beautiful Parrakeet was found, the first pair being seen at Macumba Creek. They were afterwards found throughout the trip wherever water existed. At Stevenson's Creek two black boys were preparing their supper, which consisted of nestlings of this species, which they had taken from the sprouts of the eucalypts along its margin. On May 12, whilst resting at Adminga Creek, a young bird, with its yellow bill denoting its age, and apparently enjoying its first fly, fluttered on to a branch close to our party. I then saw, and afterwards confirmed, that many of the young ones are quite as brilliant in plumage as the mature birds. Although generally in pairs, flocks of six or seven are not uncommon, probably being the parent birds and young brood. Their chief food is grass-seed, but they also display great activity in climbing amongst the foliage in search of blossom."

The sexes differ only in the female being slightly smaller and duller than the male.

In 1893 Mr. North named a new form from North-west Australia as *B. occidentalis*. It is probably a local race of *B. zonarius*, from which it differs "in having light blue instead of dark blue cheeks; in the greater extent of the conspicuous lemon-yellow of the lower portion of the breast and the whole of the abdomen, and which extends as far as the vent, instead of the deep gamboge-yellow of the abdomen only; in the verditer-green of the chest, back, wings, scapulars and interscapular region, instead of dark green, and in the absence of the narrow black band immediately below the collar." (*Records Australian Museum*, vol. ii., p. 83.)

Genus PSEPHOTUS, Gould.

This genus contains perhaps the most beautiful and, from the aviculturist's point of view, the most delightful and desirable Parrakeets that are ever brought alive to this country. The genus *Psephotus* contains eight known species, characterised by the two centre tail-feathers being longer than the others, by the absence of any yellow collar on the nape, and by the sexes differing considerably in colour, except in the case of the two "Blue-bonnet" Parrakeets, *P. hæmatorrhous* and *P. xanthorrhous*. In a wild state they feed chiefly on the seeds of various grasses, both in a green and a ripe state, and doubtless sometimes insects are eaten as well, though in captivity these are rarely touched. Canary-seed should be the staple food of these birds in captivity, and to this should be added millet, hemp and oats, the last two sparingly, and an abundance of green food during the summer months is essential. The present writer has kept three species for years, and is strongly opposed to soft food, such as bread and milk, egg and bread, and so on, as a food for these birds, except when there are young birds to be fed, when stale bread, soaked in cold water and squeezed nearly dry, is undoubtedly most beneficial, and aids the parents very considerably in their task of feeding their young.

THE RED-VENTED BLUE-BONNET PARRAKEET.

Psephotus hæmatorrhous, Bp.

This species has so often and persistently been confounded with the commoner Yellow-vented Parrakeet, that I have thought it desirable to give coloured figures of these two nearly-allied forms, so that in future aviculturists may have no difficulty in distinguishing them. The Red-vented form inhabits Southern Queensland and the northern parts of New South Wales. Gould found it in tolerable abundance in the neighbourhood of the Lower Namoi, "where it appeared to give a decided preference to those parts of the plains which were of a loose mouldly character, and with which the colour of its back so closely assimilates as to be scarcely distinguishable from it." He found it in small flocks, feeding on the seeds of various grasses.

This is a very beautiful Parrakeet, and one that would, without doubt, live as well in captivity as its congener, but it seems never to be imported nowadays, although it has probably been offered for sale here on rare occasions, and has doubtless passed for its commoner congener, with which in a wild state it most likely occasionally interbreeds, since two specimens in the National collection appear to be intermediate between the two forms; and it is interesting to note that these two birds lived in captivity in this country, one in the Zoological Gardens and the other in Mr. Wiener's aviary. As above stated, the two species of "Blue-bonnet" Parrakeets are very closely allied, but they are very distinct from the other members of the genus both in their form and habits, and in the fact of the sexes being superficially alike, whereas in the others the male and female are totally distinct.

This species has the whole of the face blue, the forehead being somewhat brighter than the cheeks; remainder of head, neck, back, scapulars and breast brownish-grey; rump like the back but slightly more olive; upper tail-coverts like the rump but with a slight reddish tinge; flanks yellow; centre of abdomen, *vent and under tail-coverts crimson*, the feathers having a narrow margin of yellow; *a broad patch of chestnut-red on the wings;* lesser wing-coverts verditer-green and blue; most of the greater wing-coverts, primary-coverts, outer webs of primaries and secondaries, and under wing-coverts blue; central tail-feathers olive-green at the base passing to blue at the tip, the outer feathers blue at the base passing to white at the tips. Total length about 15 inches.

THE YELLOW-VENTED BLUE-BONNET PARRAKEET.

Psephotus xanthorrhous, Bp.

The Yellow-vented, or common Blue-bonnet Parrakeet inhabits the south of Australia, going about in pairs and chiefly frequenting the banks of the rivers. It is fairly well known to aviculturists in this country, although sometimes several years may pass without a single living specimen being imported. It is a most desirable species, being remarkably active and engaging, but according to the present writer's experience it cannot be trusted with other birds, being one of the most spiteful of Parrakeets. A pair came into the possession of the writer on April 6, 1900. On arrival they were put into an ordinary parrot cage, but before they had been in this for five minutes both managed to squeeze between the bars, and it was some time before they could be recaptured and placed in a safer cage. These birds were soon transferred to an outdoor aviary, where they lived both summer and winter, but although on more than one occasion they seemed anxious to breed, eggs were never laid, although everything seemed favourable to their breeding, so far as their surroundings were concerned. From the first these Parrakeets were extremely timid, and although they lived in the writer's possession until the autumn of 1902, they never became much tamer than when first received. Blue-bonnets that have been hand-reared from the nest would be most delightful birds, and would undoubtedly breed in captivity; but one very seldom comes across hand-reared Australian Parrakeets nowadays.

One day some half-dozen Chinese Quails (*Excalfactoria*), recently reared in the aviary, which occupied a neighbouring compartment to the one in which the Blue-bonnets lived, managed to get into the Parrakeets' compartment in consequence of the door between becoming unfastened, and the result was that on entering the aviary I discovered three dead Quails, with their backs literally torn open, and the others with most of the feathers torn off their backs. Doubtless had I not entered until a few hours later every one of the little Quails would have been killed by the blood-thirsty Blue-bonnets.

In an interesting letter on Parrakeets published in *Notes on Cage Birds* (sec. series, p. 167), a correspondent who signs himself "Vicar," writes: "The Blue-bonnet Parrakeet, one of the prettiest of the tribe, has been called 'gentle.' I have found it a most vigorous and determined fighter when occasion has called forth its powers; having been three years in my aviary it is now friendly with all. But I have had experiences. I once turned in two strong Paradise Parrakeets, and it fought the pair for half-an-hour. It was no use to scold, nor to throw my hat at the combatants; I had to go in with my great gauze net and catch the cock Paradise, which never recovered the mauling he got; the hen had fled, and peace presently prevailed. Last year she—for the blue beauty was a hen—appeared one morning in the trees of my garden. I was startled before I was up with her well-known 'chup chup.' I failed to trap her that day, for at noon she vanished. Next morning, however, my housekeeper watched her enter the conservatory door, and shut her in. She had gnawed her way through the roof of the outdoor addition to the conservatory aviary, and had spent a very cold night without her supper, but without damage."

Mr. A. Johnson, of St. Olave's Grammar School, quoted by Dr. Greene in his *Parrots in Captivity*, remarks of this species: "They seem the mildest of inmates of the aviary, but they are really its most insidious assassins. I have found young birds with their pinions cruelly mutilated, although they were apparently safe in small cages; young Budgerigas, valuable Bourke's Parrakeets, Turquoisines, and others, dead or dying, with their wing-joints mutilated, or their heads smashed; and I never was able to trace the assassins, until one day I saw my innocent-looking pets sidle up to a delicate, graceful dove, seize him by the wing, and begin to gnaw him savagely. They will live for months with smaller birds on the most friendly terms, but in the end they will clear an aviary of all weaker than themselves, although, like true assassins, they never attack one of their own size. It is only fair to say that these are only imported birds, and some I have bred myself have not developed this murderous tendency. For hardiness, intelligence, grace, and most amusing ways, commend me above all to the Blue-bonnet, but be sure to keep him with birds who are his match in strength, or better still, in a small compartment by himself, when he will be a model of good behaviour."

In the above interesting account of his Blue-bonnets the writer incidentally records, possibly, the only case in which this species has successfully reared young in this country; at any rate, I have been unable to find any other record of success in this direction.

The Hon. Canon Dutton, writing also in *Parrots in Captivity*, evidently of birds which have been reared by hand from the nest in Australia, remarks: "I place the Blue-bonnet at the head of Paroquets as a cage bird. It is the Merry Andrew of birds. Who can describe its tricks in all their charm, amusement and infinite variety? It is a bird full of resources, and never suffers from boredom. If it has nothing else to play with, it will play with its own tail. Really to enjoy them, they are better kept singly. If they are rather like *Pulcherrimus* in harrying their wives, they are the complete opposite of *Pulcherrimus* as to timidity. No birds could be bolder, and it needs a very short time to make them perfectly familiar with their master. I do not mean to say that they like being handled Paroquets are not like Parrots and Cockatoos in this respect. The tamest of them endure handling rather than like it as a rule; and the Australian ones like it rather less than the Indian and American ones if anything. But they come forward to the edge of their cage, and are always ready for play. In fact, if I were to have to choose which of all the species of the Parrot tribe should be the only representatives of the family left on the earth, I should beg that it might be the Blue-bonnet. Mine did not make any advances to breeding."

As previously remarked, this and the preceding species differ very considerably in many ways from the other species of the genus *Psephotus*; their actions are completely different; the pairing note, which is a very soft sound in the other species, is a harsh cry in the Blue-bonnet. The sexes, moreover, in the majority of the *Psephoti*, are completely distinct as to their colourings, but in the Blue-bonnets they are alike. To those who know the birds in a living state it seems that the present classification of these birds cannot be right; and I have little doubt that if systematists could study the living birds, and not work entirely from skins, a great many weak places would be found in the present-day classification, and amongst other alterations that would be made, *P. hæmatorrhous* and *P. xanthorrhous* would occupy a new genus to themselves.

In a wild state the Blue-bonnet breeds, like other Parrakeets, in the hollow of a tree trunk, and Mr. A. J. Campbell tells us that it is also reported to breed in the cliffs of the Lower Murray River. The eggs are said to number from five to seven to a clutch.

P. xanthorrhous differs from *P. hæmatorrhous* in the possession of an olive-yellow instead of a reddish patch on the wings, and in the *vent and under tail-coverts being yellow* instead of red. Total length 12 or 13 inches.

The present species is subject to considerable variation, some specimens in the National Collection, which the present writer has been privileged to examine, from Cooper' Creek in the interior of South Australia, being very much paler in colour than the more typical specimens.

THE BEAUTIFUL PARRAKEET.

Psephotus pulcherrimus (Gould).
Coloured Figure, GOULD'S *Birds of Australia*, Vol. V., Pl. XXXIV.

This exquisite Parrakeet, sometimes called the Paradise Parrakeet, is an inhabitant of Eastern Australia, from Port Denison to New South Wales. It may be classed with the Golden-shouldered Parrakeet as the most lovely of all the Australian forms, and the sight of a living specimen, or even a skin, is enough to make the aviculturist long to add the species to his living collection. Unfortunately, however, it is at the present time hardly ever imported into this country, although there are many more aviculturists now than formerly who would be only too glad to purchase these lovely birds at prices that would make it well worth anybody's while to import them.

Gould writes: "The graceful form of this Parrakeet, combined with the extreme brilliancy of its plumage, renders it one of the most lovely of the *Psittacidæ* yet discovered; and in whatever light we regard it, whether as a beautiful ornament to our cabinets or a desirable addition to our aviaries, it is still an object of no ordinary interest." He tells us very little about the bird in a wild state, but he observes that it feeds in small families on the seeds of grasses and other plants growing on the plains; and that the crops of those examined were filled with grass seeds exclusively.

One very interesting point in connection with this species is the fact of its sometimes nesting in disused ant-hills, although it probably more often takes possession of the hole of a tree in the usual way. With reference to this singular habit Mr. A. J. Campbell writes:—

"The eggs and the first information of the interesting fact that the birds lay in ant-hillocks I received from the late Mr. George Barnard, Coomooboolaroo (Queensland), where the birds breed. Unfortunately, during my visit to that part of the country a drought existed, and consequently the birds were not laying. However, on a trip subsequently, Mr. D. Le Souëf was more successful, and was enabled to bring away an excellent photograph of an anthill, also showing the positions of the eggs in the mound.

"Dr. Carl Lumholtz observed that the nests were several miles apart, and that those examined in September contained eggs partly incubated. He proceeds to state: 'There is an irregular entrance, about two inches in diameter and about a foot above the ground. In the interior the Parrot makes an opening about a foot high and two or three feet in diameter. None of the building material is carried away, but all the cells and canals are trampled down, so that there remains simply a wall, one or two inches thick, around the whole nest. Here the female lays five white eggs. Breeding months September to December.'" (*Nests and Eggs of Australian Birds*, p. 645.)

The Hon. Canon Dutton writes: "*P. pulcherrimus*, the Paradise Paroquet, as dealers call it, is not only the most beautiful *Psephotus*, as its name says, but surely the most beautiful Paroquet that exists. The vivid emerald-green and brilliant carmine of the cock, beautifully contrasted with the grey of the rest of the plumage, make him 'a joy for ever.' But 'handsome is that handsome does,' and I regret that I cannot give any of those I have kept a good character as a cage bird. They are very shy, and the cock is much given to driving about the hen. They do not appear to have bred in captivity, but I do not think it impossible that they should do so. A pair I had were most anxious to burrow into the wall of a room in which they were. Had they done so, they would have got into a loft and escaped. So they were caged and sent to the Zoological Gardens. . . . I regretted afterwards that a box covered with tin was not fastened on the other side of the wall into which they wanted to burrow: I think they might then have bred. . .

"I have never had any trouble with *Pulcherrimus* as to health." (*Parrots in Captivity*, vol. ii., p. 31.)

The Beautiful Parrakeet was at one time—some ten

or fifteen years ago—comparatively common amongst English aviculturists, but at the time of writing these notes (April, 1903) it is impossible to obtain it, as no living specimens seem to have been imported for a number of years.

The genus *Psephotus* seems to have been but little understood in the days when the *P. pulcherrimus* was obtainable in this country, even the hardy Many-coloured Parrakeet being considered extremely difficult to keep in health for more than a few months. One writer even considered that that species and the one we are now considering were closely related to the Lories, and required the same treatment as that honey-eating family. I can only say that several aviculturists, the present writer included, have kept the Many-coloured Parrakeet for years on a simple diet of seed and green food, and have found it almost as hardy as its congener the Redrump; and it seems probable that the rarer Beautiful, or Paradise, Parrakeet would be equally easy to keep in health under similar treatment. At one time it was universally thought that the majority of the birds in this genus required such food as sop, honey, pollen-bearing flowers, and the like; which are certainly *most* unsuitable for any but the purely honey-eating Parrots. Given plain food, such as the best canary-seed, millet, a little hemp, and perhaps a few oats, and a regular supply, especially in the spring and summer, of chickweed or grass in flower, there is little doubt that the Paradise Parrakeet would prove to be no more difficult to keep in health than the Many-coloured, or the rare Golden-shouldered Parrakeets which have both been proved to be, when once acclimatised, long-livers in captivity. These lovely Parrakeets should never be kept for any length of time in a cage. If an outdoor aviary cannot be given up to them for the summer months, they are certainly worthy of a well-lighted and well-kept bird-room; and there is very little doubt that they would breed in captivity, although this most desirable event does not appear to have taken place, up to the present time, in this country. If any of my readers should be fortunate enough to secure a pair of these birds they should remember that it, sometimes at any rate, nests in ants' hills when wild, and it would not be a bad plan to supply, besides the usual logs and boxes, which should be fastened fairly high up, some substitute for ants' hills.

The adult male has the forehead bright scarlet; crown brownish-black; region round the eye reddish, the feathers being tipped with yellowish; back greyish-brown; sides of the head and neck, also the breast, bluish-green; rump and upper tail-coverts blue; a black band crosses the lower back; flanks turquoise-blue; abdomen and under tail-coverts scarlet, each feather having a yellowish edge; a large red patch on the shoulders; most of the upper wing-coverts brown; under wing-coverts blue; two central tail-feathers brown at the base, gradually passing to blue towards the tip, and ending in a black tip; outer tail-feathers pale blue with white tips, all except the pair nearest the central ones having an irregular black band towards the base.

The female and young have the crown and back much paler than the male; forehead yellowish; sides of the head and breast yellowish-grey tinged with greenish; underparts pale blue, stained with red in the centre of the abdomen; wing patch greyish, stained with red; rump and tail as in the male.

THE GOLDEN-SHOULDERED PARRAKEET.
Psephotus chrysopterygius, Gould.

This truly exquisite Parrakeet almost rivals the lovely *Pulcherrimus* itself in beauty. It is rarer than that species even in Australia. It inhabits the north of that continent, from Port Darwin to the Gulf of Carpentaria.

The late John Gould wrote, concerning this species: "One of the greatest pleasures enjoyed by the late celebrated botanist, Robert Brown, during the last thirty years of his life, was now and then to show me the drawing of a Parrakeet made by one of the brothers Bauer, from a specimen procured somewhere on the north coast of Australia, but of which no specimen was preserved at the time, and none had been sent to England, until several were brought home by Mr. Elsey, a year or two prior to Mr. Brown's death. On comparing these with the drawing made at least forty years before, no doubt remained on my mind as to its having been made from an example of this species. This, then, is one of the novelties for which we are indebted to the explorations of A. C. Gregory, Esq.; and I trust it may not be the last I shall have to characterise through the researches of this intrepid traveller. Mr. Elsey, who, as is well known, accompanied the expedition to the Victoria River, obtained three examples—a male, a female, and a young bird—all of which are now in our national collection. In the notes accompanying the specimens, Mr. Elsey states that they were procured on September 14, 1856, in lat. 18° S. and long. 141° 33′ E., and that their crops contained some monocotyledonous seeds."

Nothing further seems to have been known of this Parrakeet until 1896, when some specimens were procured at Pine Creek in the Port Darwin district by Mr. Harry Barnard, as recorded by Mr. Campbell in his book on Australian birds. The following year, however, no less than eight living specimens, all in immature plumage, arrived in London. (*Cf. Avic. Mag.*, vol. iv., p. 153.) There appears to have been but one male in this lot, and this, with one of the females, went to the Zoological Gardens in Regent's Park, where the pair have lived until the present time, quite wasted within the bars of a miserably small cage in the Parrot house. Probably other specimens went to Continental collections at the same time, for during the year 1901 a pair of extremely beautiful hybrids between this species and *Psephotus multicolor*, presumably bred in some Continental aviary, were received by the London Zoological Society, and exhibited in their living collection.

My friend, Mr. Reginald Phillipps, was so fortunate as to secure two of the specimens that arrived in London, both females; and he wrote a very interesting account of these birds in the *Avicultural Magazine* (vol. iv., p. 152). He found them to be easily kept in health on the simplest of food—canary seed and spray millet—but they were somewhat susceptible to cold, which is not to be wondered at, considering that they are inhabitants of the hottest part of Australia; and one of these birds unfortunately took a chill and died. The other one eventually paired with a male Red-rump Parrakeet, and their owner gives us the following interesting account of their nesting: "On May 14, I suddenly became aware that the Golden-shoulder must be sitting, and found she had a nest in the bird-room, close to the door; and, feeling in the log, I found it contained four eggs. As there were other birds in the bird-room I was obliged to go in occasionally; but she sat so timidly that she invariably dashed out of the room the instant I touched the handle of the door. Otherwise she sat well, never coming off the nest but for the shortest possible time. While sitting, I think she was never fed on the nest by the male Red-rump. The Red-rump, nevertheless, could not have been more watchful and attentive. By word of mouth he let her know everything that was going on in the outside world. They had a by no means meagre vocabulary, and, although of different species, understood one another perfectly. Should anyone appear, instantly a few high-pitched piercing notes were sounded in rapid succession, almost as high pitched as the squeak of the bat, which is inaudible to some ears. When that note had been uttered, the Golden-shoulder would lie like a log. Indeed, except when disturbed, I doubt if she ever left the nest until he came for her, and called her off with a few shrill whistles followed by pretty warbling notes, which she usually obeyed at once. He would then instantly feed her; and she would quickly rush off for a nibble at the green grass or something, and dart away back to her nest accompanied by her warbling mate. . . .

"But their hopes and mine were doomed to disappointment, for the four eggs were clear.

"Whether this was the fault of the individual Red-rump—an aviary-bred specimen I am told, which never seemed to have half the life and energy of my former Red-rumps and has not grown a full-length tail to this day—or whether the sterility was owing to the birds being of different species, I am not able to say. It does seem a pity that a male Golden-shoulder should be unobtainable.

"The eggs are small, of a stout oval in shape, of precisely the same length as those of the Peach-faced Lovebird, but thicker." (*Avic. Mag.*, vol. v., p. 158).

It is worthy of note that Mr. Phillipps' bird is still alive and well (May, 1903), having lived in his aviary for more than six years.

Mrs. Johnstone, of Bury St. Edmunds, was fortunate enough to obtain a pair of these lovely Parrakeets in the autumn of 1902, and writes, under date April 30, 1903: "They wintered in a warm house, the temperature of which never fell below 40° F. They are, when first imported, decidedly delicate, being thinly feathered. They are very much attached to one another, and always roost together. They eat canary-seed, white and spray millet, and are very fond of flowering grass. They feel cold acutely, but are very bright and lively, and soon get tame. They are quite harmless amongst a swarm of little birds, and are, as far as I can see, very like the Manycolours in their ways, only more delicate. They have only just been turned out into an out-door aviary, so I cannot say if they are likely to nest."

There is nothing further to be added at present respecting this beautiful Parrakeet, but I hope I may have the pleasure of recording Mrs. Johnstone's success in breeding the species in the Appendix to this volume.

The adult male has the forehead and region close around the eyes pale yellow; crown black, extending back and becoming diffused in the brown of the nape; back, scapulars, inner wing-coverts and inner secondaries greyish-brown; *a large yellow patch on the wings;* sides of the head, neck, breast and upper part of abdomen, also rump and upper tail-coverts, turquoise-blue, with a decided tinge of green on the cheeks and tail-coverts; under wing-coverts blue; centre of abdomen and under tail-coverts red barred with white; central tail-feathers green at the base, passing into deep blue towards the tip, which is black; outer tail-feathers bluish-green, tipped with white and crossed by an oblique band of black.

The female has the frontal band yellowish-white ; crown brownish ; sides of the head nearly white, washed with blue ; underparts greenish, washed with blue down to the lower abdomen and under tail-coverts, which are marked with red and white as in the male but much fainter ; back, scapulars and upper wing-coverts yellowish-green, the yellow becoming brighter on the wing-patch ; rump and upper tail-coverts bright blue ; primaries blackish, edged with blue on the outer web ; tail as in the male.

In the *Proceedings of the Zoological Society* for 1898, Professor Collett described a new species of *Psephotus*, which had been discovered in Arnhem Land, North-west Australia, and named it *P. dissimilis*. It appears to be very closely allied to *P. chrysopterygius*, from which it differs in the absence of a yellow band across the forehead ; the crown is chestnut, the lower parts verditer-blue, and the under tail-coverts orange.

THE MANY-COLOURED PARRAKEET.

Psephotus multicolor (Kuhl.).

This very delightful Parrakeet inhabits the Interior and South of Australia. Gould did not meet with it himself, but informs us that it is abundant on the plains bordering the Lachlan, the Upper Murray and the Darling. It was met with during the Horn Expedition to the Interior of Australia, and Mr. Keartland, who accompanied the expedition, gives the following note in the Report : "These birds were found near all water-holes passed. Although a number were shot, not one of the males was as brilliant

LESSER PATAGONIAN CONURE, *Cyanolyseus patagonicus* (now known as PATAGONIAN CONURE, *Cyanoliseus patagonius*); text page 53.

1. SCLATER'S HANGING PARRAKEET, *Loriculus sclateri* (now known as MOLUCCAN HANGING PARROT, *Loriculus amabilis sclateri*); text page 157.
2. GOLDEN-BACKED HANGING PARRAKEET, *Loriculus chrysonotus* (now known as PHILIPPINE HANGING PARROT, *Loriculus philippensis chrysonotus*); text page 153.

1. WHITE-WINGED PARRAKEET, *Brotogerys virescens* (now known as WHITE-WINGED PARRAKEET, *Brotogeris versicolorus*); text page 80.
2. TUI PARRAKEET, *Brotogerys tui* (now known as TUI PARRAKEET, *Brotogeris sanctithomae*); text page 85.

GOLDEN-SHOULDERED PARRAKEET, *Psephotus chrysopterygius* (now known as GOLDEN-SHOULDERED PARROT, *Psephotus chrysopterygius*); text pages 202, 281.

Opposite:
INDIAN RING-NECKED PARRAKEET, *Paleornis torquata* (now known as INDIAN RING-NECKED PARAKEET, *Psittacula krameri*); test page 101.

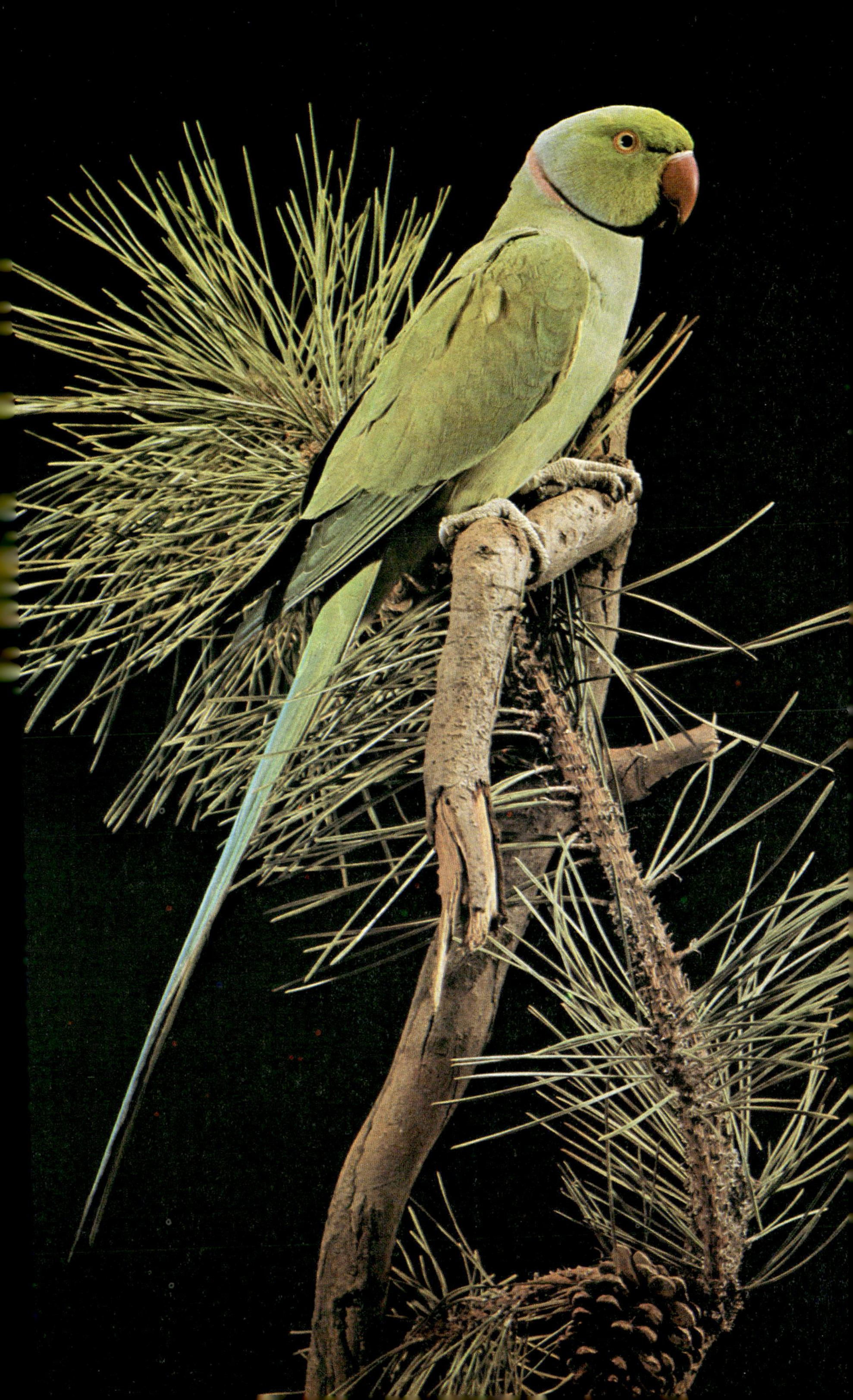

ROSELLA PARRAKEET, *Platycercus eximius* (now known as EASTERN ROSELLA, *Platycercus eximius*); text page 172.

GOLDEN-CROWNED CONURE, *Conurus aureus* (now known as PEACH-FRONTED CONURE, or HALF-MOON PARAKEET, *Aratinga aurea*); text page 47.

GREY-BREASTED PARRAKEET, *Myopsittacus monachus* (now known as MONK PARAKEET, *Myiopsitta monachus*); text page 145.

COCKATIEL, *Calopsittacus novae-hollandiae* (now known as COCKATIEL, *Nymphicus hollandicus*); text page 20.

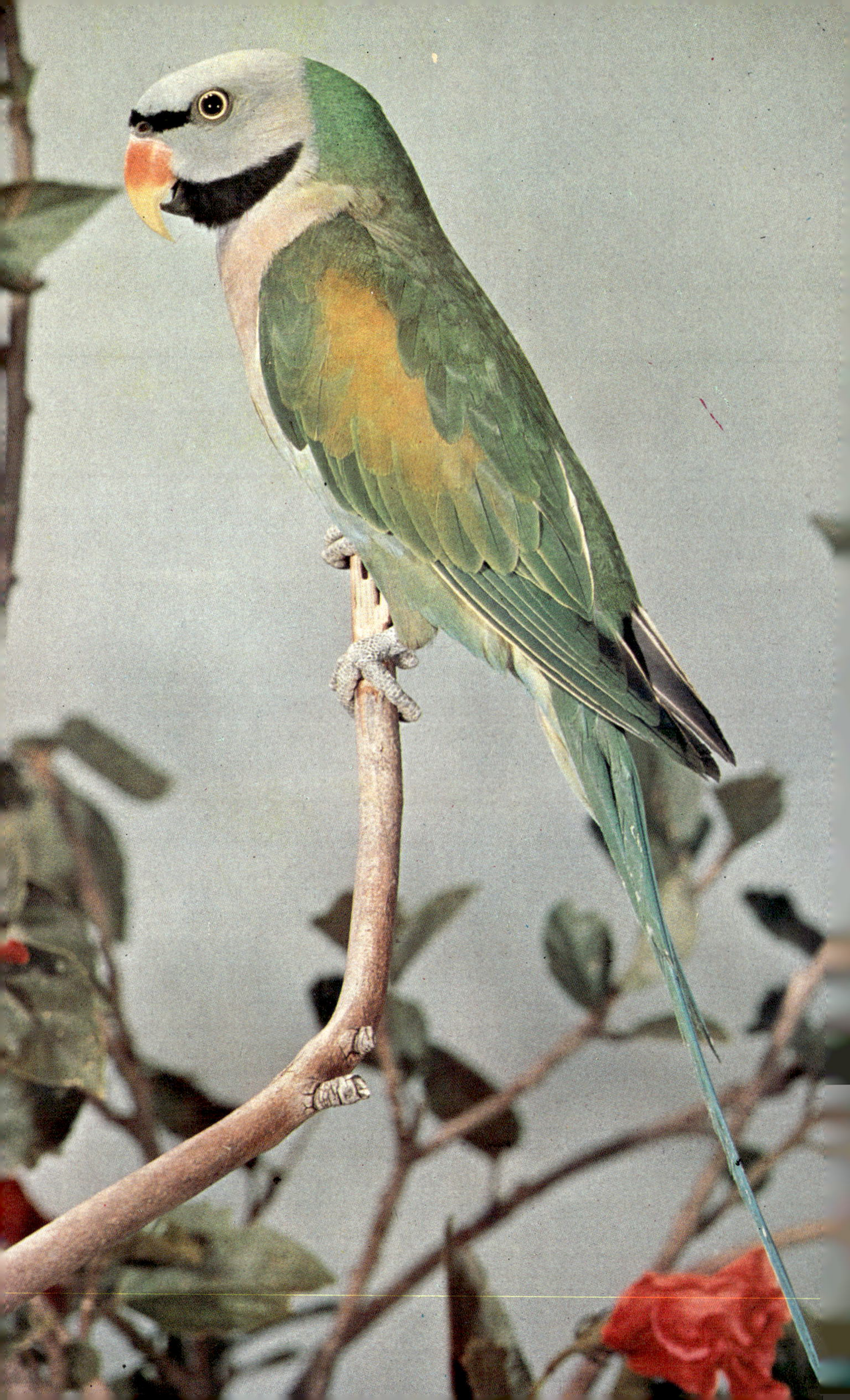

GOLDIE'S LORIKEET, *Glossopsittacus goldei*, (now known as same); text page 265.

Opposite:
JAVA PARRAKEET, *Palaeornis alexandri* (now known as MOUSTACHED PARAKEET, *Psittacula alexandri alexandri*); text page 114.

GOLDEN CONURE, *Conurus guarouba* (now known as GOLDEN CONURE, *Aratinga guarouba*); text page 30.

MASKED LOVEBIRD, *Agapornis personata*; text page 280.

MEXICAN CONURE, *Conurus holochlorus* (now known as GREEN CONURE, *Aratinga holochlora*); text page 39.

PETZ'S CONURE, *Conurus canicularis* (now known as ORANGE-FRONTED CONURE, *Aratinga canicularis*); text page 48.

ROSY-FACED LOVEBIRD, *Agapornis roseicollis* (now known as PEACH-FACED LOVEBIRD, *Agapornis roseicollis*); text page 145.

in the scarlet markings on the thighs and abdomen as those found at Murtoa and in the Mallee Scrub near the Murray. They were all in pairs, and were never seen in flocks like the Red-rumped Parrakeet (*P. hæmatonotus*). The females were all of the same modest hue as those found further south."

The Many-coloured Parrakeet is occasionally offered for sale in this country, and it is certainly very well worth obtaining, even though it be at a high price, for of all the Parrakeets that the writer has kept, the species now under notice is by far the most beautiful and delightful in every way. It must, however, be understood that he has never had the good fortune to possess either the Beautiful or the Golden-shouldered Parrakeets, which are doubtless equally desirable, though considerably more delicate. When first imported this species needs care, like every other bird on its arrival from a hot country, but when once it has become established it is almost as hardy as its congener the Red-rumped Parrakeet. During the winter months some warmth is certainly desirable, though it has been known to live and do well in a sheltered, unheated, outdoor aviary through the whole year. It certainly does not require much warmth.

My friend, Mr. A. Savage, of Rouen, bred this species successfully in his aviary in 1897, though this was not the first occasion on which young had been reared in France.

He writes as follows, in the *Avicultural Magazine* for September, 1897 : " A pair was offered for sale last autumn in the neighbourhood of Bordeaux, and being desirous of trying my luck with these beautiful birds, I purchased them at a good figure. The gentleman wrote me : 'If you wish to be successful in breeding with them, put them in an aviary alone and give plenty of green food. The latter they have had, but as I could not lodge them alone they have been, since their arrival, in an aviary with at least thirty small birds, from Waxbills up to Saffron Finches and Pekin Robins. They wintered in an outdoor aviary, as most of my birds do, but the aviary has a glass door that can be shut when the weather is very cold or damp. I ought to say though, perhaps, that a small oil-stove was burned in the aviary for about a couple of hours in the mornings of about a dozen of the worst days during the winter, not on account of the Parrakeets, but principally for the small Waxbills, which seemed to feel the winter and looked most uncomfortable. The Many-coloureds, being in the same aviary, had their share of the warmth too; but had they been alone I should not have put in the stove, the winter not being a very severe one.

"Things went on exceedingly well, and towards the beginning of May the hen began visiting the nest-boxes, and looked like nesting. The cock was most attentive, and fed her continually. A box was eventually chosen and four white eggs laid, not very large. One of the eggs was broken during incubation; I patched it over with thin gum paper, but it came to nothing; the other three all hatched and produced two hens and a cock. The two hens I still have in splendid health and plumage, but the young cock died. I attribute the loss to his having been accidentally shut out one chilly night while very young, when he caught cold, and death ensued. They left the nest at a very tender age, before they could walk properly, and days before they could fly. I put them back a time or two, but they were out again soon after and appeared determined to stop out! They were reared without any fuss or extras, the food being spray millet, canary seed, white millet, and a little hemp mixed; they had also a liberal supply of groundsel, chickweed, and flowering grass, roots with it.

"A saucer of soft food for the Finches is always in the aviary—ants' eggs, a prepared food (bought) and bread-crumbs mixed, a little boiling milk being poured over the whole just sufficient to moisten it—and this the parents were very fond of picking over while feeding their young, more on account, I fancy, of the bread and milk than the ants' eggs. I only obtained one nest, rather late, as will be seen—young hatched in June—and the parents are now moulting ; but if they could be induced to commence a little earlier, two nests might be obtained during the year. I would strongly recommend anybody who attempts breeding these Parakeets to give a liberal supply of fresh groundsel *daily*, and plenty of flowering grass, roots included, as soon as it can be got in the spring, and continue it fresh *daily* as long as it lasts ; they are extremely fond of it, and groundsel."

This species had probably never been bred in England until last year (1902), when one young bird was reared in the Rev. C. D. Farrar's aviary at Micklefield, Yorkshire. (*Cf. Avic. Mag.*, vol. viii., p. 212.) Earlier in the same year Mr. W. Fasey had two young birds hatched in his aviary which I saw myself, but these both died during a spell of exceptionally cold weather in May. Eggs were also laid in Mrs. Johnstone's aviary in Suffolk, and in my own aviary. Mr. Fasey writes me, under date April 26, 1903, to the effect that he has two young Many-colours in the nest, about a week old, and at the present moment (May 7, 1903) a pair in the present writer's possession, from which the illustration here given was drawn, have eggs on which the hen is sitting very steadily.

The proper food for the Many-coloured Parrakeet is canary-seed, white and spray millet, a little hemp, and an abundant supply of such green food as chickweed, groundsel and flowering grass. Few birds are more fond of chickweed than the present species, especially as the spring advances and the nesting season draws near. Whenever I approach the aviary my cock Many-colour flies to meet me, and his disappointment is great if I do not give him a handful of chickweed. He is very tame and will almost eat it from my hand. Several nesting boxes and logs should be fixed up in the aviary in which it is intended that a pair of these Parrakeets should breed, for the hen is not always easy to please. My own pair took a long time to decide upon a nest, eventually selecting a box about 18 inches in height by 10 inches in breadth and width, the bottom of which contains a layer of dry earthy matter similar to that found inside decaying tree-trunks. The entrance hole is near the top. In this the hen is at present sitting, appearing very seldom to feed. Immediately she leaves the nest the cock flies to her and feeds her.

The following is a description of the male Many-coloured Parrakeet: Prevailing colour bluish-green back and scapulars darker green, and the cheeks bluer; frontal band and a large patch on the wing-coverts yellow; a patch of red on the occiput; a light bluish band bordered with two blackish bands crossing the lower back; upper tail-coverts bluish-green, with a red patch in the centre; abdomen and thighs orange-red; under tail-coverts yellow; a patch of bright blue at the bend of the wing; edge of the wing and under wing-coverts deep blue, central tail-feathers deep blue, becoming green towards the base and black at the tips; the outer tail-feathers greenish at the base, becoming light blue towards the tips, which are white, and these are crossed by a blackish band near the base.

The female is very different from the male, having

the upper parts mostly brownish-grey with an olive-green tinge; *patch on the wing-coverts red;* frontal band reddish in some individuals, yellowish in others; some specimens have a faint patch of reddish on the occiput, which is absent in others; lower breast, abdomen and under-tail coverts yellowish-green, with a bluish tinge; a faint indication of red on some of the feathers of the abdomen; rump, upper tail-coverts and tail as in the male.

Total length about 12 inches.

This species is subject to much individual variation.

The sexes of the young birds can be easily distinguished when they leave the nest.

THE RED-RUMPED PARRAKEET.

Psephotus hæmatonotus, Gould.
Coloured Figure, GOULD'S *Birds of Australia*, Vol. V., Pl. XXXVI.

This species inhabits South-east and South Australia, where, according to Gould "it is more frequently seen on the ground than among the trees, and it evidently gives a decided preference to open grassy valleys and the naked crowns of hills, rather than to the wide and almost boundless plain. During winter it associates in flocks, varying from twenty to a hundred in number, which trip nimbly over the ground in search of the seeds of grasses and other plants, with which the crops of many that were shot were found to be distended. In the early morning, and not unfrequently in other parts of the day, I have often seen hundreds perched together on some leafless limb of a *Eucalyptus*, sitting in close order along the whole length of the branch, until hunger prompted them to descend to the feeding ground or the approach of a hawk caused them to disperse. Their movements on the ground are characterised by much grace and activity, and although assembled in one great mass running over the ground like Plovers, they are generally mated in pairs, a fact easily ascertained by the difference in the colouring of the sexes; the rich red mark on the rump of the male appearing, as the bright sun shines upon it, like a spot of fire."

Mr. A. J. Campbell says: "The familiar Red-backed Parrakeet is probably the most common of the graceful genus *Psephotus*, and is found in the inland or interior tracts of Eastern Australia, where at some seasons, especially during winter, they congregate in flocks of from 150 to 200 birds, making a harvest for bird-catchers. On account of its spending most of its time on the ground, it is often called the 'grass' Parrot. It makes a good cage bird, its musical whistling notes, as Gould remarks, almost approach a song."

This species is by no means rare as an aviary bird in this country, and it is very popular with aviculturists on account of its beautiful plumage, very pretty notes, engaging habits, and its readiness to nest and rear its young in our aviaries. Not only will the Red-rump breed freely in an outdoor aviary or a bird-room, but it will even nest and rear healthy broods of young in a large cage. Mr. Savage, of Rouen, succeeded in rearing numbers of young Red-rumps in a large cage in his garden. (*Cf. Avic. Mag.*, vol. ii., p. 159.)

The Red-rumped Parrakeet is perfectly hardy, and needs no artificial warmth during the winter months in this country, so long as its aviary is sheltered from the north and east winds. It generally commences breeding quite early in the year, sometimes at the end of February or beginning of March, so that it is advisable to have the nest box fixed up in some very sheltered part of the aviary Two and sometimes three broods are produced during the season. Red-rumps require an abundance of green food during the nesting season, and in addition, stale bread, soaked in cold water and then squeezed out, is much appreciated by the old birds while they are rearing young.

These Parrakeets soon become tame and are exceedingly nice birds to keep, but they ought to have an aviary to themselves as they are somewhat spiteful towards other birds.

The adult male has the face bluish-green; head emerald-green; breast yellowish-green; back and scapulars brownish-green; rump bright red; upper tail-coverts yellowish-green; abdomen yellow; vent and under tail-coverts yellowish-white; wing-coverts bluish-green; edge of the wing, primary coverts, and outer web of primaries deep blue; central tail-feathers green, becoming bluish towards the ends, and tipped with black; outer tail-feathers green at the base, becoming bluish-white towards the tip, which is white.

The female has the head, chest, back and scapulars greenish-grey; rump green; abdomen pale yellow; vent and under tail-coverts white; wing-coverts greyish-green, tinged with blue; primary-coverts and outer web of primaries dull blue.

The sex of the young bird can be readily distinguished on leaving the nest, being pale editions of the adults.

Genus NEOPHEMA, Salvad.

This genus, which comprises what are popularly termed the Grass-Parrakeets, is confined to South Australia and Tasmania. There are seven species known, differing from *Psephotus* in having the four central tail-feathers of almost equal length. The Grass-Parrakeets form perhaps the most graceful and elegant group of the Parrot tribe. Their food consists for the most part of the seeds of various grasses, in the search of which much of their time is spent upon the ground. The sexes are very much alike in plumage.

These little Parrakeets do remarkably well in captivity on a simple diet of canary- and millet-seed and green food; and the two least uncommon species (*N. elegans* and *N. pulchella*) have been known to breed quite freely in captivity.

BOURKE'S GRASS-PARRAKEET.

Neophema bourkei (Mitch.).
Coloured Figure, GOULD'S *Birds of Australia*, Vol. V., Pl. XLIII.

This curiously-marked and extremely rare Parrakeet inhabits the interior of New South Wales and South Australia. It was first discovered by Major Sir T. L. Mitchell on the banks of the river Bogan in New South Wales.

Bourke's Parrakeet is little known even in Australia, and it is an extremely rare occurrence for living specimens to be brought alive to this country, although some twenty years or so ago a few pairs seem to have been imported.

Mr. Wiener, quoted by Dr. Greene in his *Parrots in Captivity*, remarks of this species: "This delicately-tinted Australian Grass-Parrakeet is one of the most gentle birds of the Parrot tribe. It is much to be regretted that it is so rarely imported, and therefore very dear to buy. If once acclimatised these birds are very hardy, and breed freely. Mr. Groom, of Camden Town, London, had the best pair I ever saw, and kept them summer and winter in one of the open-air aviaries of his own construction, where the birds hatched a brood of young. I quote Mr. Groom's report *verbatim:* 'The egg of the *Bourkei* is about the size of a Turquoisine's egg, of roundish shape. The male bird assists in the incubation. Time: about seventeen days. Nest in wood log hollowed out for them, as they do not appear to have the power to cut away the wood like most Parrakeets do.'" The hen of the above pair seems to have died just as the young were hatched, and no case of successful breeding seems to be on record, though young are said to have been reared on the Continent. There is little doubt, however, that the species would readily breed in captivity in this country if only living specimens could be obtained.

Bourke's Parrakeet has the upper parts brown, with a reddish tinge; a pale blue band on the forehead to the eyes; cheeks pale rose-colour, each feather edged with brown; breast brown, each feather being edged with rose-colour; abdomen rose-colour; upper and under tail-coverts and flanks light blue; wings brown, with a large patch of blue in the centre; tail-feathers brown in the centre, the lateral feathers being bluish, and white towards the tips.

The female lacks the blue frontal band, and is slightly duller.

Total length $8\frac{1}{2}$ inches.

THE BLUE-WINGED GRASS-PARRAKEET.

Neophema venusta (Temm.).

Coloured Figure, GOULD'S *Birds of Australia*, Vol. V., Pl. XXXVII.

This beautiful species, which is also known as the Blue-banded Parrakeet, inhabits New South Wales, South Australia, and Tasmania. It is very seldom imported into this country nowadays, although at one time it was occasionally to be obtained. It very closely resembles the *Neophema elegans*, both species passing with bird-dealers as "Elegant Parrakeets." The Blue-winged Parrakeet is, however, quite distinct from the Elegant, the latter being more golden-green in colour, and possessing other distinguishing markings which will be pointed out further on.

Gould writes: "This bird is a summer resident in Tasmania, arriving in September and departing again in February and March. During its sojourn it takes up its abode in such open and thinly-timbered localities as are favourable for the growth of various kinds of grasses, upon the seeds of which it almost solely subsists. . . .

"The Blue-banded Grass-Parrakeet is one of the most beautiful and interesting of the *Psittacidæ*, for whether perched on the small dead branches of a low bush, or resting upon the stronger grasses, there is grace and elegance in all its actions. It runs over the ground and threads its way among the grasses with the greatest facility, and the little flocks are usually so intent upon gathering the seeds as to admit of your walking close up to them before they will rise; the whole will then get up simultaneously, uttering a feeble cry, and settling again at a short distance, or flying off to some thickly-foliaged tree, where they sit for a time and again descend to the ground."

In the *Victorian Naturalist* for 1898 (vol. xv., p. 64), Mr. Robert Hall gives a very interesting paper on the life history of this species, in which he quotes a naturalist correspondent as follows: "This Parrakeet is very regular in timing its visit, from September 14 to 21. Its first concern upon arrival is to find a suitable stump for nesting, the kind preferred being that about 1 foot in diameter and 10 feet to 22 feet high, perpendicular, and 2 feet to 3 feet of the top part hollow. This season (1897) I watched the operations of two pairs, and as their times of action were identical, a description of one will suffice: On September 28 bird No. 1 commenced preparing hole by throwing overboard every particle of charcoal and coarse wood from bottom and sides of hole. After the coarser matter was removed, the fine, dry decayed matter was carefully scraped from every hole and crevice around the inside and allowed to fall to the bottom of hole. This work continued until October 22. I visited it each day and always found a bird at work, but whether male or female, as you ask, I cannot say—perhaps both, and it is a question for future research. From October 22 to 28 one bird sat continually, and I got alarmed lest the eggs should be laid during this period, for although I visited it often five times during each day, and remained watching till after dark, during these six days I did not find the bird from the nest. However, on the 28th, the bird had flown and left one egg. A second was laid on October 30, and from then until November 19 I had no opportunity of seeing what was taking place beneath the sitter, as it could not be persuaded to leave the nest; rough measures would not do. On the 19th day broken egg-shells pointed to full incubation of one or more eggs. On November 21 and 23 more shells, with bird still keeping close on nest. On November 24 appeared five young birds, with a yellowish downy appearance, and old birds keeping close on nest till November 27, after which two young birds opened their eyes on December 1. On December 4 two young birds appeared, covered with grey, yellowish about head and tail-feathers, the latter being 1 inch long. By December 10 two had developed green over body and wings, with a little grey still remaining about the head. The remaining three, being less advanced, were partly coloured green and grey. By December 19 traces of grey had disappeared from all. The first young bird left nest on December 20. A second left on the following day, 21st. No. 3 left on the 22nd. Nos. 4 and 5 left on 23rd. Towards the end of January, and occasionally as late as the middle of February, one may see the adult birds flying from place to place, followed closely by young birds, which receive their food from the parent birds' bills. A field of standing oats is much appreciated by this species; failing this, milk thistle and flat weed (*Hypocharis*, sp.) seed come next in favour. Immigration to warmer parts begins during March, and continues to mid-April, after which no more are seen until the following spring."

The Blue-winged Grass-Parrakeet may be described as follows: Prevailing colour olive-green; forehead crossed by a band of deep blue, bordered above by a band of lighter blue; lores yellow; abdomen and under tail-coverts yellow; upper and under wing-coverts blue; central tail-feathers greenish-blue; outer tail-feathers with the base black on the inner, and blue on the outer webs, becoming yellow towards the tips. Total length about 9 inches.

The sexes are alike, but the male is, as a rule somewhat brighter than the female.

THE ELEGANT GRASS-PARRAKEET.

Neophema elegans (Gould).

Coloured Figure, GOULD'S *Birds of Australia*, Vol. V., Pl. XXXVIII.

This species is common in Western Australia, and also occurs, less abundantly, in South Australia.

"It appears to prefer the barren and sandy belts bordering the coast," writes Gould, "but occasionally resorts to the more distant interior. Flocks were constantly rising before me while traversing the salt-marshes, which stretch along the coast from Holdfast Bay to the port of Adelaide; they were feeding upon the seeds of grasses and various other plants, which were there abundant; in the middle of the day, or when disturbed, they retreated to the thick *Banksias* that grow on the sandy ridges in the immediate neighbourhood, and in such numbers, that I have seen those trees literally covered with them, intermingled with the orange-breasted species (*E. aurantia*), which, however, was far less numerous. When they rise they spread out their beautiful yellow tail-feathers to the greatest advantage."

Gilbert, quoted by Gould, remarks of this species in Western Australia: "The Elegant Grass-Parrakeet inhabits every variety of situation, but particularly where there is an abundance of grass, the seeds of which are its favourite food; it may be generally observed in small families, but at Kojenup, where there are several pools, and no other water for many miles round, I saw these birds in myriads; but although I shot a great many, they were nearly all young birds. Its flight is rapid and even, and frequently at considerable altitudes. The breeding season is in September and October."

The Elegant Parrakeet is very rarely imported into this country now-a-days, which is much to be regretted, since it is not only a very beautiful species, but one that is easily acclimatised and hardy, and, moreover, it is very ready to reproduce its kind in our aviaries.

Writing of this species and the closely-allied Turquoisine (*N. pulchella*) in captivity, Mr. John Sergeant remarks: "They, like the Pennant and Mealy Rosella, will not nest so readily unless given an aviary to themselves, although I have reared two broods of Turquoisines and one brood of Elegants in my large aviary, tenanted by nearly fifty other birds. Still, I consider this an exceptional experience and one I could not repeat with any other birds, because these two pairs were very tame, and then again, they had a very quiet corner all to themselves in which I hung their nesting logs, which were entirely hidden by heather. Given aviaries to themselves, these Parrakeets are no trouble to the aviarist, and although not so prolific as one could wish, considering their desirability as pets, they will rear at least one brood regularly each year. These little Parrakeets require a quantity of green stuff, and if they can be turned into an aviary where there is a nice lawn they will do all the better. I never give mine any addition to their seed diet, except a soft biscuit each day when they have young. Although several of my Turquoisines and Elegants have wintered out of doors, I am never going to repeat the experiment, as I lost three last winter but one, during the severe frost, and it is evident they are not quite as hardy as other Australian Parrakeets. Turquoisines and Elegants sit about eighteen days, and the young appear in about twenty-eight days. They seem to be subject to no adverse influences when once fledged, and rapidly reach maturity." (*Avic. Mag.*, vol. ii., p. 98.)

Hybrids from a male *N. elegans* and female

N. pulchella, were bred in the Zoological Gardens of London in 1879.

The Elegant Grass-Parrakeet differs from the Blue-winged species in the green colouring being of a more golden hue; in the blue frontal band extending behind the eyes; and in the blue on the wings being much less extensive. The present species is also slightly less in size than the last, being about 8½ inches in length. In other respects the two forms are alike.

The female of *N. elegans* differs from the male only in being slightly smaller and duller.

THE ORANGE-BELLIED GRASS-PARRAKEET.

Neophema chrysogastra (Lath.).

Coloured Figure, GOULD'S *Birds of Australia*, Vol. V., Pl. XXXIX.

This species, easily recognised by the rich orange colour of the abdomen, inhabits the South-east and South of Australia and Tasmania.

Gould writes: "I observed it sparingly dispersed in the neighbourhood of Hobart Town and New Norfolk, but found it in far greater abundance on the Actæon Islands, at the entrance of D'Entrecasteaux Channel. These small and uninhabited islands are covered with grasses and scrub, intermingled with a species of Barilla, nearly allied to *Atriplex halimus;* and almost the only land-bird that enlivens these solitary spots is the present beautiful Parrakeet; I frequently flushed small flocks from among the grass, when they almost immediately alighted on the Barilla bushes around me, their sparkling orange bellies forming a striking contrast with the green of the other parts of their plumage and the silvery foliage of the plant upon which they rested. I made many unsuccessful attempts to discover their breeding-places; as, however, these islands are destitute of large trees, I am induced to believe that they lay eggs in holes on the ground, or among the stones on the shore."

Mr. Campbell informs us that the nest is "usually within a small hollow spout of a fallen tree or log."

The Orange-bellied Parrakeet has been represented in the Zoological Society's collection, but is practically unknown to Aviculturists. It may be described as follows: Prevailing colour bright grass-green; forehead with a band of deep blue, margined in front and behind with a narrow line of lighter blue; lores, cheeks and breast yellowish-green, passing to greenish-yellow on the under-parts; a conspicuous patch of bright orange on the centre of the abdomen; shoulders and upper wing-coverts deep blue; central tail-feathers bluish-green, becoming more bluish towards the tip; the outer ones greenish-blue on the outer webs, blackish on the inner webs, and tipped with yellow. Total length about 8½ inches.

Female like the male but duller, and with the abdominal spot smaller.

The young are like the female but duller.

THE ROCK GRASS-PARRAKEET.

Neophema petrophila (Gould).

Coloured Figure, GOULD'S *Birds of Australia*, Vol. V., Pl. XL.

This rare species inhabits the South-west of Australia, where, according to Gilbert, "it breeds in the holes of the most precipitous cliffs, choosing in preference those facing the water and most difficult of access."

Mr. A. J. Campbell, in his *Nests and Eggs of Australian Birds*, remarks: "It is a rare picture to witness a pair of these lovely little creatures in their golden-green plumage, perched on the face of a limestone crag, amidst such romantic and rugged surroundings. I was singularly successful in securing a series of their eggs at Rottnest Island, where the birds invariably select rocky islets off the main island for breeding purposes, notably Green and Parrakeet Islands. . . . .

" The birds make no nest, but simply deposit four or five eggs under the slabs of indurated sand or limestone, where the eggs are sometimes very difficult to reach, especially if a crevice on a steep side sloping to the water's edge be selected."

The Rock Grass-Parrakeet has probably been imported alive into this country, but I can find no published record of such an event.

Prevailing colour olive-green, more yellowish on the under parts; centre of abdomen with a slight tinge of orange; frontal band deep blue, bordered in front and behind with a narrow line of lighter blue; lores, and a circle round the eyes blue; some of the wing-coverts blue; bastard-wing, primary-coverts and outer webs of primaries deep blue; central tail-feathers bluish-green; outer ones bluish-green at the base, with inner webs brownish-black, tipped with yellow. Total length $8\frac{1}{2}$ inches.

THE TURQUOISINE GRASS-PARRAKEET.
Neophema pulchella (Shaw).

This very beautiful Grass-Parrakeet is the best known of the genus, and is in every way a most desirable species from the aviculturist's point of view. It inhabits the South and South-east of Australia.

Gould writes: " All those who have traversed

the 'bush' of New South Wales will recognise in this lovely species an old favourite, for it must have often come under their notice; during my own

From *The Royal Natural History.*

TURQUOISINE GRASS-PARRAKEET. *Neophema pulchella.*

rambles in that country my attention was constantly attracted by its beautiful outspread tail and wings as it rose before me. Its sole food being the seeds of grasses and of the smaller annuals, it spends much of its time on the ground, and appears to evince a greater partiality for stony ridges than for the rich alluvial flats. When flushed it flies off to a short distance between the trees, perches on some dead branch and remains there until hunger impels it to return to the ground. I have never seen this bird congregated in large flocks like the *Euphema chrysostoma* and *E. elegans;* but usually met with it in small companies of six or eight in number."

The Turquoisine is at the present time extremely rare in this country, although it appears to have been imported somewhat frequently years ago; and it has bred in captivity in this country and on the Continent on numerous occasions. In the London Zoological Gardens alone numbers were bred between the years 1860 and 1883, but for several years past no specimen has been exhibited there. A few individuals still exist in the living collections of aviculturists, but it is extremely difficult to obtain living specimens nowadays.

Not only is the Turquoisine a very beautiful and graceful Parrakeet, but it is one of the gentlest of Parrots, and may be trusted with birds much smaller and weaker than itself. It is, moreover, hardy, and requires the simplest of treatment in captivity. A diet of canary- and millet-seed and green food such as groundsel, chickweed, flowering grass, shepherd's purse, and such like, is all that they require. Although they do not appear to feel the cold to any great extent, it is extremely unwise as well as cruel to subject them to the rigours of an English winter in an outdoor aviary. Slight warmth should certainly be given them.

The Turquoisine Grass-Parrakeet may be described thus: General colour above bright green;

face and wing-coverts bright blue; chest, abdomen and under tail-coverts yellow; a reddish-chestnut spot on the upper wing-coverts; under wing-coverts blue; four central tail-feathers green, tipped with black; the lateral ones bluish-green at the base, tipped with yellow, the inner web blackish.

The female is considerably duller in all her colours, and lacks the chestnut-red spot on the wings. Total length about 8½ inches.

THE SPLENDID GRASS-PARRAKEET.

Neophema splendida (Gould).

This is certainly the most beautiful of the genus, almost rivalling in the richness of its hues, the gorgeous *Psephoti*. It inhabits the South and South-west of Australia, but practically nothing seems to be known of its habits in a wild state. It is very closely allied to the Turquoisine, and there is little doubt that its habits are much the same. The Zoological Society of London received a pair of this exquisite Parrakeet in January, 1871, and their *List of Vertebrated Animals* contains a record of a young bird being hatched in the gardens, July 21, 1872. It is probable that no living specimen has reached this country for many years past.

The Splendid Grass-Parrakeet has the face and ear-coverts bright blue; upper parts bright green, the nape washed with blue; a patch of rich scarlet on the chest; abdomen and under tail-coverts yellow; sides green; upper wing-coverts pale blue; under wing-coverts deep blue; central tail-feathers dark green; outer tail-feathers with the base green on the outer and black on the inner webs and tipped with yellow. Total length 8 inches.

"The female differs in having the face and wing-coverts, both above and beneath, of a pale lazuline blue, and in the chest being green instead of blue" (*Gould*).

Genus CYANORHAMPHUS, Bp.

This genus contains some fourteen or fifteen known species, inhabiting New Zealand, New Caledonia, the Loyalty and Society Islands. The members have the tarsi of considerable length and spend much of their time upon the ground, feeding upon the seeds of grass and other plants. The genus is characterised by the base of the upper mandible of the bill being shining pearl grey. Five species have been represented in the Zoological Society's collection.

In captivity the food of these Parrakeets should consist of canary, millet and hemp-seed and ripe fruit. Green food, such as chickweed and groundsel, should also be given in the summer time.

THE ANTIPODES ISLAND PARRAKEET.

Cyanorhamphus unicolor, Vig.

This fine Parrakeet, probably the largest of the genus, was named by Vigors in 1831 from a specimen living in the Zoological Society's collection. Nothing was known of the locality from whence this bird came, and it remained a mystery until, some fifty-five years later, a specimen was received at the Christchurch Museum, from the Antipodes Islands.

Sir Walter Buller writes thus in the second edition of his *Birds of New Zealand* (1888).

"Captain Fairchild, of the Government steamboat 'Hinemoa, on a visit to Antipodes Island in

March, 1886, found the bird comparatively common there and brought several specimens back with him to New Zealand. One of these was forwarded to me by Sir J. Hector, and this has enabled me to add the description of the female to that of the hitherto unique specimen of the male bird in the British Museum collection. . . . . .

"Captain Fairchild, who is an excellent observer, reports that on Antipodes Island he found it inhabiting a plateau 1,320 feet above the sea. It was very tame and easily caught. He never saw it take wing, which he attributes as much to the boisterous winds that sweep over this exposed island as to its naturally feeble powers of flight. It habitually walks and climbs among the tussock-grass, reminding one of the habits of the Australian Ground-Parrot (*Pezoporus formosus*).

"Besides collecting several good specimens, Captain Fairchild brought with him to Wellington a live one. Sir James Hector sends me the following account of this interesting bird, for which he has proposed the name of *Platycercus fairchildii:* 'It is a *ground* Parrakeet, *i.e.*, a Parrakeet that resembles a Kakapo. It is twice the bulk of *P. novæ zealandiæ*, flies freely, but does not care to perch, climbs with its beak and feet, and walks in the same waddle-and-intoed fashion as the Kakapo."

The Antipodes Island Parrakeet has been represented in the Zoological Society's collection on five or six occasions, but it is an extremely rare species.

In colour this species is olive-green, brighter on the forehead, cheeks and ear-coverts, and somewhat yellowish on the rump and under-parts ; outer web of primaries bluish ; bastard wing and primary coverts with the outer webs bright blue ; under side of tail dull golden olive. Total length about 13 inches.

Female slightly smaller and paler in colour than the male.

THE NEW-ZEALAND PARRAKEET.
Cyanorhamphus novæ-zealandiæ (Sparrm.).
Coloured Figure, BULLER'S *Birds of New Zealand*.

The Red-fronted, or common New Zealand Parrakeet, is the best-known member of the genus, and although not very often to be obtained in this country, is well known to most aviculturists. Besides inhabiting the whole of the mainland of New Zealand,

Cyanorhamphus novæ-zealandiæ.

it occurs also in Auckland Island. Sir Walter Buller gives us the following account of its wild life :—

"The Red-fronted Parrakeet is very generally dispersed over the whole country—but more plentiful in the southern portion of the North Island than in the north, where the yellow-fronted species predominates. It frequents every part of the bush, but appears to prefer the outskirts, where the vegetation is low and scrubby, as also the wooded margins of creeks and rivers. It is often met with among the dense Koromiko (*Veronica*) which covers the low river-flats, or among the bushes of *Leptospermum* and other scrub. It seldom ventures beyond the shelter of the woods, unless it be to visit the farmer's fields for its tithe of grain, or to reach some distant feeding-place, when it rises rather high in the air and flies rapidly, but in a rather zig-zag course. When on the wing it utters a hurried chattering note; and when alarmed, or calling to its fellows, it emits a cry resembling the words 'twenty-eight,' with a slight emphasis on the last syllable. It often resorts to the tops of the highest trees, but may always be enticed downwards by imitating this note. It is gregarious, forming parties of from three to twelve, or more, in number, except in the breeding season, when it is generally met with in pairs.

"Its food consists chiefly of berries and seeds; but I suspect that it devours small insects and their larvæ; for I have observed flocks of a dozen or more on the ground, engaged apparently in a search of that kind. . . . . .

"When the cornfields are ready for the harvest, flocks of these gaily-coloured Parrakeets resort to them to feed on the ripe grain; and it is very pretty to see them, on alarm being given, rise in the air together and settle on a fence, or on the limb of a dead tree, to wait till the danger has passed, keeping up all the time a low, pleasant chatter.

"This species bears confinement remarkably well, and is very docile and familiar even when taken as an adult bird. It is also very intelligent, and possesses the faculty of mimicry in a high degree.

"One of these birds has been in the possession of a lady at Christchurch (Canterbury) for more than eight years. Although full grown when first caged, it has learnt to articulate several words with great clearness. It is very tame, and displays a considerable amount of intelligence—leaves its cage every day for exercise, and returns to it immediately on the appearance of a stranger. It knows its fair owner's voice, will respond to her call, and will 'shake hands' with each foot alternately in the most sedate manner. Another, in our own possession, survived confinement for more than *eleven* years, and appeared then in perfect health and strength, when it fell a victim to the household puss. This bird could articulate sentences of three or four words with great precision of accent; and the loss of so intimate a family friend was 'sincerely lamented' by all our circle.

"A hole in a decaying or dead tree affords this species a natural breeding-place, the eggs being laid on the pulverised rotten wood at the bottom; for there is no further attempt at forming a nest. The months of November and December constitute the breeding season. The eggs vary in number from three to seven. . . . Although exhibiting a preference for hollow trees, they sometimes nest in the holes or crevices of rocks. On the Upper Wanganui the natives pointed out to me a small round cavity in the perpendicular cliff forming the bank of the river, and assured me that this was the entrance to a small chamber where a pair of Parrakeets had reared their young in security for years. The eggs are very broadly oval, measuring 1·05 by ·83. They are pure white, and are very finely granulated on the surface, sometimes with minute limy excrescences near the thicker end."

The New-Zealand Parrakeet is, when acclimatised, a comparatively hardy and easily kept species, and one that will breed freely in captivity if suitably accommodated. The writer's actual experience of these birds in captivity is limited to one pair which lived in his aviary for a short time only, as the hen sickened and died a few months after her arrival. I found them perfectly harmless towards the other occupants of the aviary. They possess a curious habit, shared by the other members of the genus, of scratching for seeds, &c., in the sand, like gallinacerus birds. The Germans call this species "Ziegensittich," or Goat Parrakeet, from the peculiar note it utters, which much resembles the bleat of a goat.

My friend Mr. Savage, of Rouen, writes as follows, in the *Avicultural Magazine* * :—

"They are, as far as my experience goes, quite harmless birds, and can be lodged, without fear, in an aviary of mixed finches or Budgerigars, and this opinion is confirmed by others who have kept them on this side of the channel.

. . . . .

"I believe the importation of the New Zealand Parrakeet to be rare, both in England and on the Continent, but aviary-bred birds are frequently obtainable on this side of the Channel; such birds are quite hardy, and a good pair will breed freely without fuss or trouble. They are adult at six months, and young hatched in January have been known to breed the same year; birds hatched during the spring and summer months breed, as a rule, the next year. I believe New Zealands were the first Parrakeets, larger than Budgerigars, I ever bred. The eggs are white, as is usually the case with Parrakeets, and there are generally from four to six to the clutch. I have never had less than two, or more than four young reared per nest, but more fortunate amateurs can boast of a nest of six on more than one occasion. There are three, four, or even five nests during the year, when a good pair commence breeding early in January; but three nests have always satisfied me.

"Food is a very simple matter: Canary-seed,

---

* Vol. iv., p. 161.

white millet and oats, mixed with a sprinkling of hemp (about a couple of dozen seeds) on the top, and spray millet, is all the seed I give, whether they have young or not. Green food is, of course, necessary—chickweed in seed, and groundsel in flower, I consider the best—and they must have plenty of it when they have young to feed. As soon as the young are hatched the parents become quite bold when the green food is taken into the aviary; one cock bird I had would almost come on to my hand for it, he was in too big a hurry to wait, with the cares of his family of four on his shoulders, until it was tied up in its place. They are excellent feeders, and I never lost a young one from want of care on the part of the parents or insufficient feeding. They remain in the nest about a month, and can dash about pretty well when they leave it. This Parrakeet can be strongly recommended to any amateur wishing to 'try his hand' with a species a nick above Budgerigars."

The Hon. Canon Dutton wrote of this species as follows, in *Parrots in Captivity* (1884) :—

"It is shy and gentle, a quiet bird, and very fond of bathing. I have known three, of which two were talkers, but none of them tame enough to allow themselves to be handled. The two that talked said several sentences, but did not pick up anything fresh. They are very attractive cage-birds for anyone who likes quiet birds, but they are rather wanting in character."

Prevailing colour green, with a decided yellowish tinge on the underside; crown, lores and ear-coverts crimson; a spot of crimson on each side of the rump; outer primaries, primary-coverts and bastard wing bright blue; tail green; bill horn-colour, with a large silvery-grey patch at the base of the upper mandible. Total length about 11 inches.

The sexes are alike in plumage, but the female is somewhat smaller than the male.

SAISSET'S PARRAKEET.

Cyanorhamphus saisseti, Verr. and Des Murs.

Coloured Figure, P.Z.S., 1882, Pl. XLVI.

This is the New Caledonian form of the Red-fronted Parrakeet (*C. novæ zealandiæ*), and differs only from the typical birds in being larger (12½ inches), having a longer tail, and more yellow on the cheeks. The tail-feathers are more distinctly bluish towards the ends, and the tips are yellowish. It is said to feed on the ground on small seeds, and to travel in small flocks. "It is very partial to the ripe fruit of the paupaw, tearing away the melon-like pulp to arrive at the pungent seeds within" (Layard, *Ibis*, 1882, p. 524).

The Zoological Society of London received a living example of this species on June 28, 1882.

THE GOLDEN-CROWNED PARRAKEET.

Cyanorhamphus auriceps (Kuhl).

This very pretty little Parrakeet inhabits the whole of New Zealand, but is more plentiful in the North than in the South Island. It also occurs on Chatham Islands.

Sir Walter Buller writes: "In habits this bird closely resembles the preceding one (Red-fronted Parrakeet) but it is less gregarious, being seen generally in pairs. It loves to frequent the tutu bushes (*Coriaria ruscifolia*), to regale itself on the juicy berries of this bushy shrub; and on these occasions it is easily snared by the natives, who use for that purpose a flat noose at the end of a slender rod. When feeding on the tutu-berry the whole of the interior becomes stained of a dark purple. When the wild dock has run to seed, this pretty little Parrakeet repairs to the open fields and feasts on the ripe seeds of that noxious weed. At other seasons the berries of *Coprosma lucida*, *Fuchsia excorticata*, and other forest-shrubs, afford it a plentiful and agreeable nutriment.

"In captivity it is very gentle and tractable, but it is far inferior to the large red-fronted bird in its talking-capacity. One or two instances of its being taught to articulate words of two syllables have come to my knowledge; but as a rule the attempt to instruct it ends in failure.

"Like its congener it nests in hollow trees, and lays from five to eight eggs, resembling those of *Platycercus** *novæ zealandiæ*, but smaller. Specimens in my collection measure ·9 in. in length by ·75 in. in breadth.

"Major Mair informs me that he watched a pair of these birds breeding in the cavity of a dead tree for three successive seasons. The first year's brood numbered five, the second eight, and the third seven."

The Golden-crowned Parrakeet is, unfortunately, very seldom to be obtained alive in this country, but it is a most delightful little bird, and very ready to reproduce its kind in captivity.

Mr. G. E. Bouskill has published in the *Avicultural Magazine*,† the following interesting account of some of these Parrakeets in his possession:—

---

* *Cyanorhamphus.* † Vol. iv., p. 45.

"The habits of my Golden-crowned Parrakeets are very interesting. They are remarkably tame, and although so recently imported, will come quite close to me while feeding. When first introduced into my aviary, hardly two months ago, they made themselves at home and behaved as if they had been there all their lives. The long legs of this bird enable it to run and hop with great freedom, and it has the peculiar habit of scratching on the ground, after the manner of our common poultry. It is never tired of either running, hopping, or flying about and uttering its song (if such it can be called), and at such times it will stretch itself out with a forward motion, and then it is that the Golden-crown really looks at its best: for while it is singing, the dilating of the eye goes on and the iris becomes like a ball of fire. They are particularly fond of their bath—they quite drench themselves through, and then fly to the nearest branch to dry. Although their beaks are so long and sharp, yet they are very gentle. My Turquoisines and even Budgerigars frequently drive them away if they approach them whilst feeding.

"During their short residence in my aviary one of the cocks has paired with the hen, and on October 24 (exactly seven weeks after date of arrival) the hen bird laid her first egg; and on the 28th she was closely sitting on five pure white eggs."

The further history of this little pair appeared in the same Journal two months later,* and is as follows:—

"It was late in the season to allow my Golden-crowns to nest, and the only portion of my aviary which I could allot to them at the time was occupied by a pair of Turquoisines and a pair of Budgerigars,

---

* Vol. iv., p. 77.

the latter of which had young; but before these had left the husk the Golden-crowns had begun to prospect on their own account, and as I did not want the young Budgerigars to be turned out of their nest, I decided to put up another husk, and it was in this that the Golden-crowned Parrakeets settled down to nest.

"The hen built a cup-shaped nest, using the fibre off the inside of the cocoa-nut husk,* and in this she laid five pure white eggs, which were very round, and, I think, large for the size of the bird (they almost equalled in size the egg of the Rosella). The female alone incubated the eggs, and a most dutiful parent she was, rarely leaving her nest except to be fed by her mate. Incubation lasted about twenty-one days from the laying of the first egg. As I stated in my last paper, the first egg was laid on October 24, and the fifth on the 28th; this would fix the time of hatching to be about November 14. You can imagine how anxious I was when November 5 arrived, for my neighbours had their children to please and could not be expected to study my birds. I was greatly afraid that the illuminations and flashes of light would frighten the hen bird off her nest, and so let the precious eggs get cold; to obviate this, I covered the glass portion of the aviary with dust sheets; the loud reports I could not keep out, and so far as noise was concerned, the birds had to take their chance. I have read somewhere that 'a loud report or the

---

* These birds do not naturally build any nest, but simply hollow out a saucer-shaped depression, for the reception of their eggs, in the rotten wood of the inside of some hollow trunk or branch of a tree, in the same way as almost all other Parrots do. In the above instance the nest was probably "built" accidentally by the bird in endeavouring to hollow out a depression in a very fibrous material.

slamming of a door will kill young birds in the shell;' mine, however, had a fair test in this respect on November 5 last. But the hen Golden-crown was not so easily startled, and proved herself a most assiduous sitter.

"When first hatched the young were covered with a dirty yellow down; they grew very rapidly; and during the first week the hen bird did not leave them much, but the cock bird fed her both while she brooded her young and when she came off for a little exercise. As the young got stronger, she left them more frequently, and when about ten days old both birds entered the nest to feed their young. They began to feather when about fourteen days old, and were fully fledged when about a month old. The young did not leave the nest until they were five weeks old. They were then much like their parents, except that the crimson band above the upper mandible was hardly perceptible, and the patch of golden-yellow less bright, the red under the wings was just indicated, and the beak was flesh colour, being rather darker at the tip. The young were reared on canary, hemp, and millet seed, and in addition, about thirty to forty mealworms per diem, and stale bread soaked in cold water and then squeezed nearly dry."*

The prevailing colour of this species is bright grass-green, the under-parts being paler and more yellowish; a band of crimson across the forehead; crown bright golden-yellow; bastard wing and primary-coverts deep blue; a red spot on the sides of the rump; tail green. Total length about 9 inches.

The sexes are alike in colour, but the female is slightly smaller than the male.

---

* Mr. Bouskill informs me that he has bred *Cyanorhamphus auriceps* each year since 1898.

THE ALPINE PARRAKEET.

Cyanorhamphus malherbei, Souancé.

This species was named *Platycercus alpinus* by Sir Walter Buller, but it had previously been described by Souancé as *C. malherbei*. It very closely resembles the Golden-crowned Parrakeet, but differs in being smaller, the frontal band being *orange*, and the crown paler yellow. The under-parts moreover are not tinged with yellow, and the spot on the sides of the rump is *orange*. It inhabits the South Island of New Zealand.

Sir W. Buller writes: "The present bird was originally described by me, from specimens obtained in the forests of the Southern Alps, at an elevation of from 2,000 to 2,500 feet. In its native haunts it may be found frequenting the alpine scrub, in pairs or in small parties, and is very tame and fearless. It is by no means uncommon in the wooded hills surrounding Nelson.

"Mr. Reischek met with this little Parrakeet in the scrub on the summit of Mount Alexander (above Lake Brunner); and he met with the species again on the Hen, where he shot two, and on the Little Barrier, where he observed another pair on the highest peak and killed the male. It does not exist on the opposite mainland, nor indeed, so far as I am aware, in any part of the North Island.

"At Nelson I saw many caged birds of this species, and one in particular was remarkable for the clear manner in which it articulated the words 'pretty Dick,' repeating them all day long in the most untiring way."

This species has been represented in the Zoological Society's collection.

Genus NYMPHICUS, Wagl.

Two species only are known to belong to this genus, in which the head is ornamented by a crest. Both species are rare as cage-birds in this country, and very little seems to be understood as to their correct treatment. Both appear to be decidedly delicate.

THE HORNED PARRAKEET.

Nymphicus cornutus (Gm.).

This very rare Parrakeet is confined to the island of New Caledonia and is only imported alive to this country on extremely rare occasions. I once saw a very fine specimen in a small bird-shop in Dover.

H. Grönvold, del.

Nymphicus cornutus.

Mr. Layard gives us the following insight into its wild life :—

"This crested Parrot, which is peculiar to New Caledonia, is found in all the forest region, frequenting trees in flower or fruit. It usually flies in pairs, though often several pairs may be found feeding on the same tree. They are very partial to the candle nut fruit and to the blossoms of the *Erythrina*. We have seen them on the ground on fallen fruits and berries, but they do not usually resort thither. They nest in holes in trees, and we obtained their eggs on October 15. They are dirty white, rough, four in number, similarly shaped at each end, and much rounded: axis 12, diam. 10." (*Ibis*, 1882, p. 524.)

The diet of these Parrakeets in captivity is little understood, but the usual seeds should certainly form the staple food, and a little ripe fruit should be given every day. I should also be inclined to give them occasionally milk-sop, as recommended for Lorikeets.

The prevailing colour is green, becoming yellowish on the under-parts; feathers on the top of the head black with crimson tips; crest consisting of *two* long feathers, black with red tips; ear-coverts and nape yellow; face and cheeks black; bastard wing, primary coverts and primaries blue; tail above blue, below blackish; irides orange. Total length about 14 inches. The sexes are alike in plumage.

THE UVÆAN PARRAKEET.

Nymphicus uvæensis, Layard.

This species inhabits the Loyalty Islands, and its habits appear to be similar to those of its congener. It is imported rather more freely than the New Caledonian bird, which it resembles in its extreme delicacy. The Hon. Canon Dutton, referring to this species, remarks: "To look at their bills you would say they were seed-eaters; but I bought a lot of eight once, which *looked* healthy enough. They all died, one after the other, of digestion troubles, and I have had other specimens, which I have kept for twelve months or so, but then they have died. They have never been kept very long in the Zoological Gardens. I cannot but think they would live longer, if we knew how to feed them correctly." (*Avic. Mag.*, vol. vi., p. 245.)

The sexes of the Uvæan Parrakeet are outwardly alike, though the male is, as a rule, a little larger than the female. They may be described thus: Prevailing colour grass-green, somewhat yellowish on the under-parts; crest, consisting of *six* upturned feathers, dark green; feathers of the forehead tipped with red; bastard wing, primary coverts and primaries dark blue; central tail-feathers green, becoming blue towards the tips, outer tail-feathers blue; irides orange. Total length about $12\frac{1}{2}$ inches.

Genus NANODES, Vig. and Horsf.

THE SWIFT PARRAKEET.
Nanodes discolor (Shaw).
Coloured Figure, GOULD'S *Birds of Australia*, Vol. V., Pl. XLVII.

This is the sole representative of the genus, and differs from all other species in this sub-family, in which Count Salvadori has placed it, in the possession of a brush-tongue, which would seem to show that its proper place is among the *Loriidæ*. In fact, in its habits and manner of living it closely resembles the Lorikeets, and in captivity requires much the same treatment as other brushed-tongued Parrots, though seed should form a considerable part of its diet.

The Swift Parrakeet, or Lorikeet, inhabits the South-east and South of Australia and Tasmania, varying its locality according to the season and the supply of its favourite food—the honey of the flowering *Eucalyptus*. Gould gives a delightful account of this species, which I cannot do better than reproduce here: he writes: "This elegant Lorikeet is a migratory species, passing the summer and breeding-season only in the more southern parts of the Australian continent and Tasmania, and retiring northward for the remainder of the year. During September and the four following months, it is not only abundant in all the gum-forests of Tasmania, but is very common in the shrubberies and gardens at Hobart Town. It is frequently to be seen on the gum-trees bordering the streets, within a few feet of the heads of the passing inhabitants, and so intent upon gathering the honey from the fresh-blown flowers which daily expand, as almost entirely to disregard their presence. The tree to which it is so eagerly attracted is the *Eucalyptus gibbosus*, cultivated specimens of which appear to have finer blossoms than those in their native forests. It is certainly the finest of the *Eucalypti* I have ever seen, and when its pendant branches are covered with thick clusters of pale yellow blossoms, it presents a most beautiful appearance; these blossoms are so charged with saccharine matter that the birds soon fill themselves with honey, even to their very throats: several of those I shot, upon being held up by the feet, discharged from their mouths a small stream of this liquid to the amount of a dessertspoonful. Small flocks of from four to twenty in number are also frequently to be seen passing over the town, chasing each other, like the Swift of Europe, whence, in all probability, has arisen its colonial name. Sometimes these flights appear to be taken for the sake of exercise, or in the mere playfulness of disposition, while at others the birds are passing from one garden to another, or proceeding from the town to the forests at the foot of Mount Wellington, or *vice versâ*. Their plumage so closely assimilates in colour to the leaves of the trees they frequent, and they, moreover, creep so quietly, yet actively, from branch to branch, clinging in every possible position, that were it not for their movements and the trembling of the leaves, it would be difficult to perceive them without a minute examination of the tree upon which they have alighted.

"In its actions and manners it is closely allied to the *Trichoglossi*, but differs from them in some few particulars, which are more perceptible in captivity than in a state of nature; it has neither the musky smell nor the jumping motions of the *Trichoglossi*. I have never observed it to alight upon the ground, or elsewhere than among the branches."

The chief colour of the Swift Parrakeet is green, lighter and more yellowish on the under-side; forehead, throat, anterior part of cheeks and under wing-coverts scarlet; a band of yellow on the cheeks, bordering the red; crown and sides of the head blue, deeper on the crown; flanks and under tail-coverts scarlet, the latter edged with greenish-yellow; bend of the wing red; primary wing-coverts blue; tail brownish-red changing to blue towards the tips.

The female is like the male, but less bright and slightly smaller.

Genus MELOPSITTACUS, Gould.

THE BUDGERIGAR, OR UNDULATED GRASS-PARRAKEET.

Melopsittacus undulatus (Shaw).
Coloured Figure, GOULD'S *Birds of Australia*, Vol. V., Pl. XLIV.

The Budgerigar, Betcherrygah, Undulated Grass-Parrakeet, Warbling Grass-Parrakeet, or Shell Parrakeet, inhabits the greater part of Australia. It is gregarious and migratory, but the vast flocks that used to appear in the south in the spring are rarely seen nowadays in consequence of the grassy plains of former days being now used for feeding stock and growing crops.

Gould writes: " On arriving at Brezi to the north of the Liverpool Plains in the beginning of December, I found myself surrounded by numbers breeding in all the hollow spouts of the large *Eucalypti* bordering the Mokai ; and on crossing the plains between that river and the Peel, in the direction of the Turi Mountain, I saw them in flocks of thousands. Their flight is remarkably straight and rapid, and is generally accompanied by a screeching noise. During the heat of the day, when flocks of them are sitting motionless among the leaves of the gum-trees, they are with difficulty detected. . . .

" In a state of nature they feed exclusively upon grass-seeds, with which their crops are always found crammed."

Mr. Campbell writes : " Where are the flocks of these lovely little Parrakeets, that from the far interior used periodically to visit Victoria and other parts of Southern Australia when the grass seeds were ripening ? ' Because their primitive feeding grounds have been destroyed by the depasturing of other flocks (stock),' is the significant reply of an old and experienced bird trapper."

The same authority proceeds : " During the Calvert Expedition (1896) to the North-west, throughout the whole of the country traversed these birds were noted. They were breeding in July and August, and numbers of eggs and young birds were seen. On July 26 Mr. G. L. Jones took young birds fully fledged from a hollow limb, in which he found four nests. Two of the latter contained fresh eggs.

Other nestlings were seen on August 26. As these birds require to drink frequently, their presence was always noted and their course watched. They travel immense distances to feed, and in the vicinity of Johanna Springs flocks of several thousands were seen going to some favourite feeding place soon after sunrise. On three occasions Mr. Keartland saw a beautiful yellow bird flying in the flock. These abnormal birds were described as being as richly coloured as Norwich Canaries."

This beautiful little Parrakeet is one of the commonest foreign birds kept by aviculturists both in this country and on the continent, and is a general favourite wherever it is known, not only on account of its beautiful plumage and pretty ways, but from the extraordinary rapidity with which it will produce brood after brood of young birds, and rear them with far less trouble to their owner than any other kind of small bird; in fact, several aviculturists have given up keeping Budgerigars on account of the enormous extent to which they multiply and the difficulty experienced in disposing of the young quickly enough. Anyone can breed Budgerigars to almost any extent who possesses a good-sized outdoor aviary. Here some half-dozen or so pairs will produce anything up to a hundred young in the course of a year, commencing to nest about January or February and producing brood after brood, consisting of from four to eight or even ten, throughout the entire year. Young Budgerigars that have been hatched in January or February will themselves commence to breed in June or July, so that it can well be imagined that their numbers increase to a most astonishing extent in a very short time; and, moreover, I have never found that the young produced by birds that were themselves but a few months old were in any way weak or imperfect.

It has often been stated that aviary-bred Budgerigars are inferior to imported birds, but I think this statement is often far from true. There is no doubt whatever that birds bred in artificially heated rooms during the winter months are anything but robust, and most liable to be affected by excessive loss of feathers—"French moult"—but I can positively affirm that Budgerigars that have been bred during the summer months in large outdoor aviaries in England, providing of course that inbreeding is not permitted, are just as fine and healthy birds as any that were ever seen in Australia; in fact, I would go further and say that one breeder has, to my knowledge, by carefully selecting his breeding stock, produced birds that are considerably finer than any imported birds.

By careful selection and in-breeding the well-known yellow variety of the Budgerigar has been produced. It is by no means so handsome a bird as the ordinary form, neither is it so hardy or so prolific. That this variety occurs occasionally in a wild state is proved by yellow birds having been observed by the Calvert Expedition, as mentioned above.

A few years ago the breeding of Budgerigars was a decidedly profitable hobby, as the young could readily be disposed of at ten or twelve shillings a pair, but so common have they now become that it is often difficult to realise half those prices for young birds, and adult specimens can generally be obtained at about seven shillings a pair. Even at these prices, however, a schoolboy may do far worse than invest his spare pocket-money in a few pairs of Budgerigars if he can give them a suitable aviary. Budgerigars will thrive perfectly well on a diet of canary and millet seed, or canary seed only, but when they have young to feed they should also be supplied with stale bread that has been soaked for about a minute in cold water and then squeezed nearly dry. Green food, such as groundsel and chickweed, should also be supplied, unless grass is allowed to grow in the aviary, in which case other green food will be unnecessary. The most suitable form of aviary for Budgerigars consists of a large dry shed, with a wire flight of about equal size attached. In the covered part should be hung the nesting receptacles, such as cocoanut husks, or small boxes. Personally I have found boxes preferable to husks, for the reason that the eggs very often get thrown out of the latter. The boxes should be about seven inches in height by about five or six inches in width and depth, and the bottom should be slightly hollowed so that the eggs cannot roll about as they would do if this were flat. An entrance hole, about an inch and a quarter in diameter, should be bored near the top of the box, and just below this a perch fixed for the birds to alight upon before entering. Budgerigars are perfectly hardy and require no artificial warmth during the coldest weather providing their aviary is sheltered and dry. Young birds, if taken from the nest a few days before they would naturally leave it, can very easily be tamed and trained to make really delightful pets. I have known several that had completely lost every particle of fear of human beings, and would fly to their owner when called, or allow themselves to be carried all over the house on his hand, head or shoulder. All that is necessary is to cage the young bird just before it would otherwise leave the nest, and handle and caress it as much as possible. For the first day or two it will be unable to crack seed and must be fed by hand on soaked bread and seed that has been shelled. In a couple of days or so it will take seed from the fingers and crack it itself, though it may not seem to understand how to descend from the perch and take the seed from the ground. In about a week's time it will feed itself perfectly, and the more it is handled and petted the tamer will it become. A specimen so tamed was photographed on the writer's hand, and its portrait appears on the title-page of this volume.

The plumage of the sexes is alike in the adults, but they can be readily distinguished by the nostrils which are bright blue in the male and brown in the female. The plumage is as follows: Crown, throat and lower part of cheeks bright yellow; nape, ear-coverts, back and wing-coverts greenish-yellow, each feather with a band of black; on each cheek an oblique band of blue, below which are three distinct spots of black; underparts vivid green; tail blue. Total length about $7\frac{1}{2}$ inches.

In the young birds the black stripes extend over the whole of the forehead and crown, and the colours are less brilliant.

Genus PEZOPORUS, Illig.

THE GROUND, OR SWAMP PARRAKEET.

Pezoporus terrestris (Shaw).
Coloured Figure, GOULD'S *Birds of Australia*, Vol. V., Pl. XLVI.

This species inhabits South and Western Australia and Tasmania, but is far rarer at the present time than formerly on account of the extent to which the waste lands have been cultivated, and predatory animals introduced; and Mr. Campbell tells us that it is likely soon to become extinct.

Gould writes: "So far as I could learn, it is everywhere a stationary species. Having very frequently met with it in a state of nature, I am enabled to state that in its actions it differs from every other known species of its family. Whether the power of perching is entirely denied to it or not I am uncertain, but I never saw it fly into a tree, nor could I ever force it to take shelter on the branches. It usually frequents either sandy sterile districts covered with tufts of rank grass and herbage, or low swampy flats

From *Cassell's Book of Birds.*
GROUND PARRAKEET. *Pezoporus terrestris.*

abounding with rushes and other kinds of vegetation peculiar to such situations. From its very recluse habits and great powers of running it is seldom or ever seen until it is flushed, and then only for a short time, as it soon pitches again and runs off to a place of seclusion. On the approach of danger it crouches on the earth or runs stealthily through the grasses, and, from the strong scent it emits, dogs road and point as dead to it as they do to ordinary game-birds; consequently, when shooting over swampy land in Australia, the sportsman is never certain whether a parrakeet, a quail, or a snipe will rise to the point of his dog. It flies with great rapidity, frequently making several zigzag turns in the short distance of a hundred yards, which it seldom exceeds without again pitching to the ground."

Mr. A. J. Campbell informs us that the nest is "a somewhat deep hollow in the ground, evenly lined with fine grass, &c., under a tussock of grass—usually a button-grass tussock in Tasmania. A nest in the Australian Museum is composed of rushes and wire-grass, bitten into suitable lengths, bent and roughly interwoven into a platform about $4\frac{1}{2}$ inches in diameter and about half an inch thick." Three or four round white eggs are laid to a clutch. The food of this species consists of the seeds of grasses and other vegetation.

Although the Ground Parrakeet has been kept in the Zoological Gardens, it is quite unknown to present-day aviculturists, and as it appears to be becoming rare in its native country, there would seem to be very little chance of its ever being imported to any extent, which is much to be regretted, seeing that it is a particularly interesting species about which much still remains to be learnt.

The prevailing colour is green above, yellowish-green below, spotted and barred with black and yellow; *a conspicuous band of dark orange on the forehead;* each quill with a yellow spot; central tail-feathers green, barred with yellow; outer tail-feathers yellow, barred with dark green. Total length $12\frac{1}{2}$ inches.

The sexes are alike in colour in the adults, but the young lack the frontal band.

Genus GEOPSITTACUS, Gould.

THE NIGHT PARRAKEET.

Geopsittacus occidentalis, Gould
Coloured Figure, GOULD'S *Birds of Australia*, Suppl., Pl. LXVI.

This species occurs in South and Western Australia; it was considered by Gould to be not only specifically, but generically distinct from *Pezoporus*, and ornithologists have one and all followed him. "In *Pezoporus*," writes Gould, "the proportions of the head, bill, body, wings and tail are evenly balanced, the legs are especially adapted for running over the ground, and the claws, particularly that of the outer hind toe, are remarkably long; while in the bird under consideration, the head is disproportionately large, the mandibles short and robust, the nostrils high and round, the *tarsi* and toes short and delicate, and the nails unusually diminutive when compared with those of other Parrakeets; to complete the differences seen in the anomalous bird, the wings are large and long, while the tail is very short. The whole contour of *Pezoporus* is graceful and elegant: the present bird, on the other hand, is short and dumpy, and much reminds me of a diminutive *Strigops*."

A most interesting account of this species was read by the late Mr. F. W. Andrew, before the Royal Society of South Australia in 1893, and is quoted by Mr. A. J. Campbell* as follows: "During the day

---

* *Nests and Eggs of Australian Birds*, p. 660.

this bird lies concealed in the inside of a tussock or bunch of porcupine grass (*Triodia*), the inside being pulled out and a snug retreat formed for its protection. Here also its rough nest is formed, and four white eggs laid. When the dark shades of evening have fairly set in, it comes out to feed, but generally flies direct to the nearest water, which is often a considerable distance from its nest; in some instances I have known them fly a distance of four or five miles. After drinking and shaking themselves up a little, they fly off to feed on the seeds of the porcupine grass, returning to water two or three times during the night.

" The name given to this bird by the aborigines is 'Myrrlumbing,' from the supposed resemblance of their whistling note to the sound of that word. They have also a very peculiar croaking note of alarm whilst at the water, which much resembles the loud croak of a frog. On one occasion one of these Parrots was caught in a hut, where it had apparently been attracted by the light of a bush lamp; it was put into a box, with a handful of dry grass. On examination the next morning the bird could not be seen; it had placed the dry grass in a heap and had drawn out the inside straw by straw until it had formed a hole, in which it had concealed itself.

"These birds are pretty generally distributed through the north and north-west of this colony; they come and go according to the nature of the season. When the early season is wet, the porcupine grass flourishes and bears large quantities of seed, on which the bird feeds; but if on the contrary the season is a dry one, the grass does not seed, and no birds are to be seen."

The Night Parrakeet has the upper parts olive-green, spotted and streaked with black and yellow; abdomen yellow, with irregular black bands at the sides; under tail-coverts yellow; wings greyish-brown; tail blackish, with yellow bands. Total length about 9½ inches. The sexes are alike.

This species has been represented in the Zoological Society's Gardens.

APPENDIX.

THE RED-CROWNED, OR VARIED LORIKEET.

Ptilosclera versicolor (Vig.).

One of the objects of the present work is to treat of every species, comprised under the title, that has ever been imported alive into Great Britain; but when writing of the Loriidæ the species now under notice was absolutely unknown in a living state in Europe, so was not mentioned. Since then, however, on November 15, 1902, to be exact, some eight or nine pairs were received in London by Mr. Hamlyn, the well-known bird dealer in St. George Street, London Docks. Aware of my fondness for rare Parrakeets, Mr. Hamlyn sent a pair down to me the evening of their arrival, which I was glad to be able to secure. One pair went at the same time to the Zoological Gardens, and the others were distributed amongst various aviculturists in different parts of the country. Some of these birds had the characteristic red on the head conspicuously developed, while in others it was almost absent, and by some the red-crowned birds were taken to be males and the others females. Knowing, however, how difficult it is to distinguish the sex of Lorikeets, I had little faith in this difference and took those without the red crowns to be merely immature birds. With most of the Lorikeets the colours increase in depth and brilliance with age, an old female often being more highly coloured than a younger male; and so I believe it to be with *Ptilosclera*. My own pair were evidently quite young when obtained, and although I have not the least doubt that they were a true pair, neither became so well coloured as the adult bird in the accompanying plate. The series of skins in the British Musuem entirely fails to help one to arrive at any definite conclusions as to distinguishing the sexes of this species, as they are almost all bad specimens and unsexed.

I found this species very shy and nervous, and not nearly so active or interesting as any other Lorikeets I have kept. It does not appear to be particularly delicate. My pair absolutely refused to eat seed, but took to sweetened milk-sop readily. They were particularly fond of sweet-water grapes, but did not care much for other fresh fruit, although they would sometimes nibble at preserved raisins and figs. I finally parted with them, in exchange for some other birds.

The Varied Lorikeet has its home in Northern and Western Australia, "where," Gould informs us, "its suctorial mode of feeding leads it, like the other members of the genus, to frequent the flowery *Eucalypti*." Gilbert, quoted by Gould, says that it "congregates in immense numbers; and when a flock is on the wing their movements are so regular and simultaneous it might easily be mistaken for a cloud passing rapidly along, were it not for the utterance of the usual piercing scream, which is frequently so loud as to be almost deafening. They feed on the topmost branches of the *Eucalypti* and *Melaleucæ*. I observed them to be extremely abundant during the month of August on all the small islands in Van Diemen's Gulf."

The following interesting letter, dated November 2, 1902, appears in the *Emu* (vol. ii., p. 218), above the signature of Mr. F. L. Berney, and refers to this species in North Queensland: "I am forwarding a skin of a Lorikeet (female) obtained on the river here, where during the past month it has been numerous, feeding on the honey of the bauhinia blossoms and the river gums. Never saw it on the ground except when down at water. It apparently lives almost entirely on honey. One we caught, and which has taken very kindly to captivity, is reported never to eat seed, but to subsist on sugar and water, with perhaps now and again a small portion of bread soaked in sugar and water. I examined three specimens recently that suicided in a well. They were all females, and, like the one I skinned, contained in their ovaries only very minute eggs. The bird sent fell into the sheep water-trough. I rescued it (only to make a specimen), when it squealed so vigorously that in an instant I was standing in a cloud of the Parrots, which settled on my arms, hands, shoulders, and hat till they weighed down the broad felt brim of the latter, almost to shut out my sight. There must have been two or three dozen on me. It was a wonderfully pretty sight, and I should much have liked to have caught the picture with a camera."

According to Mr. A. J. Campbell, the nest and eggs are as yet undescribed.

Prevailing colour green, with yellowish streaks over almost the entire body; forehead and crown bright red; back of the head greyish-blue; ear-coverts yellow; breast vinous-red; quills yellowish on the outer web; tail green, edged with yellow. The immature birds are more streaked with yellow, and have the forehead and lores only red. Total length about 8 inches.

Page 60.

THE RED-BELLIED CONURE.
Pyrrhura vittata (Shaw).

I am informed that some of these Conures were offered for sale in London in 1898; and three specimens, two males and one female, were obtained by the writer on August 24th, 1903. The two males commenced at once to fight for the possession of the female, and one had to be removed. The pair are extremely affectionate to one another and the male frequently feeds the female, and there would seem to be every prospect of their breeding.

Page 71.

THE LINEOLATED PARRAKEET.
Bolborhynchus lineolatus (Cass.).

This species, which has always been a rare importation into Europe, has recently been brought over somewhat freely by a dealer who makes a speciality of South American birds. The present writer has obtained a pair, and finds them extremely quiet and gentle little birds.

Page 123.

THE BLACK-TAILED PARRAKEET.
Polytelis melanura (Vig.).

Mrs. Johnstone, of Bury St. Edmunds, has this year (1903), succeeded in breeding this species in her aviary, one young bird being reared.

Page 158.

MASTERS'S PARRAKEET.
Platycercus mastersianus, Ramsay.

Mr. Frank Finn recently suggested to me that this was merely a variety of Pennant's Parrakeet. I have therefore carefully examined the specimen living in the Zoological Society's Gardens, and I find that its plumage has altered very considerably within the last few months. The blue on the back and under parts has given place to the red of the mature Pennant, and the only difference I could detect between this bird and a Pennant in a neighbouring cage with which I compared it, was in the yellow centres to some of the tail-feathers; this colour, however, is not so extensive as when the bird was figured in the *Proceedings of the Zoological Society*. The colored plate there given is now totally unlike the bird from which it was drawn. I have no hesitation whatever in saying that this is not a good species, but merely an abnormal variety of *Platycercus elegans*.

PAGE 163.

THE YELLOW-RUMPED PARRAKEET.
Platycercus flaveolus, Gould.

A pair of these fine Parrakeets nested in Mr. Fasey's aviaries at Snaresbrook during the present summer (1903), and two young birds were hatched, but died in the nest when about three weeks old.

PAGE 170.

THE RED-MANTLED PARRAKEET.
Platycercus erythropeplus, Salvad.

In writing of this species, I stated that it was the opinion of some ornithologists that it was merely a hybrid between *Platycercus elegans* and *P. eximius*, and I also remarked that "it should not be at all difficult to solve the problem once and for all by any aviculturist who possesses aviary accommodation for experimenting in hybridising Parrakeets." In the *Avicultural Magazine* for August, 1903, Mrs. Johnstone published the following communication, which, I think, quite settles the question: "Mr. Cocksedge, in his aviaries at Beyton, bred two fine Red-mantled Parrakeets from a cock Pennant and a hen Red Rosella. These nested and hatched two young ones, but they died when a few days old.

.   .   .   .   .

"They passed into my possession and I had them some time, but I parted with them at the end of last year. I have had frequent nests of this cross in my aviaries. This year two, but in only one case were the eggs fertile, but the young birds (two) were killed by a weasel about two weeks after they left the nest."

PAGE 183.
BARNARD'S PARRAKEET.
Barnardius barnardi (Vig. and Horsf.).

This species has bred again this year (1903) in Mrs. Johnstone's aviary; and Mr. Fasey has obtained young hybrids between this species and the Yellow-naped Parrakeet (*Barnardius semitorquatus*).

PAGE 206.
THE MANY-COLOURED PARRAKEET.
Psephotus multicolor (Kuhl).

This beautiful Parrakeet has bred successfully this year in Mr. Fasey's and in my own aviaries; in each case three young birds have been reared, two males and one female with Mr. Fasey, and three females with me. Mr. Fasey kindly allowed me to see his young birds the day after they left the nest, and the sexes were then clearly distinguishable, the cocks showing more bluish-green on the face than the hens, and a distinct yellow band on the wing.

In my own aviary, an upright box with the entrance-hole near the top was chosen. On the bottom of the box was a layer of dry earth, about one inch deep, in which the hen hollowed out a slight depression and deposited three eggs. She commenced to sit on April 30, and the third egg hatched on May 22. The first young bird left the nest on June 20, the second on the 21st, and the third not until the 28th of the month. I have never seen young birds stronger on the wing than these young Many-colours were immediately they left the nest. The parents continued to feed the young for nearly a month after they had flown, although they were perfectly capable of feeding themselves when they had been out a fortnight or less.

While nesting, and when the young were being reared, the adult birds were most impatient for green food, especially chickweed and groundsel, although there was abundance of grass growing in the aviary. Soft food of all kinds was rejected.

The birds showed no inclination to breed a second time, which is rather strange when it is remembered that the nearly-allied Red-rumped Parrakeet (*Psephotus hæmatonotus*) will frequently rear three broods in a season.

THE SOLITARY OR RUFFED LORIKEET.

Calliptilus solitarius (Lath.).
Coloured Figure, MIVART'S *Loriidæ*, Pl. XXV.

In November, 1911, several of these very beautiful Lorikeets were brought from the Fiji Islands by Dr. Philip Manson-Bahr. It may be described as bright green on the back, red below, with a very dark blue cap and a band of the same colour on the abdomen. The feathers of the neck are very long and pointed, and of a vivid green, and below these is a narrow band of similarly shaped feathers of bright red, these long feathers forming a ruff on the back of the neck.

Mr. E. L. Layard, writing of this species in the *Proceedings of the Zoological Society* in 1875, observes " This lovely little bird, called ' Kula ' by the natives, is found throughout the [Fiji] islands, its favourite food being the flowers of the *Erythrina* when in bloom, or those of the cocoanut when others fail. . . . They are trapped in great numbers by the natives for sale to the Tongans and Samoans, who periodically pluck them, their crimson feathers being much used for ornamentation. Europeans find much difficulty in keeping them alive, even for a short period ; but I am told the native girls chew sugar-cane and berries and allow the birds to feed from their lips."

This species appears to be very susceptible to cold, but not difficult as regards their feeding, since Dr. Bahr was very successful in bringing them home on a diet of oatmeal porridge and condensed milk.

JOHNSTONE'S LORIKEET.

Trichoglossus johnstoniæ, Hartert.
Coloured Figure, *Avicultural Magazine*, Jan., 1906. p. 83.

In a collecting trip undertaken by Mr. Walter Goodfellow in 1903, to the mountains of Mindanao, a species of Lorikeet was discovered at an altitude of some 8,000 feet, which proved to be new to science, and was described at a meeting of the British Ornithologist Club in October of that year, being named after Mrs. Johnstone, a well-known aviculturist, on whose behalf Mr. Goodfellow had undertaken several expeditions.

In 1905 Mr. Goodfellow succeeded in bringing home living specimens of this Lorikeet, a pair of which subsequently bred in Mrs. Johnstone's aviaries at Groombridge, the event being recorded in the *Avicultural Magazine* of November, 1906.

The prevailing colour of this species is grass-green, the feathers of the under surface being dull sulphur-yellow, margined with green. The forehead is dark rosy red, as also is the upper part of the cheeks and the space surrounding the lower mandible, while a line of dark purplish brown runs from the eyes backwards to the nape. The bill is red and the legs and feet grey.

THE BLACK-THROATED LORIKEET.

Trichoglossus nigrigularis, G. R. Gray.
Coloured Figure, *Avicultural Magazine*, November, 1905.

This beautiful Lorikeet occurs in the South of New Guinea and the Aru and Ké Islands. It is very closely allied to the Green-naped Lorikeet (*Trichoglossus cyanogrammus*) of Western New Guinea, described at page 5. It differs from the latter species in having less purple on the occiput and narrower transverse bands on the feathers of the breast. The red colour of the breast is also of a slightly more orange hue, and the abdomen is darker. It is common in the Aru Islands, and was first imported by Mr. Walter Goodfellow in 1904, and has been included in some of the later collections of birds that have come from that district. Mr. W. A. Harding, describing a pair of this species which came into his possession soon after their first arrival in 1904, says that "Their habits in captivity generally resembled those of a pair of Swainson's Lorikeets inhabiting an adjoining cage. They performed in a rather exaggerated degree, the same amusing antics, acrobatic feats and quaint dances, but were less noisy and of a more gentle disposition."

PAGE 4.

FORSTEN'S LORIKEET, *Trichoglossus forsteni* was bred successfully in 1905 by Mrs. Mitchell, as recorded in the *Avicultural Magazine* of November in that year. The young bird is described as follows :—
" The plumage is just like that of its parents, the rose-red on the breast and under wing-coverts, and the green on the wing is quite as light as in the adults. The head is rather duller, and the eye is dark, without the red light the old birds have. The underpart of the body is well-feathered and just the colouring of the parents, but grey down shows amongst the red feathers on the breast."

ROSENBERG'S LORIKEET.

Trichoglossus rosenbergi, Schleg.
Coloured Figure, Mivart's *Loriidæ*, Pl. XXXVIII.

This Lorikeet inhabits Misori Island and North-west New Guinea, and a single example was imported by Mr. Frost in 1920.

It has a blue head, becoming purple towards the occiput, a narrow red band on the occiput, and a yellowish-green band, sometimes mingled with red, on the nape. The breast and lower abdomen are red, the feathers edged with dark blue.

WEBER'S LORIKEET.

Psitteuteles weberi, Büttikofer.

This Lorikeet, from the Island of Flores, was described by Dr. Büttikofer in Max Weber's *Zoologische Ergebnisse einer Reise in Neiderländisch Ost-Indien* in 1894, and well figured in colour by Keulemans. It was only known by specimens in the Leyden Museum until 1898, when a series was received by the Tring Museum.

In 1904 a living specimen was obtained by Mrs. Johnstone, of Groombridge, who described it as "a lively and interesting bird, which reminded me much of the Blue Mountain Lorikeet, having the same lively manner and quick, alert movements. The colouring was a harmony of green: blue-green head, leaf-green back, and yellow-green bar across the breast and nape. The eye was ruby colour and the beak a coral-red. He made great advances to a hen Perfect Lorikeet, and performed the curious love-dance which is peculiar to most of the Lorikeets. He rarely screamed; in fact his note was not unpleasant unless alarmed, when it became unpleasantly shrill."

GOLDIE'S LORIKEET, *Glossopsittacus goldiei,* of S.E. New Guinea, **THE PURPLE-CROWNED LORIKEET,** *G. porphyrocephalus,* of Western and South Australia, and the **LITTLE LORIKEET,** *G. pusillus* of Eastern Australia and Tasmania, have very probably been imported on rare occasions.

STELLA'S LORIKEET.

Charmosyna stellæ, A. B. Meyer.
Coloured Figure, Mivart's *Loriidæ,* Pl. LVIII.

This very beautiful Lorikeet occurs in South-east New Guinea, and was first imported by Mr. Goodfellow in 1908, for Mr. Brook, in whose aviaries young were reared. Not only is it adorned with most brilliant colours, but it is of a very slender and elegant shape, with long pointed tail. It may be described as follows :—Prevailing colour of the male, carmine red; back and wings dark green; a collection of long feathers on the occiput, lilac blue; nape black; rump bluish purple; lower breast, sides of abdomen and thighs blackish purple; middle of abdomen, under tail and under wing-coverts crimson; tail dark green, the two middle feathers passing into orange-red and then into yellow at the tips, the outer feathers yellow at the tips and crimson on the base of the inner webs. The bill is red and the feet orange. The female has the lower back and sides of the rump bright yellow.

WILHELMINA'S LORIKEET, *Hypocharmosyna wilhelminæ* (A. B. Meyer), the **PLEASING LORIKEET**, *H. placens* (Temm.), and the **FAIR LORIKEET**, *Charmosynopsis pulchella* (Gray), three very beautiful species from New Guinea, were obtained by Mr. Walter Goodfellow in 1908. Of the first, a single example was secured, but died before reaching our shores. Of the second, a single example, and of the third, eight individuals reached this country alive, and a young bird was reared in Mr. Brook's aviaries.

WEDDELL'S CONURE.

Conurus weddelli, Deville.

This Conure inhabits the interior of Brazil, Amazonia, Bolivia and Ecuador. A living example was included in a collection of Conures imported by Messrs. Chapman in 1925, and probably others have arrived with collections from Brazil.

The head is greyish-brown, the feathers tipped with dull blue; the throat and upper breast green with bluish reflections; the lower breast, abdomen and under wing-coverts yellowish-green; quills deep blue; tail, above blue, the feathers green at the base; upper parts green with an olive tinge.

The sexes are alike.

WHITLEY'S CONURE.

Conurus (Aratinga) whitleyi, Kinnear.
Coloured Figure, Avicultural Magazine, 1926.

A large Conure in the collection of Mr. Herbert Whitley, of Paignton, Devonshire, was pronounced by a conference of ornithologists to belong to an unnamed species. It had been purchased from the well-known London dealer, Mr. Chapman, and had probably come from Brazil. Mr. N. B. Kinnear, of the British Museum (Natural History), described this bird in the *Bulletin of the British Ornithologists' Club,* Vol. XLVI., page 82. He gives its generic title as *Aratinga,* a name which is said to have priority to, and which, therefore, must supersede that of *Conurus.* The formal description is as follows :—

" *Aratinga whitleyi,* sp. nov.

" Head, neck, back and wing-coverts grass-green with a yellowish tinge ; forehead flame-coloured, turning to yellow posteriorly. Rump saffron-yellow, with a greenish tinge ; upper side of tail with outer webs of feathers verditer-blue, edged with black, inner webs green tinged with bluish, under side of tail black. Primaries blue ; secondaries with outer webs green, inner blue ; under wing-coverts greenish yellow. Throat and neck smoky-green ; abdomen orange, turning to flame-colour in the middle ; thighs greenish-yellow, with a flame-coloured patch just above the tarsus. Iris greyish-grown ; naked skin round the eye pearl-grey ; tarsus and feet flesh-colour.

" Total length, 408 mm., wing 216."

PAGE 37.

THE RED-HEADED CONURE *(Conurus rubrolarvatus)* was successfully bred by Mr. Shore-Bailey at Westbury in 1925, and the event recorded in the *Avicultural Magazine* for December of that year. He there writes:—"Quite early in June they took possession of one of my nesting-boxes, and on the 16th the first egg was laid. Four was the clutch, and of these two were hatched on or about the 19th July. I was away on holiday at the time, so cannot describe the young ones in down. When I returned . . . as far as I could see they were covered with greenish down, the heads only being feathered. They were then about three weeks old. A fortnight later I had another look; they were feathered nearly all over, those on the back and wings being marked very much like those of the Lineated Parrakeet, with faint transverse barrings. On 1st September . . . on lifting the lid of the box, both birds flew out. They were quite strong on the wing. To my surprise the barrings on the upper feathers had disappeared, and they were uniform bright green all over, and but for their smaller size could not be distinguished from my White-eyed Parrots (*Conurus leucophthalmus*). I suppose they will not get their red heads until their second or third year."

PAGE 60.

Several specimens of the **RED-BELLIED CONURE** *(Conurus vittata)*, have been imported during recent years, and in 1924 a pair owned by Mr. W. Shore-Bailey successfully reared young in his aviaries at Westbury. He describes the event as follows:—
" About the middle of July I missed the hen, and on looking into the nest-box found her sitting on five eggs, and on the 24th four young ones were hatched. Both parents fed them, and they grew fairly fast; but there was little sign of feathering until they were nearly a month old, then the white around the eye began to show, and a week later their heads were feathered and wings well grown, but it was not until 13th September

that the first youngster left the nest. It was exactly like its parents, and active and strong on the wing. Three others left the nest in due course, all very nice birds. From the first they nibbled away at apples, of which they are very fond, although both parents fed them for a week or two after they left the nesting box, to which, by the way, they regularly retreated at night. These little conures are charming birds and as playful as monkeys, but I can quite imagine that they would do some mischief in a sparsely planted aviary."

AZARA'S CONURE, *Pyrrhura chiripepe* (Vieill.), which inhabits Paraguay and Colombia, appears to be a geographical race of *P. vittata* (page 60) of Brazil. The two are, in fact, with difficulty distinguished from one another, the principal difference being in the greater extent of the red on the tail and lower back in *P. vittata.*

Mr. W. Shore-Bailey secured some Conures in 1922, which were pronounced by the authorities at the British Museum to belong to this species or race. A pair of these bred successfully in his aviaries in 1923, one young bird being reared.

THE GUIANA PARROTLET.

Psittacula guianensis (Sw.).

When this work was first published, only one species of the genus *Psittacula* had been imported, namely, the well-known Passerine Parrotlet *P. passerina* (page 73). Since then, however, three other forms have reached this country alive.

The Guiana Parrotlet occurs in Amazona, Venezuela, Colombia, Trinidad and probably in Guiana, though this appears to be uncertain, in spite of its name. It has been imported on several occasions in recent years. In size and disposition it resembles the Passerine Parrotlet, but it differs from that species in having the upper tail-coverts, in the male, emerald green instead of blue, the lower back and rump are slightly shaded with blue in old examples. The innermost primary-coverts are blue. The female is entirely green.

Examples of the **CELESTIAL PARROTLET**, *Psittacula cœlestis* (referred to on page 72), were imported by Mr. Walter Goodfellow in September, 1915. The male has the rump ultramarine blue, and a blue streak behind the eye. The female has no blue whatever. It inhabits Ecuador and Peru.

The **BLUE-RUMPED PARROTLET**, *P. cyanopygia,* from Western Mexico, has also been imported. The male has the rump turquoise blue, that of the female being bright green.

THE ARU PARRAKEET.
Geoffroyus aruensis (Gray).

Of the twenty or more species of the genus *Geoffroyus,* which are distributed throughout the Moluccas, the Papuan Islands and the Timor group, only one appears to have been imported into this country, Mr. Walter Goodfellow having successfully brought home some two or three young examples of *G. aruensis* in 1925. In all of the species of this genus the colour is green, and in the majority the male has a red head tinged with blue on the hinder part. *G. aruensis* has also a brown spot on the wing-coverts, the upper mandible of the bill being orange-red and the lower mandible black. The female has the head brown. Total length, about nine and three-quarter inches, of which the tail occupies less than three inches.

EVERETT'S GREAT-BILLED PARRAKEET.
Tanygnathus everetti, Tweed.
Coloured Figure, Cat. B. Brit. Mus., XX., Pl. X.

A living specimen of this Parrakeet was obtained by Mrs. Johnstone in 1903, from the Philippine Islands. It may be distinguished from other members of the genus (page 90) by the bright blue edges to the feathers of the upper back and the deep turquoise-blue of the lower back and upper tail-coverts.

LAYARD'S PARRAKEET.
Palæornis calthropæ (Layard).
Coloured Figure, LEGGE, *Birds of Ceylon*, Pl. 6.

This is one of the most beautiful of the group of " ring-necked " Parrakeets, and is confined to the island of Ceylon, where it appears to be numerous in the forest-covered hills. It has very seldom been imported to Europe, and the author has only seen two or three living specimens.

Colonel Legge, in his *Birds of Ceylon*, gives the following account of *Palæornis calthropæ* :—

" Layard's Parrakeet frequents the outskirts and open places in the interior of forests, patna-woods, wooded gorges, and glades in the vicinity of hills ; it associates in moderately-sized flocks, and is a very noisy and restless bird, uttering its harsh ' crake ' on the wing, as it dashes up and down the magnificent valleys and forest-clad glens of the Ceylon mountains, and enlivens these romantic solitudes with its swift and headlong flight. It is entirely arboreal in its habits, settling in flocks among the leaves of its favourite trees, and silently devouring the fruit-seeds and buds on which it subsists. It is very partial to the wild fig, the fruit of the Kanda-tree, the wild cinnamon-tree, and the flowers of the Bomba-tree. After feeding in the mornings it becomes garrulous, assembling in small parties in shady trees, and keeping up a chattering note ; towards evening it commences to feed again, and before going to roost roams about in small flocks, constantly uttering its loud, harsh note, and settling frequently on the tops of conspicuous and lofty trees. In the Singha-Rajah forest their presence at evening was more conspicuous than that of any other bird ; they darted up and down the deep gorges and across the small Kurrakan clearings in the forest, keeping up an incessant din ; now and then they rested on the top of some dead tree standing in the cheena, and then suddenly glanced off, shooting with arrow-like speed between the trees of the forest, again to appear as they swept up the valley and away over the top of the gloomy jungle."

This species is somewhat less in size than the well-known Ring-necked Parrakeet, *P. torquata,* with a considerably shorter tail. It may be described as follows :—Head, nape and back bluish-grey, becoming more distinctly blue on the rump and upper tail-coverts. The forehead, lores and fore-part of the cheeks green ; a broad green collar and the underpart of the same colour ; a narrow bluish ring separates the grey of the head from the green collar ; on each side of the neck is a broad black stripe or ' moustache ' ; wings green, scapulars greenish grey ; smaller wing-coverts greyish blue, the median coverts yellowish green ; tail blue above, yellowish underneath, and tipped with yellow. Iris white, upper mandible of the male coral-red with a yellowish tip, lower mandible dusky red. Legs and feet plumbeous.

The female is very much like the male, but duller in colour, with the bill dusky black.

PAGE 111.

The **DERBYAN PARRAKEET,** *Palæornis derbyana*. In July, 1924, Mr. John Frostick obtained from a ship hailing from China, a large Parrakeet which he identified by comparison with specimens in the British Museum as *Palæornis salvadorii,* of Oustalet. This bird went subsequently into the possession of the late Mrs. Dalton-Burgess, and at her death into that of Mr. Hedges, who exhibited it at a bird show at the Crystal Palace in February, 1926.

At the Tring Museum there is a good series of specimens both of *P. derbyana* and of the so-called *P. salvadorii,* and a careful comparison of these reveals the fact that the two cannot be distinguished from one another, and the name given to these birds by Oustalet must be regarded as a synonym of *P. derbyana*. In this species, the original description of which was taken from a female, the sexes differ considerably, the male having the under-surface a blue-violet, or almost a plum-colour, whereas that of the female is of a much more lavender colour. A coloured plate of the male, taken from the living specimen in Mr. Hedges's possession, appeared in the *Avicultural Magazine* for June, 1926.

THE GREEN-WINGED KING PARRAKEET.
Aprosmictus chloropterus, Ramsay.
Coloured Figure, GOULD, *B. New Guinea*, Vol. V., Pl. 9.

This very beautiful Parrakeet inhabits the south-east of New Guinea and was described by Dr. Ramsay in the *Proceedings of the Linnean Society of New South Wales* in 1879. The first living specimens brought to this country were two males, obtained by Mr. Walter Goodfellow in 1909. These were acquired by the Zoological Society of London and lived for several years in the Regent's Park Gardens. Another was brought home by Mr. Goodfellow in 1925.

The following is a description of this fine species :—

Male.—Head, neck and under-surface carmine-red ; nape, rump, upper tail-coverts and under wing-coverts bright blue ; upper back and scapulars black, tinged with green ; wings dark green ; a yellowish-green patch on the wings ; edge of the wing blue ; tail above dark blue with a greenish tinge towards the base ; quills and underside of tail black ; bill blackish with the base of the upper mandible red. Feet black.

Female.—Green, the feathers of the throat and breast edged with red ; the abdomen red ; rump and upper tail-coverts blue ; central tail-feathers dark green, becoming blue towards the tips ; the outer tail-feathers blue, green at the base and tipped with rose-red.

Two other species of *Aprosmictus* have been imported : *A. amboinensis* from Amboina and Ceram, and *A. sulaensis* from Sula Island.

THE TAVIUNI PARRAKEET.

Pyrrhulopsis taviunensis, Layard.

This species is closely allied to the Tabuan Parrakeet referred to on page 136. It is confined to the Fijian island of Taviuni, and differs from *tabuensis* in being smaller and lacking the blue collar on the nape. It was first imported by Dr. Manson-Bahr, in 1911, and others have reached this country more recently.

THE ABYSSINIAN LOVEBIRD.

Agapornis taranta (Stanley).
Coloured Figure, Avicultural Magazine, November, 1909.

This fine Lovebird inhabits north-east Africa, from Abyssinia to Shoa. It is said to live in families of some six to ten individuals, and to be found both in the plains and at elevations up to 10,000 feet. Their flight is usually high and rapid and they frequent the tops of the trees.

This species was apparently first imported into Europe in 1906, when a few examples reached Germany, one or two reaching England in 1909. It remained very rare in collections until 1923, when a London dealer imported a considerable number, and it is now a comparatively common aviary bird.

It was first bred in captivity in 1925, both in England and on the Continent. In Germany, Herr Schütze was successful in rearing young, and recorded his experience as follows :—" At the end of January, the female remained in the nesting box and appeared to be incubating. On the 17th of February I made an examination ; result, three almost round eggs. Another inspection on the 23rd showed two young ones hatched out, the third egg being infertile. The incubation period appears to be about 18 days, but I cannot give it exactly. The female very seldom left the box, and then only for a short time, but she was diligently fed by the male. From the 26th of February onwards the female was more frequently outside the nesting-box. The male as yet did not feed the young direct, only the female, and she the young, which cried out loudly. This changed at the beginning of March, when the male took part in the feeding of the young. On March 16th the young were almost covered with feathers, and when removed made no complaint, but squatted on the ground. On the 19th of March they looked out of the box for the first time, but a further ten days elapsed before the first young one, apparently a female, left the nest. In size and colour it resembled the old female, but the red of the bill was paler. The second young one followed it on the 2nd of April, also a female. On April 9th the young began to feed themselves, but were still diligently fed by their parents. On April 27th they were able to look after themselves and eat anything, though they still begged for food from the old ones."

Herr Schütze supplied his birds with a mixture of soft-food (hard-boiled egg, ants' pupæ and bread made with eggs and milk) during the rearing of the young, which took to it readily on leaving the nest. He made the very interesting discovery that this Lovebird apparently does not construct a nest like the other species of *Agapornis* do, but "the female plucks feathers from her breast at the outset of breeding and uses these as a nest foundation."

The sexes of this Lovebird differ in colouration.

Male.—Green, the forehead, lores and a ring round the eyes red; primary feathers brown, secondaries bastard-wing and primary-coverts black. Tail green, with a broad band of black near the extremity, the inner web of the lateral feathers yellowish towards the base. The bill is bright red and the feet grey.

Female.—Lacks the red colouring on the head.

FISCHER'S LOVEBIRD.

Agapornis fischeri, Reichenow.
Coloured Figure, Avicultural Magazine, July, 1926.

This species inhabits the country bordering the Victoria Nyanza and was first brought to this country by Mr. K. V. Painter, together with specimens of

A. personata in 1925. It is one of the group in which the face is rosy-red, and is closely allied to *A. roseicollis* on the one hand and *A. lilianæ* on the other. Mr. Painter's birds were taken to the United States, and, so far as the author is aware, no others have ever been imported to Europe alive.

This species, in which the sexes are alike, differs from *A. lilianæ* chiefly in its upper tail-coverts being blue. The following is its description : The forehead deep orange red, fading into rose-red on the cheeks and throat ; top of the head olive-green, tinged with reddish on the occiput ; hind neck reddish-yellow ; throat yellowish ; back and wings grass-green ; underparts paler green ; upper tail-coverts bright ultramarine blue ; central tail-feathers green, the outer ones red at the base, green in the middle, and pale-blue at the tip and with a black band before the blue tip. The bill is coral red, the cere and naked skin round the eyes white, and the feet grey.

THE NYASA LOVEBIRD.
Agapornis lilianæ, Shelley.
Coloured Figure, Avicultural Magazine, July, 1926.

A considerable number of Lovebirds belonging to this species arrived in London in February, 1926, this being the first importation of living examples of this bird, which was described by the late Captain Shelley in 1894, and named after Miss Lilian Lutley Sclater. It occurs on the banks of the Shiré River in Nyasaland, and in a few localities on the Zambesi and the Luangwa Valley. In the *Ibis* for 1864, Sir John Kirk wrote of this Lovebird, which he then believed to be *A. roseicollis* : " Found in one spot, limited to about twenty miles, on the Shiré, between Nyasa and the rapids. It was never seen elsewhere, but was found there on two occasions. It is gregarious." Captain Boyd Alexander met with *A. lilianæ* near Chicowa, and at Chishomba, some thirty miles up the river, and also at Zumbo. He described it as frequenting enclosed country overgrown with mimosa-bush, in flocks which sometimes numbered as many as twenty birds. " At Zumbo," he writes, " this species was fairly numerous within a small area of country, outside of which it was not found. Throughout the days small flocks would continually visit the water and travel back again, the same way as they had come, to some thick retreat among the undergrowth of acacia, and in their journey they were ever uttering their rounds of cries, almost in unison, but so shrill that they almost set one's teeth on edge.

" A half-cast at Matacania, just below Zumbo, had a number of these Lovebirds in an aviary. They did not seem to mind confinement."

This Lovebird promises to thrive well in captivity and to be a very free breeder, those recently imported commencing to build their nests almost immediately they were given suitable accommodation.

Dr. Maurice Amsler, writing in the *Avicultural Magazine* for May, 1926, remarks :—

" My own pair were kept in a small wire cage for a few days, but the moment I placed them in a large box cage some three feet long with a nest box attached they disappeared into the nest, and at once started to make nesting material of their perches.

" Nothing came amiss to them; sticks as thick as a lead pencil, millet sprigs, hay, twigs, and more especially bark, which they chewed off green willow twigs. These birds are in a living room, and I have had many opportunities of watching them, yet I have never seen them put their nesting material under their rump feathers as do the Peach-faced and Black-cheeked Lovebirds. Both sexes incubate, sometimes separately, more often together, building continues after the laying of the first egg. I counted up to five, after which it was impossible to get a view of the nest cavity without seriously disturbing the nest and possibly breaking the eggs.

"*A. lilianæ* is often called Nyasa ' Peach-faced ' Lovebird. This is a misnomer, I feel sure, as the species is much more closely allied to the Black-cheeked (*A. nigrigenis*); its size, shape, quick movements, white circum-orbital zone, and especially its call and alarm notes constantly renewed, are of the Black-cheeked Lovebirds which we all bred so freely some years ago."

A. lilianæ is about equal in size to the well-known Red-faced Lovebird of West Africa. The head and throat are rosy brick-red, brighter on the forehead, the back of the head and hind neck greenish-yellow; lower throat with a yellowish tinge; inner web of tail-feathers, all but the middle pair, red, with a black band near the extremity. The remainder of the plumage, including the rump, is grass-green. The bill is rosy-red and a broad ring of naked skin of a whitish hue surrounds the eyes. The sexes are superficially alike.*

THE BLACK-CHEEKED LOVEBIRD.
Agapornis nigrigenis, W. L. Sclater.
Coloured Figure, Avicultural Magazine, October, 1908.

This Lovebird was described in 1906 from specimens obtained by Dr. A. H. B. Kirkman in North-west Rhodesia in 1904. In 1908 a number were imported into Europe and since that time several have been bred in captivity, though not enough to establish the species as an aviary bird and it became scarce, but in June, 1926, a large number were imported by

* A collection from Northern Rhodesia which reached London in July, 1926, consisting chiefly of *Agapornis lilianæ* and *A. nigrigenis*, contained in addition a number of birds that were undoubtedly wild-caught hybrids between these two species.

Mr. Chapman. The late Mr. Reginald Phillipps was apparently the first to breed this species in England, and published an exhaustive account of the event in the *Avicultural Magazine* of October and November, 1908. The habits of the species do not differ materially from those of the other species of the genus. A nest, composed of small sticks, grass and strips of green bark is built in a hollow log or box, a habit common to the genus. The eggs, generally four in number, are white and smooth in texture, and the young, on leaving the nest, resemble their parents in colouration, though they are less bright in hue.

The following is a description of this beautiful Lovebird, in which the sexes are alike in plumage: General colour grass-green; forehead and crown sienna-brown; hinder part of the head and neck washed with yellowish-olive; sides of the face and throat blackish-brown; lower throat salmon-red; tail dark green, all of the feathers, except the central pair, having a red stripe near the base and a black bar near the extremity, which is bluish; the quills are dusky with a wash of blue on the outer webs. The bill is rosy-red with a broad whitish cere, and surrounding the eyes is a broad circle of bare whitish skin. The colour of the iris differs in the two sexes according to the late Mr. Reginald Phillipps, that of the male being pale yellow-brown, and of the female dark yellow-brown.

THE MASKED LOVEBIRD.
Agapornis personata, Reichenow.
Coloured Figure, Avicultural Magazine, July, 1926.

This very distinct and beautiful Lovebird inhabits East Africa from the Victoria Nyanza to Ugogo. So far as the author is aware, it has only once been imported at the date of writing (July, 1926), but with increased intercourse with its native land there is a prospect of others arriving. Mr. K. V. Painter, an enthusiastic American aviculturist, brought three living specimens of this Lovebird to London, *en route* for the United States, in 1925, and the present writer had the privilege of seeing and identifying them. Mr. Painter was subsequently successful in breeding them in his aviary at Cleveland, Ohio. He writes that his three birds were put into a large flying cage of which the inside part was about 14 feet square and ten feet high, with an outside flight of about the same size. He had no idea of any young ones coming until they suddenly appeared from the breeding boxes, "full grown and almost in mature plumage, their plumage is so like that of their parents that they are hardly distinguishable, excepting that the colours are a little fainter."

This species is easily distinguished by its blackish face and broad yellow collar. It is an extremely handsome bird, and may be described as follows :—Face (forehead, lores and anterior part of cheeks) deep brownish-black ; a broad band on the hind neck and throat yellow ; back and wings green ; upper breast reddish-orange ; upper tail-coverts pale blue ; two central tail-feathers green, the remainder orange at the base, green in the middle, then a black band and a yellowish tip. Bill coral-red ; cere white ; the feet lead-colour.

THE HOODED PARRAKEET.

Psephotus dissimilis, Collett.
Coloured Figure, MATHEWS, *B. of Australia*, Vol. VI., Pl. 314.

In the years 1909 and 1910 a number of Parrakeets were imported that were thought to belong to the species known as the Golden-shouldered Parrakeet *Psephotus chrysopterygius* (*antea* page 202). In that species the male has a distinct frontal band of yellow, which, however, was wanting in the newly imported birds, which proved to belong to a species described by Professor Collett in the *Proceedings of the Zoological Society for* 1898. He describes the forehead, lores and crown as dark chestnut, which is misleading, as, in fully adult birds, at least, these are black. This mistake in the original description led the late Mr. North to believe this black-hooded form to be undescribed, and to confer upon it the name of *P. cucullatus*. There is, however, no doubt that Collett's description refers to the species under notice.

Mr. Gregory Mathews, in his *Birds of Australia* places *P. dissimilis* in the synonymy of *P. chrysopterygius*, an arrangement which will not appeal to those who have known the two forms in the living state.

The golden-fronted form which was described by Gould as long ago as 1857, appears to be restricted to the central parts of Northern Queensland, but it had been lost sight of for many years except for a few birds which reached Europe alive in 1896, though from what exact locality these came was a mystery. However, in 1922, Mr. W. McLennan, who was collecting on behalf of Mr. H. L. White, re-discovered *P. chrysopterygius* at Coen, North Queensland, where they were breeding in tall ant-hills. Several young birds were secured and safely conveyed to Taronga Park, Sydney, where there were at the time a number of specimens of the Hooded Parrakeet (*P. dissimilis*) from the Northern Territory. Thus were the two forms placed side-by-side and a unique opportunity presented of comparing the difference, if any, not only in their colouring, but also in their habits and voice. Such a comparison was made by Mr. A. S. Le Souef, of the Taronga Zoological Park, and Mr. J. R. Kinghorn, of the Australian Museum, Sydney, and the result published as a paper in the *Emu* of July, 1924. From this there would appear to be no doubt whatever that the two are perfectly distinct species. The authors write:—" On comparing the two species, both with living specimens and skins in the Museum, we find that *P. chrysopterygius* is distinctly smaller and more slender that *P. dissimilis;* furthermore, it is much more active and perky, and has, in addition to the typical ' cluck-cluck ' note, a soft and pleasing whistle resembling ' joee-joee,' with an occasional ' jeeo,' neither of which have we heard uttered by *P. dissimilis,* the note of which is rather harsh.

" In *P. chrysopterygius* the head feathers, especially those on the fore-part of the crown, can be raised in the form of a crest, while *P. dissimilis* shows no disposition to raise these feathers."

The Hooded Parrakeet may be described as follows:—

Male.—Feathers, lores, crown, and a band extending down the nape to the mantle, black; cheeks and whole of the under-surface verdita-blue; the abdomen greenish-blue; under tail-coverts red; mantle greyish-brown; rump bright blue; upper tail-coverts yellowish-green; a large golden-yellow band, starting from the point of the shoulder and covering the lesser, median and greater wing-coverts; the quills black, edged with a bluish tint; two central tail-feathers olive-green at the base, passing into brownish-black at the extremity; the second pair bluish-green with lighter tips and blackish on the inner webs; the outer tail-feathers light bluish-green, crossed by a blackish band.

Female.—Forehead and crown greyish-olive; cheeks grey; upper surface and breast yellowish-green; abdomen bluish-green; rump, upper and under tail-coverts as in the male, but paler. According to Le Souef and Kinghorn, *P. dissimilis* is slightly larger in all its dimensions than *P. chrysopterygius*.

The **NORFOLK ISLAND PARRAKEET**, *Cyanorhamphus cooki*, Gray, is a local form of the Red-fronted Parrakeet (*C. novæ-zealandiæ*) described at page 229. It differs from the form occurring on the mainland in being larger and in possessing a stronger bill. The Marquis of Tavistock obtained two pairs in 1924.

The **BUDGERIGAR** *(Melopsittacus undulatus)*. When the article on this popular Parrakeet was written (page 244), the only abnormally coloured variety known in this country was the yellow Budgerigar, but in the year 1910 great excitement was caused amongst aviculturists by the appearance at a bird-show in London of a sky-blue variety. This was the first time that this very beautiful mutant had been seen in this country, but it seems to have originated in Belgium as long ago as 1882 in the aviaries of M. Limbosch.

In the blue variety of the Budgerigar the yellow pigment has disappeared, and thus we see that all those areas of the plumage which in the normal bird are yellow, are pure white, and all those parts that would be green in nature are blue. The variety is now so well known that it is being bred by many amateurs, while in France one firm alone is producing it in hundreds. The Olive Budgerigar is another established variety which breeds true to type. It has probably been produced by a careful admixture of the green and yellow forms.

By crossing the various coloured varieties of these Parrakeets and carefully selecting the offspring, other tints have been established, such as the cobalt and the grey.

The so-called White Budgerigar is generally nothing more than a very washed-out blue, and the anxiety of some amateurs to produce it has resulted in the deterioration of the original sky-blue variety.

INDEX.

Abyssinian Lovebird, 275.
acuticaudatus, Conurus. 28.
adelaidæ, Platycercus. 162.
Adelaide Parrakeet, 162.
adelaidensis, Platycercus. 159, 162.
æruginosus, Conurus. 44.
affinis, Palæornis. 119.
African Ring-necked Parrakeet, 104
Agapornis, 72, 139, 275.
  ,, *cana*, 141.
  ,, *fischeri*, 276.
  ,, *lilianæ*, 277.
  ,, *nigrigenis*, 279.
  ,, *personata*, 280.
  ,, *pullaria*, 143.
  ,, *roseicollis*, 145.
  ,, *taranta*, 275.
albirostris, Tanygnathus. 93.
Alexandra Parrakeet, 125.
alexandræ, Polyetlis. 121, 125.
  ,, *Spathopterus.* 125.
alexandri, Palæornis. 95, 114.
Alexandrine Parrakeet, 95, 96.
Alexandrine Parrakeet, Cinghalese, 96.
Alexandrine Parrakeet, Great-billed. 100.
Alexandrine Parrakeet, Indo-Burmese. 99.
Alexandrine Parrakeet, Nepalese. 98
All-Green Parrakeet, 79.
Alpine Parrakeet, 239.
alpinus, Platycercus. 239.
amathusia, Platycercus. 168.
amboinensis, Aprosmictus. 274.
Andaman Parrakeet, 119.
Antipodes Island Parrakeet, 227, 228.
Aprosmictus, 131.
  ,, *amboinensis*, 274.
  ,, *chloropterus*, 273.
  ,, *cyanopygius*, 132.
  ,, *sulaensis*, 274,
Aratinga whitleyi, 267.

Aru Parrakeet, 270.
aruensis, Geoffroyus, 270.
aurantia, Euphema. 219.
aureus, Conurus. 47.
auricapillus, Conurus. 35.
auriceps, Cyanorhamphus. 234.
Australian Grass-Parrakeet, 214.
  ,, Ground-Parrot, 228.
Azara's Conure, 269.
Aztec Conure, 41.
aztec, Conurus. 41.

Banded Parrakeet, 112.
Bank-Parrot, 54.
barnardi, Barnardius. 183, 260.
Barnardius, 183.
  ,, *barnardi*, 183, 260.
  ,, *macgillivrayi*, 187.
  ,, *occidentalis*, 190.
  ,, *semitorquatus*, 187, 260.
  ,, *zonarius*, 189.
Barnard's Parrakeet, 183, 260.
barrabandi, Polytelis. 121, 175.
Barraband's Parrakeet, 121, 175.
Bauer's Parrakeet, 189.
Beautiful Parrakeet, 197, 207.
Black-headed Conure, 36.
  ,, -tailed Parrakeet, 123, 258.
  ,, -throated Lorikeet, 263.
Blood-winged Parrakeet, 129.
Blossom-headed Parrakeet, 93, 104.
Blue-banded Parrakeet, 216.
Blue-bonnet Parrakeet, 167, 169, 191, 193.
Blue-bonnet Parrakeet, Red-vented, 191.
Blue-bonnet Parrakeet, Yellow-vented, 193.
Blue-cheeked Parrakeet, 168.
  ,, -crowned Conure, 28.
  ,, ,, Parrakeet, 91.
  ,, ,, Hanging-Parrakeet, 155
  ,, -faced Lorikeet, 4.

INDEX

Blue Mountain Lories, 9.
„ „ Lory, 6.
„ -rumped Parrakeet, 138.
„ „ Parrotlet, 270.
„ -winged Conure, 62.
„ „ Grass-Parrakeet, 216.
„ „ Love-bird, 73.
„ „ Parrotlet, 76
Blyth's Nicobar Parrakeet, 115.
Bolborhynchus, 71.
„ *lineolatus*, 71, 258.
bourkei, Neophema, 214.
Bourke's Grass-Parrakeet, 214.
„ Parrakeet, 195.
Brotogerys, 77.
„ *chiriri*, 79.
„ *chrysopterus*, 85.
„ *jugularis*, 82.
„ *pyrrhopterus*, 81.
„ *tirica*, 79.
„ *tui*, 85.
„ *tuipara*, 82, 83.
„ *virescens*, 80.
browni, Platycercus, 168.
Brown's Parrakeet, 168.
Brown-throated Conure, 44.
Budgerigar, 244, 284.
„ Blue, 284.
Burmese Slaty-headed Parrakeet, 109.
byroni, Cyanolyseus, 53, 57.

Cacatuidæ, 20.
cactorum, Conurus, 41.
Cactus Conure, 41.
cœlestis, Psittacula. 72.
Calliptilus solitarius, 261.
Calopsittacinæ, 20.
Calopsittacus novæ-hollandiæ, 20, 175.
calthropæ, Palæornis. 271.
cana, Agapornis. 141.
Canary-winged Parrakeet, 79.
caniceps, Palæornis. 115.
canicularis, Conurus. 48.
Carolina Conure, 48.

carolinensis, Conuropsis. 48.
Ceylon Lorikeet, 154.
Ceylonese Hanging-Parrakeet, 154
Charmosyna stellæ, 265.
Charmosynopsis pulchella, 266.
Chilian Conure, 58.
chiriri, Brotogerys. 79.
chlorolepidotus, Psitteuteles. 14.
chloropterus, Aprosmictus. 273.
chrysogastra, Neophema. 221.
chrysonotus, Loriculus. 153.
chrysopterus, Brotogerys. 85.
chrysopterygius, Psephotus. 202, 281.
chrysostoma, Euphema. 225.
Cinghalese Alexandrine Parrakeet, 96.
coccineopterus, Ptistes. 129.
Cockatiel, 20, 123, 175.
Cockatoo Parrakeet, 123.
concinnus, Glossopsittacus. 17, 84.
Conure, Azara's. 269.
„ Aztec. 41.
„ Black-headed. 36.
„ Blue-crowned. 28.
„ Blue-winged. 62.
„ Brown-throated. 44.
„ Cactus. 41.
„ Carolina. 48.
„ Chilian. 58.
„ Golden. 30.
„ „ -crowned. 47.
„ „ -headed. 35.
„ Greater Patagonian. 57.
„ Green. 39.
„ Jendaya. 32, 34.
„ Lesser Patagonian. 53.
„ Mexican. 39.
„ Pearly. 62.
„ Petz's. 48.
„ Red-bellied. 60, 258, 268.
„ „ -eared. 59.
„ „ -faced Conure, 37.
„ „ -headed. 37, 267.
„ „ -throated. 40.
„ St. Thomas'. 46.
„ Sharp-tailed. 28,

INDEX

Conure, Wagler's. 38.
,, Weddell's. 266.
,, White-eared. 61.
,, Whitley's. 267.
,, Yellow. 32.
,, ,, -headed. 33.
Conures, 26.
Conurinæ, 26, 72.
Conuropsis, 48.
,, *carolinensis*, 48.
Conurus, 28, 48.
,, *acuticaudatus*, 28.
,, *æruginosus*, 44.
,, *aureus*, 47.
,, *auricapillus*, 35.
,, *aztec*, 41.
,, *cactorum*, 41, 42.
,, *canicularis*, 48.
,, *chiripepe*, 269.
,, *guarouba*, 30, 32.
,, *hæmorrhous*, 28.
,, *holochlorus*, 39, 40.
,, *jendaya*, 33.
,, *leucophthalmus*, 39.
,, *luteus*, 32.
,, *nenday*, 36.
,, *patagonus*, 66.
,, *pertinax*, 46.
,, *rubrolarvatus*, 37, 267.
,, *rubritorques*, 40.
,, *solstitialis*, 32.
,, *wagleri*, 38, 39.
,, *weddelli*, 266.
cooki, Cyanorhamphus, 284.
cornutus, Nymphicus. 240.
Crimson-winged Parrakeet, 129.
cruentata, Pyrrhura. 59.
cucullatus, Psephotus. 282.
cyanocephala, Palæornis. 94, 104.
cyanogrammus, Trichoglossus. 5.
Cyanolyseus, 53.
,, *byroni*, 53, 57.
,, *patagonicus*, 53, 57.
cyanopygius, Aprosmictus. 132.
Cyanorhamphus, 227.
,, *auriceps*, 234.

Cyanorhamphus cooki, 284.
,, *malherbei*, 239.
,, *novæ-zealandiæ*, 229, 234.
,, *saisseti*, 234.
,, *unicolor*, 227.

derbyana, Palæornis. 111, 112, 273.
Derbyan Parrakeet, 111, 273.
discolor, Nanodes, 242.
dissimilis, Psephotus. 206, 281.
docilis, Palæornis. 104.

Earl of Derby's Parrakeet, 178.
" El Chocoyo," 39.
elegans, Neophema. 219.
,, Platycercus. 159, 259.
,, ,, var. *nigrescens*. 159.
Elegant Grass-Parrakeet, 219.
,, Parrakeet, 216.
eques, Palæornis. 100.
erythropeplus, Platycercus. 170, 259
erythropterus, Ptistes 129
eupatria, Palæornis 96,
Euphema aurantia, 219
,, *chrysostoma*, 225
,, *elegans*, 225
euteles, Psitteuteles 13
Everett's Parrakeet, 271.
everetti, Tanygnathus. 271.
eximius, Platycercus. 172.

fairchildii, Platycercus. 228.
fasciata, Palæornis. 112.
ferruginea, Microsittace. 58.
finschi, Palæornis. 109.
fischeri, Agapornis. 276.
flaveolus, Platycercus. 163, 259.
flaviventris, Platycercus. 164, 172.
formosus, Pezoporus. 228.
forsteni, Trichoglossus. 4, 264.
Forsten's Lorikeet, 4, 264.

galgulus, Loriculus. 155.
Geoffroyus aruensis,
Geopsittacus, 252.
,, *occidentalis*, 252.

Glossopsittacus, 16.
,, *concinnus,* 17, 84.
,, *goldiei,* 265.
,, *porphyrocephalus,* 265.
,, *pusillus,* 265.
Goat Parrakeet, 232.
goldiei, Glossopsittacus. 265.
Golden-backed Hanging-Parrakeet, 153.
Golden Conure, 30.
,, -crowned Conure, 47.
,, - ,, Parrakeet, 234.
,, -fronted Parrakeet, 83.
,, -headed Conure, 35.
,, - ,, Parrakeet, 166.
,, -shouldered Parrakeet, 202.
,, -winged Parrakeet, 85.
Grass-Parrakeet, Australian. 214.
,, - ,, Blue-winged. 216.
,, - ,, Bourke's, 214.
,, - ,, Elegant. 219.
,, - ,, Orange-bellied. 221.
,, - ,, Rock. 222.
,, - ,, Splendid. 226.
,, - ,, Turquoisine. 223.
Great-billed Parrakeet, 91.
,, - ,, Alexandrine Parrakeet, 100.
Greater Patagonian Conure, 57.
Green Conure, 39.
" ,, Leek," 121.
,, -naped Lorikeet, 5.
,, Parrakeet, 164.
,, Parrot, 165.
,, -winged King Parrakeet, 273.
Grey-breasted Parrakeet, 63.
,, -headed Lovebird, 141.
Ground-Parrakeet, 249.
guarouba, Conurus. 30,
Guiana Parrotlet, 269.
guianensis, Psittacula.

hæmorrhous, Conurus. 28.
hæmatorrhous, Psephotus. 191.
hæmatodes, Trichoglossus. 4.

hæmatonotus, Psephotus. 211.
Half-moon Parrakeet, 47.
Hanging-Parrakeet, 150.
Hanging-Parrakeet, Blue-crowned. 155.
Hanging-Parrakeet, Ceylonese. 154.
Hanging-Parrakeet, Golden-backed, 153.
Hanging-Parrakeet, Sclater's. 157.
Hanging-Parrakeet, Vernal, 151.
Henicognathus, 57.
,, *leptorhynchus,* 57.
holochlorus, Conurus. 39.
Hooded Parrakeet, 281.
Horned Parrakeet, 240.
Hybrids.
Barnardius barnardi × B. *semitorquatus.* 176, 260.
Neophema elegans, × *N. pulchella.* 221.
Platycercus elegans × *P. eximius.* 176, 260.
P. eximius × *Psephotus hæmatonotus.* 176.
P. eximius × *Calopsittacus novæhollandiæ,* 175.
P. eximius × *P. pallidiceps,* 176.
Polytelis barrabandi × *Platycercus eximius,* 175.
Hypocharmosyna placens, 266.
,, *wilhelminæ,* 266.

icterotis, Platycercus. 178.
incertus, Psittinus. 138.
Indian Ring-necked Parrakeet, 101.
indicus, Loriculus. 154.
indoburmanica, Palæornis. 99.
Indo-Burmese Alexandrine Parrakeet, 99.

Javan Parrakeet, 114.
Jendaia, 33.
Jendaya Conure, 33.
jendaia, Conurus. 33.
Johnstone's Lorikeet, 262.
johnstoniæ, Trichoglossus.
jugularis, Brotogerys, 82.

INDEX

King Parrakeet, 132.
,, ,, Green-winged. 273.

Layard's Parrakeet, 271.
leptorhynchus, Henicognathus. 57.
Lesser Patagonian Conure, 53.
leucophthalmus, Conurus. 39.
leucotis, Pyrrhura. 61.
lilianæ, Agapornis, 277.
Lineolated Parrakeet, 71, 258.
lineolatus Bolborhynchus. 71, 258.
Little Lorikeet, 265.
longicauda, Palæornis. 120.
Long-tailed Parrakeet, 120.
Loriculus, 150.
,, *chrysonotus,* 153.
,, *galgulus,* 155.
,, *indicus,* 154.
,, *sclateri,* 157.
,, *vernalis,* 151.
Loriidæ, 1.
Lorikeet, Black-throated. 263.
,, Blue-faced. 4.
,, Blue Mountain. 9.
,, Ceylon. 154.
,, Forsten's. 4, 264.
,, Goldie's. 265.
,, Green-naped. 5.
,, Johnstone's. 262.
,, Little. 265.
,, Mitchell's. 6.
,, Musky. 17.
,, Ornate. 11.
,, Perfect. 13.
,, Pleasing. 266.
,, Purple-crowned. 265.
,, Red-collared. 10.
,, Red-crowned. 255.
,, Rosenberg's. 264.
,, Ruffed. 261.
,, Scaly-breasted. 14.
,, Solitary. 261.
,, Stella's. 265.
,, Swainson's. 6.
,, Swift. 242.
,, Varied. 255.

Lorikeet, Weber's. 264.
,, Wilhelmina's. 266.
Lovebird, Abyssinian. 275.
,, Black-cheeked. 279.
,, Fischer's. 276.
,, Grey-headed. 141.
,, Madagascar. 141.
,, Masked. 280.
,, Nyasa. 277.
,, Red-faced. 143, 145.
,, Rosy-faced. 145.
,, South American. 73.
Lucian Parakeet, 116.
luteus, Conurus. 32.
luzonensis, Tanygnathus. 91.

macgillivrayi, Barnardius. 187.
Madagascar Love-bird, 141.
magnirostris, Palæornis. 100.
Malabar Parrakeet, 109.
malherbei, Cyanorhamphus. 239.
Many-coloured Parrakeet, 206, 260.
Masked Parrakeet, 136.
mastersianus, Platycercus. 158, 259.
Master's Parrakeet, 158, 259.
Mauritius Ring-necked Parrakeet, 100.
Mealy Rosella, 165.
magalorhynchus, Tanygnathus. 91.
melanura, Polytelis. 123, 258.
Melopsittacus, 244.
,, *undulatus,* 244, 283.
Mexican Conure, 39.
Micrositlace, 58.
,, *ferruginea,* 58.
Mitchell's Lorikeet, 6.
mitchelli, Trichoglossus. 6.
modesta, Palæornis. 116.
monachus, Myopsittacus. 63.
Monk Parrakeet, 63.
Moreton Bay Rosella, 165.
Moustache Parrakeet, 112.
muelleri, Tanygnathus. 93.
Mueller's Parrakeet, 93.
multicolor, Psephotus. 206, 260.
Musky Lorikeet, 17.

INDEX

Myopsittacus, 63.
  ,, *monachus*, 63.

Nandy Parrakeet, 36.
Nanodes, 157, 242.
  ,, *discolor*, 242.
Nasiterna, 25.
Nasiterninæ, 25.
nenday, Conurus. 36.
Nenday Parrakeet, 36.
Neophema bourkei, 214.
  ,, *chryosgastra*, 221.
  ,, *elegans*, 219.
  ,, *petrophila*, 222.
  ,, *pulchella*, 220, 221, 223.
  ,, *splendida*, 226.
  ,, *venusta*, 216.
nepalensis, Palæornis. 98.
Nepalese Alexandrine Parrakeet, 98.
New Zealand Parrakeet, 229.
Nicobar Parrakeet, 117.
  ,,   ,, Blyth's. 115.
nicobarica, Palæornis. 117.
Night Parrakeet, 252.
nigrigenis, Agapornis. 279.
nigrigularis, Trichoglossus. 263.
Norfolk Island Parrakeet, 284.
novæ-hollandiæ, Calopsittacus. 20.
  ,, - ,, *Trichoglossus*. 6, 10.
  ,, *-zealandiæ, Cyanorhamphus*. 229.
Nymphicus, 240.
  ,, *cornutus*, 240.
  ,, *uvæensis*, 241.

occidentalis, Barnardius. 190.
  ,, *Geopsittacus*. 252.
Orange-bellied Grass Parrakeet, 221.
  ,, -flanked Parrakeet, 81.
Ornate Lorikeet, 11.
ornatus, Trichoglossus. 11.

Palæornis, 93.
  ,, *affinis*, 119.
  ,, *alexandri*, 114.
  ,, *calthropæ*, 271.

Palæornis caniceps, 115.
  ,, *cyanocephala*, 104.
  ,, *derbyana*, 111.
  ,, *docilis*, 104.
  ,, *eques*, 100.
  ,, *eupatria*, 96.
  ,, *fasciata*, 112.
  ,, *finschi*, 109.
  ,, *indoburmanica*, 99.
  ,, *longicauda*, 120.
  ,, *magnirostris*, 100.
  ,, *modesta*, 116.
  ,, *nepalensis*, 98.
  ,, *nicobarica*, 117.
  ,, *peristerodes*, 109.
  ,, *rosa*, 106.
  ,, *salvadorii*, 273.
  ,, *schisticeps*, 107.
  ,, *torquata*, 101.
  ,, *tytleri*, 119.
Palæornithinæ, 90.
Pale-headed Rosella, 165, 166.
pallidiceps, Platycercus. 165.
Paradise Parrakeet, 197.
Paroquet, Rose-ringed. 101.
Parrakeet, Adelaide. 162.
  ,, African Ring-necked. 104.
  ,, Alexandra. 125.
  ,, Alexandrine. 95, 96.
  ,, All-green. 79.
  ,, Alpine. 239.
  ,, Andaman. 119.
  ,, Antipodes Island. 227, 228.
  ,, Aru. 270.
  ,, Banded. 112.
  ,, Barnard's. 183, 260.
  ,, Barraband's. 121, 175.
  ,, Bauer's. 189.
  ,, Beautiful. 197, 207.
  ,, Black-tailed. 123, 258.
  ,, Blood-winged. 129.
  ,, Blossom-headed. 93, 104
  ,, Blue-banded. 216.
  ,, ,, -bonnet. 167, 169, 191, 193.

INDEX

Parrakeet, Blue-cheeked. 168.
,, ,, -crowned. 91.
,, ,, - ,, Hanging-. 155.
,, ,, -rumped. 138.
,, ,, -winged Grass-. 216
,, Blyth's Nicobar. 115.
,, Bourke's. 195.
,, ,, Grass-. 214.
,, Brown's. 168.
,, Burmese Slaty-headed. 109.
,, Canary-winged. 79.
,, Ceylonese Hanging-. 154
,, Cinghalese Alexandrine. 96.
,, Cockatoo. 123.
,, Crimson. 165.
,, ,, -winged. 129.
,, Derbyan. 111.
,, Earl of Derby's. 178.
,, Elegant, 216.
,, ,, Grass-. 219.
,, Everett's Great-billed. 271.
,, Goat. 232.
,, Golden-backed Hanging-. 153.
,, Golden-crowned. 234.
,, ,, -fronted. 83.
,, ,, -headed. 166.
,, ,, -shouldered. 202.
,, ,, -winged. 85.
,, Great-billed. 91.
,, ,, - ,, Alexandrine. 100.
,, Green. 164.
,, Green-winged King. 273.
,, Grey-breasted. 63.
,, Ground. 249.
,, Half-Moon. 47.
,, Hooded. 281.
,, Horned. 240.
,, Indian Ring-necked. 101
,, Indo-Burmese Alexandrine. 99.
,, Javan. 114.

Parrakeet, King. 132.
,, Layard's. 271.
,, Lineolated. 71, 258.
,, Long-tailed. 120.
,, Lucian. 116.
,, Malabar. 109.
,, Many-coloured. 206, 260
,, Masked. 136.
,, Masters'. 158, 259.
,, Mauritius Ring-necked, 100.
,, Mealy Rosella. 165.
,, Monk. 63.
,, Moustache. 112.
,, Mueller's. 93.
,, Nandy or Nenday. 36.
,, Nepalese Alexandrine. 98.
,, New Zealand. 229.
,, Nicobar. 117.
,, Night. 252.
,, Norfolk Island. 284.
,, Orange-bellied Grass-. 221.
,, Orange-flanked. 81.
,, Pale-headed. 165.
,, Paradise. 197.
,, Passerine. 73.
,, Pennant's. 159, 258.
,, Pileated. 179.
,, Port Lincoln. 189.
,, Quaker. 63, 70.
,, Queen of Bavaria, 30.
,, Red-backed. 212.
,, ,, -capped. 179.
,, ,, -fronted. 229.
,, ,, -mantled. 170.
,, ,, -rumped. 211.
,, ,, -shining. 135.
,, ,, -vented Blue-bonnet. 191.
,, ,, -winged. 129.
,, Ring-necked. 100.
,, Rock-Grass. 222.
,, Rose-hill. 172.
,, Rosella. 172, 260.

Parrakeet, Rosy-headed. 106.
,, Saisset's. 234.
,, Sclater's Hanging-. 157.
,, Shell. 244.
,, Slaty-headed. 107.
,, Slight-billed, 57.
,, Smutty. 168.
,, Splendid Grass-. 226.
,, Stanley. 178.
,, Swamp. 249.
,, Swift. 242.
,, Tabuan. 136.
,, Tovi. 82.
,, Tui. 85.
,, Tuipara. 83.
,, Turquoisine Grass-. 223.
,, Twenty-eight. 189.
,, Undulated Grass-. 244.
,, Uvæan. 241.
,, Vernal Hanging-. 151.
,, Warbling Grass-. 244.
,, Western Rosella. 178.
,, White-winged. 80.
,, Yellow, 163.
,, ,, -bellied. 164.
,, ,, -cheeked. 178.
,, ,, -mantled. 177.
,, ,, -naped. 187, 260
,, ,, -rumped. 163, 259.
,, Yellow-vented. 191.
Parrakeet, Yellow-vented Blue-bonnet. 193.
Parrot, Australian Ground-. 228.
,, Bank-. 54.
,, Grass. 212.
,, Green. 165.
,, Grey and Yellow Topknotted. 22.
Parrotlet, Blue-rumped. 270.
,, ,, -winged. 76.
,, Celestial. 270.
,, Guiana. 269.
,, Passerine. 73, 75.
Parrots, Pigmy. 25.
passerina, Psittacula. 72, 73.

Passerine Parrotlet, 73, 75.
Patagonian Conure, Greater. 57.
,, ,, Lesser. 53, 55.
patagonicus, Cyanolyseus. 53, 57.
patagonus, Conurus. 66.
" Paviches," 81.
Peach-faced Lovebird, 149, 204
Pearly Conure, 62.
pennantii, Platycercus. 160.
Pennant's Parrakeet, 159, 170, 259, 260.
Perfect Lorikeet, 13, 14.
peristerodes, Palæornis. 109.
perlata, Pyrrhura. 62.
personata, Agapornis. 280.
,, *Pyrrhulopsis.* 136.
pertinax, Conurus. 46.
petrophila, Neophema. 222.
Petz's Conure, 48.
Pezoporus, formosus, 228.
,, *terrestris,* 249.
picta, Pyrrhura, 62.
Pigmy Parrots, 25.
Pileated Parrakeet, 179.
placens, Hypocharmosyna. 266.
Platycercinæ, 157.
Platycercus, adelaidæ, 162.
,, *adelaidensis,* 159, 162.
,, *alpinus,* 239.
,, *amathusia,* 168.
,, *browni,* 168.
,, *elegans,* 159, 259.
,, ,, var. *nigrescens* 159.
,, *erythropeplus,* 170, 259.
,, *eximius,* 172.
,, *fairchildii,* 228.
,, *flaveolus,* 163, 259.
,, *flaviventris,* 164, 172.
,, *icterotis,* 178.
,, *mastersianus,* 158, 259.
,, *pallidiceps,* 165.
,, *pennantii,* 160.
,, *semitorquatus,* 188.
,, *splendidus,* 177.
Pleasing Lorikeet, 266.

INDEX

Polytelis alexandræ, 121, 125.
 ,, *barrabandi*, 121. 175.
 ,, *melanura*, 123, 258.
porphyrocephalus, Glossopsittacus.
 265.
Porphyrocephalus, 179.
 ,, *spurius*, 179.
Port Lincoln Parrakeet, 189.
Psephotus chrysopterygius, 202, 281.
 ,, *cucullatus*, 282.
 ,, *dissimilis*, 206, 281.
 ,, *hæmatonotus*, 211.
 ,, *hæmatorrhous*, 191.
 ,, *multicolor*, 206, 260.
 ,, *pulcherrimus*, 197.
 ,, *xanthorrhous*, 191, 193.
Psittacula, 72.
 ,, *cœlestis*, 72, 270.
 ,, *cyanopygia*, 270.
 ,, *guianensis*, 269.
 ,, *passerina*, 73.
Psitteuteles, 13.
 ,, *chlorolepidotus*, 14.
 ,, *euteles*, 13.
 ,, *weberi*, 264.
Psittinus, 138.
 ,, *incertus*, 138.
Ptilosclera versicolor, 255.
Ptistes, 129, 132.
 ,, *coccineopterus*, 129.
 ,, *erythropterus*, 129.
pulchella, Charmosynopsis, 266.
 ,, *Neophema*. 220, 221. 223.
pulcherrimus, Psephotus. 197
pullaria, Agapornis. 143.
Purple-crowned Lorikeet, 265.
pusillus, Glossopsittacus. 265.
pyrrhopterus, Brotogerys. 81.
Pyrrhulopsis, 134.
 ,, *personata*, 136.
 ,, *personatus*, 135.
 ,, *splendens*, 135.
 ,, *tabuensis*, 136.
 ,, *taviunensis*. 274.
Pyrrhura, 59.
 ,, *chiripepe*, 269.

Pyrrhura cruentata, 59.
 ,, *leucotis*, 61.
 ,, *perlata*, 62.
 ,, *picta*, 62.
 ,, *vittata*, 60, 258, 268.

Quaker Parrakeet, 63.
Quarrion, 22.
Queen of Bavaria Parrakeet, 30.

Red-backed Parrakeet, 212.
 ,, -bellied Conure, 60.
 ,, -capped Parrakeet, 179.
 ,, -collared Lorikeet, 10.
 ,, -crowned Lorikeet, 255.
 ,, -eared Conure, 59.
 ,, -faced Conure, 37.
 ,, ,, Lovebird, 143.
 ,, -fronted Parrakeet, 229.
 ,, -headed Conure, 37.
 ,, -mantled Parrakeet, 170.
 ,, Rosella, 167.
 ,, -rumped Parrakeet, 211.
 ,, Shining Parrakeet, 135.
 ,, -throated Conure, 40.
 ,, -vented Blue-bonnet, 191.
 ,, -winged Lory, 129.
 ,, - ,, Parrakeet, 129.
Ring-necked Parrakeet, African. 104.
 ,, - ,, ,, Indian. 101.
Ring-necked Parrakeet, Mauritius.
 100.
Rock Grass-Parrakeet, 222.
Rock Pebbler, 123.
 ,, Pepler, 123.
rosa, Palæornis. 106.
Rose-hill Parrakeet, 172.
roseicollis, Agapornis, 145.
Rosella Mealy, 165.
 ,, Moreton Bay. 165.
 ,, Pale-headed. 165.
 ,, Parrakeet, 172, 260.
 ,, ,, Western. 178.
Rosenberg's Lorikeet, 264.
rosenbergi, Trichoglossus. 264.
Rose-ringed Paroquet, 101.

Rosy-faced Lovebird, 145.
„ -headed Parrakeet, 106.
rubritorques, Conurus. 40.
„ *Trichoglossus.* 10.
rubrolarvatus, Conurus. 37, 38.
Ruffed Lorikeet, 261.

St. Thomas' Conure, 46.
saisseti, Cyanorhamphus. 234.
Saisset's Parrakeet, 234.
salvadorii, Palæornis. 273.
Scaly-breasted Lorikeet, 14.
schisticeps, Palæornis. 107.
sclateri, Loriculus. 157.
Sclater's Hanging Parrakeet, 157.
semitorquatus, Barnardius. 187, 260.
Sharp-tailed Conure, 28.
Shell Parrakeet, 244.
sivalensis, Palæornis. 115.
Slaty-headed Parrakeet, 107.
„ - „ „ Burmese, 109.
Slight-billed Parrakeet, 57.
Smutty Parrakeet, 168.
Solitary Lorikeet, 261..
solitarius, Calloptilus. 261.
solstitialis, Conurus. 32.
South American Love-bird, 73.
Spathopterus, 124.
„ *alexandræ,* 125.
splendens, Pyrrhulopsis. 135.
Splendid Grass Parrakeet, 226.
splendida, Neophema. 226.
splendidus, Platycercus. 177.
spurius, Porphyrocephalus. 179.
Stanley Parrakeet, 178.
stellæ, Charmosyna. 265.
Stella's Lorikeet, 265.
sulaensis, Aprosmictus. 274.
Swainson's Lorikeet, 6.
Swamp Parrakeet, 249.
Swift Lorikeet, 242.
„ Parrakeet, 242.

Tabuan Parrakeet, 136.
tabuensis, Pyrrhulopsis. 136.

Tanygnathus, 90.
„ *albirostris,* 93.
„ *everetti,* 271.
„ *luzonensis,* 91.
„ *megalorhynchus,* 91.
„ *muelleri,* 93.
taviunensis, Pyrrhulopsis. 274.
taranta, Agapornis. 275.
Taviuni Parrakeet, 274.
terrestris, Pezoporus. 249.
tirica, Brotogerys. 79.
torquata, Palæornis. 101.
Tovi Parrakeet, 82.
Trichoglossus, 4.
„ *cyanogrammus,* 5.
„ *forsteni,* 4, 264.
„ *hæmatodes,* 4.
„ *johnstoniæ,*
„ *mitchelli,* 6.
„ *multicolor,* 15.
„ *nigrigularis,*
„ *novæ-hollandiæ* 6.
„ *ornatus,* 11.
„ *rosenbergi,* 264
„ *rubritorques,* 10.
tui, Brotogerys. 85.
Tui Parrakeet, 85.
tuipara, Brotogerys. 83.
Tuipara Parrakeet, 83.
Turquoisine Grass-Parrakeet, 223.
" Twenty-eight Parrakeet," 187.
tytleri, Palæornis. 119.

Undulated Grass-Parrakeet, 244.
undulatus, Melopsittacus. 22, 283.
unicolor, Cyanorhamphus. 227.
Uvæan Parrakeet, 241.
uvæensis, Nymphicus. 241.

Varied Lorikeet, 255.
venusta, Neophema. 216.
Vernal Hanging-Parrakeet, 151.
vernalis, Loriculus. 151.
versicolor, Ptilosclera. 255.
virescens, Brotogerys. 80.
vittata, Pyrrhura. 60, 258, 268.

INDEX

wagleri, Conurus. 38.
Wagler's Conure, 38.
weberi, Psitteuteles. 264.
Weber's Lorikeet, 264.
weddelli, Conurus. 266.
Weddell's Conure, 266.
Western Rosella Parrakeet, 178.
White-eared Conure, 61.
,, -winged Parrakeet, 80.
whitleyi, Conurus. 267.
Whitley's Conure, 267.
wilhelminæ, Hypocharmosyna. 266.
Wilhelmina's Lorikeet, 266.

xanthorrhous, Psephotus. 191, 193.

Yellow-bellied Parrakeet, 164.
,, Conure, 32.
,, -cheeked Parrakeet, 178.
,, -headed Conure. 33.
,, -mantled Parrakeet 177.
,, -naped Parrakeet, 187, 260
,, Parrakeet, 163.
,, -rumped Parrakeet, 163, 259.
,, -vented Parrakeet, 191.
,, - ,, Blue-bonnet, 193.

zonarius Barnardius. 189.

Index of Current Nomenclature

Because many of both the taxonomic and common names of the birds discussed in this book have changed since the book was first published in the 1920's, we are including here an index to the nomenclature currently used.

In the following list the first set of taxonomic and common name used for each bird agrees with its usage in the text; the succeeding set of names is the current taxonomic and common name for the same bird. The page number following each group of names refers to the page(s) on which a discussion of the bird begins. The list is arranged alphabetically in accordance with the taxonomic names used in the text.

Agapornis cana, Madagascar Lovebird = *Agapornis cana,* Madagascar Lovebird. (Page 141)

Agapornis fischeri, Fischer's Lovebird = *Agapornis fischeri,* Fischer's Lovebird. (Page 276)

Agapornis lilianae, Nyasa Lovebird = *Agapornis lilianae,* Nyasa Lovebird. (Page 277)

Agapornis nigrigenis, Black-Cheeked Lovebird = *Agapornis nigrigenis,* Black-Cheeked Lovebird. (Page 279)

Agapornis personata, Masked Lovebird = *Agapornis personata,* Masked Lovebird. (Page 280)

Agapornis pullaria, Red-Faced Lovebird = *Agapornis pullaria,* Red-Faced Lovebird. (Page 143)

Agapornis roseicollis, Rosy-Faced Lovebird = *Agapornis roseicollis,* Peach-Faced Lovebird. (Page 145)

Agapornis taranta, Abyssinian Lovebird = *Agapornis taranta,* Abyssinian Lovebird. (Page 275)

Aprosmictus amboinensis, Amboina King Parrakeet = *Alisterus amboinensis,* Amboina King Parrot. (Page 274)

Aprosmictus chloropterus, Green-Winged King Parrakeet = *Alisterus chloropterus,* Green-Winged King Parrot. (Page 273)

Aprosmictus cyanopygius, King Parrakeet = *Alisterus scapularis scapularis,* Australian King Parrot. (Page 132)

Aprosmictus sulaensis, King Parrakeet = *Alisterus amboinensis sulaensis,* Amboina King Parrot. (Page 274)

Barnardius barnardi, Barnard's Parrakeet = *Barnardius barnardi,* Mallee Ringneck Parrot. (Page 183, 260)

Barnardius semitorquatus, Yellow-Naped Parrakeet = *Barnardius zonarius semitorquatus,* Twenty-eight Parrot. (Page 187)

Barnardius zonarius, Bauer's Parrakeet = *Barnardius zonarius,* Port Lincoln Parrot. (Page 189)

Bolborhynchus lineolatus, Lineolated Parrakeet = *Bolborhynchus lineola,* Barred Parakeet. (Pages 71, 258)

Brotogerys chiriri, Canary-Winged Parrakeet = *Brotogeris versicolorus chiriri,* Canary-Winged Parrakeet. (Page 79)

Brotogerys chrysopterus, Golden-Winged Parrakeet = *Brotogeris chrysopterus,* Golden-Winged Parakeet. (Page 85)

Brotogerys jugularis, Tovi Parrakeet = *Brotogeris jugularis,* Orange-Chinned Parakeet. (Page 82)

Brotogerys pyrrhopterus, Orange-Flanked Parrakeet = *Brotogeris pyrrhopterus,* Grey-Cheeked Parakeet. (Page 81)
Brotogerys tirica, All-Green Parrakeet = *Brotogeris tirica,* Plain Parakeet. Page (79)
Brotogerys tui, Tui Parrakeet = *Brotogeris sanctithomae,* Tui Parakeet. (Page 85)
Brotogerys tuipara, Golden-Fronted Parrakeet = *Brotogeris chrysopterus tuipara,* Golden-Winged Parakeet. (Page 83)
Brotogerys virescens, White-Winged Parrakeet = *Brotogeris versicoluruswhite,* Winged Parakeet. (Page 80)
Calliptilus solitarius, Solitary or Ruffed Lorikeet = *Phigys soliterius,* Collared Lory. (Page 261)
Calopsittacus novae-hollandiae, Cockatiel = *Nymphicus hollandicus,* Cockatiel. (Page 20)
Charmosyna stellae, Stella's Lorikeet = *Charmosyna papou goliathina,* Stella's Lory. (Page 265)
Charmosynopsis pulchella, Fair Lorikeet = *Charmosyna pulchella,* Fairy Lorikeet. (Page 266)
Conuropsis carolinensis, Carolina Conure = *Conuropsis carolinensis,* Carolina Parakeet. Now extinct. (Page 48)
Conurus aeruginosus, Brown-Throated Conure = *Aratinga pertinax,* Brown-Throated Conure. (Page 44)
Conurus aztec, Aztec Conure = *Aratinga nana astec,* Aztec Conure. (Page 41)
Conurus acuticaudatus, Sharp-Tailed Conure = *Aratinga acuticaudata,* Blue-Crowned Conure. (Page 28)
Conurus aureus, Golden-Crowned Conure = *Aratinga aurea,* Peach-Fronted Conure or Half-Moon Parrakeet. (Page 47)
Conurus auricapillus, Golden-Headed Conure = *Aratinga auricapilla,* Golden-Capped Conure. (Page 35)
Conurus cactorum, Cactus Conure = *Aratinga cactorum,* Cactus Conure. Page 41)
Conurus canicularis, Petz's Conure = *Aratinga canicularis,* Orange-Fronted Conure. (Page 48)
Conurus guarouba, Golden Conure = *Aratinga guarouba,* Golden Conure. Page 30)
Conurus haemorrhous, Blue-Crowned Conure = *Aratinga acuticaudata haemorrhous,* Blue-Crowned Conure. (Page 28)
Conurus holochlorus, Mexican Conure = *Aratinga holochlora,* Green Conure. (Page 39)
Conurus jendaya, Yellow-Headed Conure = *Aratinga jandaya,* Jandaya Conure. (Page 33)
Conurus leucophthalmus, Green Conure = *Aratinga leucophthalmus,* White-Eyed Conure. (Page 39)
Conurus nenday, Black-Headed Conure = *Nandayus nenday,* Nanday Conure. (Page 36)
Conurus pertinax, St. Thomas Conure = *Aratinga pertinax pertinax,* Brown-Throated Conure. (Page 46)

Conurus rubritorques, Red-Throated Conure = *Aratinga holochlora rubritorquis,* Green Conure species. (Page 40)
Conurus rubrolarvatus, Red-Headed Conure = *Aratinga erythrogenys,* Red-Masked Conure. (Page 37, 267)
Conurus solstitialis, Yellow Conure = *Aratinga solstitialis,* Sun Conure. (Page 32)
Conurus wagleri, Wagler's Conure = *Aratinga wagleri,* Red-Fronted Conure. (Page 38)
Conurus weddelli, Weddell's Conure = *Aratinga weddellii,* Dusky-Headed Conure. (Page 266)
Conurus whitleyi, Whitley's Conure = *Cyanoliseus whitleyi,* Whitley's Conure. Almost certainly a hybrid of the Patagonian Conure. (Page 267)
Cyanolyseus byroni, Greater Patagonian Conure = *Cyanoliseus patagonius byroni,* Patagonian Conure. (Page 57)
Cyanolyseus patagonicus, Lesser Patagonian Conure = *Cyanoliseus patagonius,* Patagonian Conure. (Page 53)
Cyanorhamphus auriceps, Golden-Crowned Parrakeet = *Cyanorhamphus auriceps,* Yellow-Fronted Parakeet. (Page 234)
Cyanorhamphus cooki, Norfolk Island Parrakeet = *Cyanorhamphus novaesealandiae cookii,* Red-Fronted Parakeet. (Page 284)
Cyanorhamphus malherbei, Alpine Parrakeet = *Cyanorhampus malherbei,* Orange-Fronted Parakeet. (Page 239)
Cyanorhamphus novae-zealandiae, New Zealand Parrakeet = *Cyanorhamphus novaezealandiae,* Red-Fronted Parakeet. (Page 229)
Cyanorhamphus saisseti, Saisset's Parrakeet = *Cyanorhamphus novaezealandiae saissetti,* Red-Fronted Parakeet. (Page 234)
Cyanorhamphus unicolor, Antipodes Island Parrakeet = *Cyanorhamphus unicolor,* Antipodes Green Parakeet. (Page 227)
Geoffroyus aruensis, Aru Parrakeet = *Geoffroyus geoffroyi aruensis,* Red-Cheeked Parrot. (Page 270)
Geopsittacus occidentalis, Night Parrakeet = *Geopsittacus occidentalis,* Night Parrot. (Page 252)
Glossopsittacus concinnus, Musky Lorikeet = *Glossopsitta concinna,* Musk Lorikeet. (Page 17)
Glossopsittacus porphyrocephalus, Purple-Crowned Lorikeet = *Glossopsitta porphyrocephala,* Purple-Crowned Lorikeet. (Page 265)
Glossopsittacus pusillus, Little Lorikeet = *Glossopsitta pusilla,* Little Lorikeet. (Page 265)
Henicognathus leptorhynchus, Slight-Billed Parrakeet = *Enicognathus leptorhynchus,* Slender-Billed Conure. (Page 57)
Hypocharmosyna placens, Pleasing Lorikeet = *Charmosyna placentis subpalcens,* Red-Flanked Lorikeet. (Page 266)
Hypocharmosyna wilhelminae, Wilhelmina's Lorikeet = *Charmosyna wilhelminae,* Wilhelmina's Lorikeet. (Page 266)
Loriculus chrysonotus, Golden-Backed Hanging Parrakeet = *Loriculus philippensis chrysonotus,* Phillipine Hanging Parrot. (Page 153)
Loriculus galgulus, Blue-Crowned Hanging Parrakeet = *Loriculus galgulus,* Blue-Crowned Hanging Parrot. (Page 155)

Loriculus indicus, Ceylonese Hanging Parrakeet = *Loriculus beryllinus*, Ceylon Hanging Parrot. (Page 154)
Loriculus sclateri, Sclater's Hanging Parrakeet = *Loriculus amabilis sclateri*, Moluccan Hanging Parrot. (Page 157)
Loriculus vernalis, Vernal Hanging Parrakeet = *Loriculus vernalis*, Vernal Hanging Parrot. (Page 151)
Melopsittacus undulatus, Budgerigar, or Undulated Grass Parrakeet = *Melopsittacus undulatus*, Budgerigar. (Pages 244, 284)
Microsittace ferruginea, Chilian Conure = *Enicognathus ferrugineus*, Austral Conure. (Page 58)
Myopsittacus monachus, Grey-Breasted Parrakeet = *Myiopsitta monachus*, Monk Parakeet. (Page 63)
Nanodes discolor, Swift Parrakeet = *Lathamus discolor*, Swift Parrot. (Page 242)
Neophema bourkei, Bourke's Grass-Parrakeet = *Neophema bourkii*, Bourke's Parrot. (Page 214)
Neophema chrysogastra, Orange-Bellied Grass-Parrakeet = *Neophema chrysogaster*, Orange-Bellied Parrot. (Page 221)
Neophema elegans, Elegant Grass-Parrakeet = *Neophema elegans*, Elegant Parrot. (Page 219)
Neophema pulchella, Turquoisine Grass-Parrakeet = *Neophema pulchella*, Turquoise Parrot. (Page 223)
Neophema petrophila, Rock Grass-Parrakeet = *Neophema petrophila*, Rock Parrot. (Page 222)
Neophema splendida, Splendid Grass-Parrakeet = *Neophema splendida*, Scarlet-Chested Parrot. (Page 226)
Neophema venusta, Blue-Winged Grass-Parrakeet = *Neophema chrysostoma*, Blue-Winged Parrot. (Page 216)
Nymphicus cornutus, Horned Parrakeet = *Eunymphicus cornutus*, Horned Parrakeet. (Page 240)
Nymphicus uvaeensis, Uvaean Parrakeet = *Eunymphicus cornutus uvaeensis*, Horned Parrakeet. (Page 241)
Palaeornis alexandri, Java Parrakeet = *Psittacula alexandri alexandri*, Moustached Parakeet. (Page 114)
Palaeornis calthropae, Layard's Parrakeet = *Psittacula calthorpae*, Emerald-Collared Parakeet. (Page 271)
Palaeornis caniceps, Blyth's Nicobar Parrakeet = *Psittacula caniceps*, Blyth's Parakeet. (Page 115)
Palaeornis cyanocephala, Blossom-Headed Parrakeet = *Psittacula cyanocephala*, Plum-Headed Parakeet. (Page 104)
Palaeornis derbyana, Derbyan Parrakeet = *Psittacula derbiana*, Derbyan Parakeet. (Pages 111, 273)
Palaeornis docilis, African Rina-Necked Parrakeet = *Psittacula krameri krameri*, Rose-Ringed Parakeet. (Page 104)
Palaeornis eques, Mauritus Ring-Necked Parrakeet = *Psittacula echo*, Mauritus Parakeet. (Page 100)
Palaeornis eupatria, Cinghalese Alexandrine Parrakeet = *Psittacula eupatria*, Alexandrine Parakeet. (Page 96)

Palaeornis fasciata, Banded Parrakeet = *Psittacula alexandri fasciata*, Moustached Parakeet. (Page 112)

Palaeornis finschi, Burmese Slaty-Headed Parrakeet = *Psittacula himalayana finschii*, Slaty-Headed Parakeet. (Page 109)

Palaeornis indoburmanica, Indo-Burmese Alexandrine Parrakeet = *Psittacula eupatrai avensis*, Alexandrine Parakeet. (Page 99)

Palaeornis longicauda, Long-Tailed Parrakeet = *Psittacula longicauda longicauda*, Long-Tailed Parakeet. (Page 120)

Palaeornis maginrostris, Great Billed Alexandrine Parrakeet = *Psittacula eupatria maginrostris*, Alexandrine Parakeet. (Page 100)

Palaeornis modesta, Lucian Parrakeet = *Psittacula longicauda modesta*, Long-Tailed Parakeet. (Page 116)

Palaeornis nepalensis, Nepalese Alexandrine Parrakeet = *Psittacula eupatria nipalensis*, Alexandrine Parakeet. (Page 98)

Palaeornis nicobarica, Nicobar Parrakeet = *Psittacula longicauda nicobarica*, Long-Tailed Parakeet. (Page 117)

Palaeornis peristerodes, Malabar Parrakeet = *Psittacula columboides*, Malabar Parakeet. (Page 109)

Palaeornis rosa, Rosy-Headed Parrakeet = *Psittacula roseata*, Blossom-Headed Parakeet. (Page 106)

Palaeornis schistceps, Slaty-Headed Parrakeet = *Psittacula himalayana*, Slaty-Headed Parakeet. (Page 107)

Palaeornis torquata, Indian Ring-Necked Parrakeet = *Psittacula krameri*, Indian Ring-Necked Parakeet. (Page 101)

Palaeornis tytleri, Andaman Parrakeet = *Psittacula longicauda tytleri*, Long-Tailed Parakeet. (Page 119)

Pezoporus terrestris, Ground, or Swamp Parrakeet = *Pezoporus wallicus*, Ground Parrot. (Page 249)

Platycercus adelaidae, Adelaide Parrakeet = *Platycercus adelaidae*, Adelaide Rosella. (Page 162)

Platycercus amathusia, Blue-Cheeked Parrakeet = *Platycercus adscitus adscitus*, Pale-Headed Rosella. (Page 168)

Platycercus browni, Brown's Parrakeet = *Platycercus venustus*, Northern Rosella. (Page 168)

Platycercus elegans, Pennant's Parrakeet = *Platycercus elegans*, Crimson Rosella. (Page 157)

Platycercus erythtopeplus, Red-Mantled Parrakeet = *Platycercus eximius eximius*, Eastern Rosella. (Pages 170, 259)

Platycercus eximius, Rosella Parrakeet = *Platycercus eximius*, Eastern Rosella. (Page 172)

Platycercus flaveolus, Yellow-Rumped Parrakeet = *Platycercus flaveolus*, Yellow Rosella. (Pages 163, 259)

Plathcercus flaviventris, Yellow-Bellied Parrakeet = *Platycercus elegans melanopstra*. (Page 164)

Platycercus icterotis, Stanley Parrakeet = *Platycercus icterotis*, Western Rosella. (Page 178)

Platycercus mastersianus, Master's Parrakeet = *Platycercus elegans elegans*, Crimson Rosella. (Pages 158, 258)

Platycercus pallidiceps, Pale-Headed Rosella = *Platycercus adscitus palliceps*, Pale-Headed Rosella. (Page 165)
Platycercus splendidus, Yellow-Mantled Parrakeet = *Platycercus elegans nigriscens*, Crimson Rosella. (Page 177)
Polytelis barrabandi, Barraband's Parrakeet = *Polytelis swainsonni*, Barraband's Parrot or Superb Parrot. (Page 121)
Polytelis melanura, Black-Tailed Parrakeet = *Polytelis anthopeplus*, Regent Parrot (Rock Pepler). (Pages 123, 258)
Porphycephalus spurius, Pileated Parrakeet = *Purpureicephalus spurius*, Red-Capped Parrot. (Page 179)
Psephotus chrysopterygius, Golden-Shouldered Parrakeet = *Psephotus chrysopterygius*, Golden-Shouldered Parrot. (Pages 202, 281)
Psephotus dissimilis, Hooded Parrakeet = *Psephotus chrysopterygius dissimilis*, Hooded Parrot. (Pages 206, 281)
Psephotus haematonotus, Red-Rumped Parrakeet = *Psephotus haematonotus*, Red-Rumped Parrot. (Page 211)
Psephotus haematorrhous, Red-Vented Blue-Bonnet Parrakeet = *Psephotus haematogaster haematorrhous*, Blue-Bonnet. (Page 191)
Psephotus multicolor, Many-Colored Parrakeet = *Psephtous varius*, Mulga Parrot. (Pages 206, 260)
Psephotus pulcherrimus, Beautiful Parrakeet = *Psephotus pulcherrimus* Paradise Parrot. (Page 197)
Psephotus xanthorrhous, Yellow-Vented Blue-Bonnet Parrakeet = *Psephotus haematogaster*, Blue Bonnet. (Page 193)
Psittacula coelestis, Celestial Parrotlet = *Forpus coelestis*, Pacific Parrotlet. (Pages 72, 270)
Psittacula cyanopygia, Blue-Rumped Parrotlet = *Forpus cyanopygius*, Mexican Parrotlet. (Page 270)
Psittacula guianensis, Guiana Parrotlet = *Forpus passerinus viridissimus*, Green-Rumped Parrotlet. (Page 269)
Psittacula passerina, Passerine Parrotlet = *Forpus passerinus*, Green-Rumped Parrotlet. (Page 73)
Psitteules chlotolepidotus, Scaly-Breasted Lorikeet = *Trichoglossus chlorolepidotus*, Scaly-Breasted Lorikeet. (Page 14)
Psitteuteles euteles, Perfect Lorikeet = *Trichoglossus euteles*, Perfect Lorikeet. (Page 13)
Psitteuteles weberi, Weber's Lorikeet = *Trichoglossus haematodus weberi*, Weber's Lorikeet. (Page 264)
Psittinus incertus, Blue-Rumped Parrakeet = *Psittinus cyanurus*, Blue-Rumped Parrot. (Page 138)
Ptilosclera versicolor, Red-Crowned, or Varied Lorikeet = *Trichoglossus versicolor*, Varied Lorikeet. (Page 255)
Ptistes erythropterus, Crimson-Winged Parrakeet = *Aprosmictus erythropterus*, Red-Winged Parrot. (Page 129)
Pyrrhylopsis personata, Masked Parrakeet = *Prosopeia personata*, Masked Shining Parrot. (Page 136)
Pyrrhulopsis splendens, Red Shining Parrakeet = *Prosopeia tabuensis splendens*, Red Shining Parrot. (Page 135)

Pyrrhulopsis tabuensis, Tabuan Parrakeet = *Prosopeia tabuensis,* Red Shining Parrot. (Page 136)

Pyrrhulopsis taviunensis, Taviuni Parrakeet = *Prosopeia tabuensis taviunensis,* Red Shining Parrot. (Page 274)

Pyrrhura chiripcpe, Azara's Conure = *Pyrrhura frontalis chiripepe,* Maroon-Bellied Conure. (Page 269)

Pyrrhura cruentata, Red-Eared Conure = *Pyrrhura cruentata,* Blue-Throated Conure. (Page 59)

Pyrrhura leucotis, White-Eared Conure = *Pyrrhura leucotis,* White-Eared Conure. (Page 61)

Pyrrhura perlata, Pearly Conure = *Pyrrhura perlata,* Pearly Conure. (Page 62)

Pyrrhura picta, Blue-Winged Conure = *Pyrrhura picta,* Painted Conure. (Page 62)

Pyrrhura vittata, Red-Bellied Conure = *Pyrrhura rhodogaster,* Crimson Bellied Conure. (Page 60, 258)

Spathopterus alexandrae, Alexandra Parrakeet = *Polytelis alexandrae,* Princess Parrot. (Page 125)

Tanygnathus everetti, Everett's Great-Billed Parrakeet = *Tanygnathus sumatranus everetti,* Müller's Parrot. (Page 271)

Tanygnathus luzonensis, Blue-Crowned Parrakeet = *Tanygnathus lucionensis,* Blue-Naped Parrot. (Page 91)

Tanygnathus megalorhynchus, Great-Billed Parrakeet = *Tanygnathus megalorynchos,* Great-Billed Parrot. (Page 91)

Tanygnathus muelleri, Mueller's Parrakeet = *Tanygnathus sumatranus,* Müller's Parrot. (Page 93)

Trichoglossus cyanogrammus, Green-Naped Lorikeet = *Trichoglossus haematodus flavicans,* Olive-Green Lorikeet. (Page 5)

Trichoglossus forsteni, Forsten's Lorikeet = *Trichoglossus haematodus forsteni,* Forsten's Lorikeet. (Page 4)

Trichoglossus haematodes, Blue-Faced Lorikeet = *Trichoglossus haematodus,* Rainbow Lory. (Page 4)

Trichoglossus johnstoniae, Johnstone's Lorikeet = *Trichoglossus johnstoniae,* Johnstone's Lorikeet. (Page 262)

Trichoglossus mitchelli, Mitchell's Lorikeet = *Trichoglossus haematodus mitchelli,* Mitchell's Lorikeet. (Page 6)

Trichoglossus nigrigularis, Black-Throated Lorikeet = *Trichoglossus heamatodus nigrigularis,* Rainbow Lory. (Page 263)

Trichoglossus novae-hollandae, Swainson's Lorikeet = *Trichoglossus haematodus moluccanus,* Swainson's Lorikeet, or Blue-Mountain Lorikeet, or Rainbow Lorikeet. (Page 6)

Trichoglossus ornatus, Orante Lorikeet = *Trichoglossus ornatus,* Ornate Lory. (Page 11)

Trichoglossus rosenbergi, Rosenberg's Lorikeet = *Trichoglossus haematodus rosenbergii,* Rainbow Lory. (Page 264)

Trichoglossus rubritorques, Red-Collared Lorikeet = *Trichoglossus haematodus rubritorquis,* Red-Collared Lorikeet, or Rainbow Lory. (Page 10)